Death Metal Music

Death Metal Music

*The Passion and Politics
of a Subculture*

NATALIE J. PURCELL

McFarland & Company, Inc., Publishers
Jefferson, North Carolina, and London

LIBRARY OF CONGRESS CATALOGUING-IN-PUBLICATION DATA

Purcell, Natalie J.
　　Death Metal music : the passion and politics of a subculture / Natalie J. Purcell.
　　　　p.　　cm.
　　Includes bibliographical references and index.

　　ISBN-13: 978-0-7864-1585-4
　　softcover : 50# alkaline paper ∞

　　1. Heavy metal (Music)—History and criticism.　I. Title.
ML3534.P91　2003
781.66—dc21　　　　　　　　　　　　　　　　　　　2003007616

British Library cataloguing data are available

©2003 Natalie J. Purcell. All rights reserved

No part of this book may be reproduced or transmitted in any form or by any means, electronic or mechanical, including photocopying or recording, or by any information storage and retrieval system, without permission in writing from the publisher.

On the front cover: Sean McGrath of Impaled.

Manufactured in the United States of America

McFarland & Company, Inc., Publishers
　Box 611, Jefferson, North Carolina 28640
　　www.mcfarlandpub.com

Acknowledgments

This book is dedicated to all those in the Death Metal scene who generously gave their time and effort to this project. Thank you so much to the research assistants and to every interviewee who devoted time and thought to this endeavor: Pete, Killjoy, Kyle, King, Paul, Jeremy, John L., John G., Erik, Seth, Adrianne, Rob, John D., Brian, and Dana.

Special thanks are extended to Matt Medeiros for supporting this project from the start, to Jason Netherton and Matt Harvey for providing a wealth of advice and information, to Iris Duran for lending a critical eye and a helping hand, and to Bill for his help and generosity.

Above all, this project owes a debt to my political science professors at Seton Hall University, whose open-minded enthusiasm and support made it possible. I am especially indebted to Dr. Mary Boutilier, Dr. Jo-Renee Formicola, and Dr. Jeffrey Togman.

On a more personal note, this book was composed in a time of significant stress, and there were many times when I doubted my ability to get through it. Were it not for the kindness of my dear friends from SHU and from good old Kearny, N.J., this book wouldn't be here. The legal advice of Linda Mowad, Janice Sylvia, Janet Bayer, Griselda Morillo Manjarres, Bridget Bocchino, and others was invaluable to this project. Bridget and Griselda, your wisdom and intelligence have meant the world to me. Mikey R., I thank you for your kindness and your inspiring spirit. Mike H., you have helped me in so many ways; your listening ear, your wise words, and your pure heart are gifts I am so grateful to have received.

Sean, Nicole, Sandy, Ricky, Sergio, my grandparents, my parents, my sister, and so many others also deserve my gratitude, for they played small but deeply significant roles in the completion of this work.

Contents

Acknowledgments v
Preface 1

I: DEFINING DEATH METAL

   1. The Genre and Its Sub-Genres 9
   2. Fundamental Dynamics of the Scene 25
   3. Lyrical Content 39

II: THE HISTORY OF THE DEATH METAL SCENE

   4. Origins: 1984–1988 53
   5. Rise and Fall: 1989–1994 58
   6. The Present: 1995–2002 68

III: DEATH METAL AND AMERICAN POLITICIANS

   7. The Skeleton in America's Closet 79
   8. The Politics of Censorship 83
   9. Content Regulation Today and Tomorrow 89

IV: CONFRONTING THE CONSUMERS OF CARNAGE

   10. Facing the Demon 97
   11. Demographics 99
   12. Attitudes 116

13. Philosophy and Ethics	123
14. Behavior	133
15. Concluding Opinions on Death Metal and Violence	139

V: THE MIND OF THE METAL HEAD AND THE HEART OF THE UNDERGROUND

16. The Subcultural Phenomenon	151
17. Rebellion and Religion	163
18. Horror, Gore, Porn, and the American Mind	170

EPILOGUE

Personal Reflections on Death Metal	187
Appendix A: Project Goals, Implications, and Methodology	195
Appendix B: Topics of Focus and Research Hypotheses	198
Appendix C: Coded Survey	205
Appendix D: Sample Interview Questions	216
Appendix E: Criticism of Methods and Suggestions for Future Research	219
Notes	223
Bibliography	227
Index	233

Preface

This book invites readers to visit the music, the experience, and the fans of a dark subculture. Rich in interviews with major scene personalities—from rock stars and radio hosts to the average adolescent fan—it approaches the subculture from every inside angle. At the same time, the book addresses current tendencies of politicians, conservative groups, and typical Americans to attribute youth violence and the destruction of social values to entertainment forms with violent themes. Death Metal is among the most disturbing and despised forms of such entertainment.

Is it possible that a thorough investigation of the Death Metal scene might cast doubt upon the usual assumptions about Death Metal fans? If so, then it is possible to challenge censorship advocates. To this end, the book investigates the demographic trends, attitudes, philosophical beliefs, ethical systems, and behavioral patterns within the scene.

Finally, this work seeks to situate the Death Metal scene in the larger social order. With its extreme depictions of violence, gore, and seemingly all that is antisocial, the Death Metal community proves an intense microcosm for the subcultural phenomenon and lends insight into the psychological and social functions of forbidden or illicit entertainment forms. This analysis of the Death Metal scene provides a key to comprehending deviant tendencies in contemporary culture at large.

The Death Metal scene extends far beyond the boundaries of the United States, and many of the most important contributors to the Death Metal scene are European. Nonetheless, the sample for this study was taken from American Death Metal musicians and fans, and the book will focus on the Death Metal scene in the United States.

The book is divided into six primary sections. Part I discusses the music itself, with an emphasis on the lyrical content that is most often criticized. The nature of Death Metal music is analyzed and the different subgenres of the scene are explored. This section also looks at the activity and atmosphere of Death Metal shows themselves, as well as the appearance and behavior of show attendees.

Part II describes the history of the Death Metal scene. It is divided into three chapters marking significant periods in the history of Death Metal: 1984–1988, 1989–1994, and 1995–2002. This history is related through the experiences of the major bands of each period as the scene evolved. Much of this information is derived from interviews with key musicians and scene personalities.*

Part III introduces the politics of censorship and delves into the controversy surrounding the scene. The first chapter, *The Skeleton in America's Closet*, describes popular opinions about the destructive potential of Death Metal music and the negative behavior of its fans. The second and third chapters of the section describe the politics of media censorship in the United States and speculate about censorship prospects for Death Metal music and other forms of violent entertainment.

Part IV tests the validity of the opinions of would-be censors using data obtained through research. This lengthy section analyzes the research findings, their implications, and their relationship to existing literature on metal fans. The second chapter of the section contains a report and analysis of all of the demographic data gathered from the surveys, interviews, and direct observations. It addresses topics such as age, gender, race, socioeconomic status, education levels, employment rate, family situation, and depression. A third chapter focuses on the attitudes of Death Metal fans toward social institutions and life in general. This chapter analyzes views on religion, marriage, politics, and capitalism, as well as perceived chances of success and ideological orientation. The fourth chapter in Part IV contains data on the philosophical and ethical traits of the study population. Personal metaphysical views, faith, ethical systems, and "metal philosophy" itself are examined here. The remaining chapters in the section are perhaps the most socially relevant chapter of this study. They look at the behavior of metal fans, reporting statistics on sexual activity, alcohol use, drug use, and violent behavior.

In assessing the findings reported in Part IV, it is important to keep an accurate understanding of the nature of the study, its methods, and its aims. There should be no attempts to generalize on the basis of the information gathered and reported here. Field research, snowball sampling, and haphazard nationwide surveys proved the best methods to use for the purposes of this study. These methods, however, are not reliable tools in the social sciences and do not permit the drawing of even vague conclusions. Therefore, the purpose of this study is not to draw conclusions, but rather to raise new questions and to cast doubt on some existing and unwarranted conclusions about the population of Death Metal fans.

Part V takes us inside the mind of the metal head and the heart of the underground. In light of the analysis of metal fans thus far undertaken, the first chapter examines the reasons why persons choose to become involved in the Death Metal scene, analyzing the nature and value of the subcultural phenomenon. The second chapter speculates as to the meaning of the rebellious anti-religious nature of many Death Metal lyrics, and the third chapter discusses the significance of horror, gore, and porn (all dominant Death Metal themes) in American culture.

The Epilogue contains reflections on the author's personal experience of Death Metal and her conclusions about the role and value of the Death Metal scene in America. The book closes with several appendices that students and researchers may find of interest. Appendix A explains the project's goals, implications, and methodology. (Methods of data collection included examinations of surveys, metal CDs, and interviews with fans and musicians.) Appendix B will be of interest to those who wish to analyze the process of operationalization and the correlation between expected findings and actual findings. Appendices C and D present the research instruments utilized to collect data: a coded sample survey and sample interviews. Appendix E contains a criticism of the research methods employed, and suggestions for further research in the area of Death Metal.

In summary, this work will explore nearly every aspect of the American Death Metal scene, including its most vile elements. To challenge censors, metal's "worst" elements are precisely what must be embraced and understood. This study will not attempt to prove that Death Metal is a positive thing in spite of its offensive content. Instead, it will research the most horrific content in order to see if it does indeed have negative or positive effects. This project aims at pure honesty and full disclosure. Some of its content may be offensive because it will be entirely uncensored. This is exactly what Americans must confront if they wish to understand the music and the people who love it.

In the course of this study, the reader will encounter a number of names repeatedly. These are those persons who participated in the in-depth interviews and were willing to be identified by name. It seems appropriate to give the reader a preliminary introduction to these persons and to explain their relationship to the metal scene.

Adrianne Buchta, 21, is a devoted Death Metal fan from Jersey City, New Jersey. A college student and communications major, Adrianne is a DJ at Seton Hall University's Pirate Radio Station, WSOU. This is the most successful college radio station in the nation. Until recently, WSOU featured a hard rock format and played Death Metal music.

Iris Duran, 22, resides in New Jersey and is a well-known figure in the East Coast Death Metal Scene. Iris, a graduate of Seton Hall University, is known for her former work as the DJ of Monday Night Mayhem, the exclusively Death and Black Metal show on SHU's WSOU.

John Dreisbach, 20, is a metal fan and musician from Philadelphia, Pennsylvania. He is currently a member of the Death Metal band With Immortality. John plays the drums and is skilled in the technical composition of Death Metal music.

King Fowley, 33, who resides in Arlington, Virginia, knows the metal scene as no one else. A revered scene personality for many years, Fowley is best known for his work as the vocalist and drummer for Deceased. Fowley has been involved in various other metal bands, including October 31st and Doomstone.

John Gallagher of Maryland is a respected Death Metal guitarist and vocalist. One of the founding members of the band Dying Fetus in 1991, Gallagher remains a part of the band today.

Rob George, 20, is a metal fan from northern Connecticut. He has worked as an active volunteer for Nuclear Blast America, a music label that has produced a great deal of Death Metal music. Rob George is currently a business major at Seton Hall University and a DJ at the WSOU radio station.

Peter Helmkamp, 32, is a Death Metal musician residing in Tampa, Florida. He is known for his work in bands such as Order from Chaos (1989–1995) and Angelcorpse (1995–2000). Originally from Kansas City, Helmkamp earned a BA in history from the University of Missouri, Kansas City, and currently works for a major mobile phone company. His present musical endeavor is Terror Organ.

Brian Jimenez, 21, is a devoted metal head and musician from Union, New Jersey. He is a graduate of a New Jersey media and communications technical school. Brian has played drums for a number of bands, including Funebrarum.

Killjoy is a prominent Death Metal vocalist, whose work has helped to define the very lyrical and musical nature of the genre. He is most known for his past and present involvement in the band Necrophagia. Killjoy's current bands also include Wurdulak, Ravenous, Enoch, Hellpig, Amicuss, and Viking Crown. For more information on Killjoy and his musical endeavors, visit www.necrophagia.com and www.baphometrecords.com.

John J. Longstreth, 25, is a notable musician currently residing in Kansas. He now plays drums for the band Origin, and is known for his work with Angelcorpse.

Matthew Medeiros, 23, is a student, musician, DJ, and metal fan from New Jersey. Medeiros is pursuing a philosophy degree at Rutgers University and is currently the metal director of 90.3 WVPH, a position which gives him industry contact as well as early access to upcoming releases from across all metal genres. His radio show, Audio Apocalypse, has given him the opportunity to interview legendary acts such as Cannibal Corpse and Six Feet Under. As a skilled guitarist and songwriter, Medeiros has been involved in music composition, performance, and touring with several bands including Keokarnia and Eschaton.

Nefarious plays bass and performs vocals for the Chicago-based band Macabre. Macabre—a band still composed entirely of its original members—has provided fans with innovative "murder metal" since 1985. Nefarious also plays acoustic guitar for the Macabre Minstrels.

Jason Netherton, 29, currently resides in Washington, D.C. Netherton has an MA in International Communication and a BA in International Politics from the American University. He is a musician, lyricist, and songwriter best known for his previous work in the Death Metal band Dying Fetus. Netherton is currently involved in another Metal/Grindcore band, Misery Index. In addition to his musical endeavors, he operates and contributes social commentary to the website Demockery.org. Jason has been active in the labor movement and has worked with various organizations promoting workers' rights.

Seth Newton, 24, is a Death/Black Metal musician residing in northern Virginia. He currently plays bass, guitar, and keyboards, and does backing vocals for the band Witch-Hunt.

Paul Ryan, 28, has performed guitar and vocals for the band Origin on Relapse Records since 1993.

Karl Sanders, 38, resides in Greenville, South Carolina. Sanders is famous for his work as guitarist and vocalist for the band Nile, one of the most respected bands to recently achieve prominence in the Death Metal scene.

Erik Sayenga, 24, is a drummer living in northern Virginia. Sayenga, who composes the music of the Black Metal band Witch-Hunt, has done studio work for Aurora Borealis and is best known for his current position as drummer for the band Dying Fetus.

Kyle Severn, 31, is a metal drummer and carpenter from Ohio. Severn is best known for his work as the drummer of the seminal Death Metal band Incantation. He is a devoted metal fan who has been and continues to be involved in numerous bands, including Wolfen Society, Acheron, and Funerus.

Jeremy Turner, 27, is a musician from Topeka, Kansas. He is currently a guitarist and vocalist of the band Origin. Turner is a vocational school graduate and a certified welder.

Bill "Zebub" is the editor-in-chief of the most widely circulated international Black and Death Metal magazine, *The Grimoire of Exalted Deeds*. Bill is from Clifton, New Jersey, and is somewhat of an icon in the metal scene of the United States. His work can be viewed at www.thegrimoire.com, and the magazine can be ordered by writing to Grimoire of Exalted Deeds, PO Box 1987, Clifton, NJ 07011.

Several other fans and musicians who did not provide their names for publication were interviewed. The aforementioned persons, however, were involved in in-depth interviews that form the heart of this analysis. Their personal experiences and insights were invaluable to the success of this project. The ample cooperation and friendly assistance offered by so many Death Metal fans and musicians speaks positively about their culture and their attitudes. Because attaining even a remotely representative sample for this study was difficult, it was necessary to rely on snowball sampling methods that demanded cooperation and mass e-mailings to strangers scattered across the United States. The lengthy surveys were sent via e-mail with a plea for readers to complete and return them. It was natural to wonder whether anyone would be willing to devote to a stranger the significant portion of time it would take to fill out one of the surveys.

Such apprehension underestimated the unity and allegiance of metal fans. It seems that when people feel as though they are despised or condemned, they will unite to support one another. Not only was a decent response rate achieved, but along with the returned surveys came a number of e-mails in defense of the scene and notes reporting that respondents had forwarded the survey to metal fans they knew in order to help out with the project. This enthusiastic response and remarkable degree of cooperation says a great deal about the Death Metal scene and the persons involved in it.

Part I
Defining Death Metal

1

The Genre and Its Sub-Genres

This chapter contains a very rough definition of Death Metal for those entirely unfamiliar with it, followed by a detailed discussion of the nature of the genre and the various sub-genres of Death Metal.* Death Metal music is usually fast, low, powerful, intense, and played very loudly. The guitars are often tuned down. A great deal of Death Metal consists of speedy, chaotic guitar riffs such as those found in the music of Cannibal Corpse or most Death Metal bands hailing from Florida. Other bands play slow, deep, repetitive tunes with resounding and spooky guitars. In Death Metal, drums are often very dominant and very fast. Hyper double-bass blast beats, which mimic the sound of a machine gun firing, are common and are utilized frequently. Many New York style bands like Suffocation, Dying Fetus, and Internal Bleeding are slam-oriented and bass-based; this sort of music promotes dancing with rapid shifts from low and slow to fast and blast. In general, Death Metal music is very extreme. Lyrics and vocals aside, this is not the sort of music one would ever hear on a commercial radio station or on MTV.

The lyrics and vocals, which would strike the casual listener before anything else, only augment the extremity of the music. In society at large, Death Metal is probably best known for its vocals. Those who are outside of the scene typically classify it according to the vocals, ignoring the definite trends in the instrumental music itself. (Such classification might irk some metal fans, who are insulted whenever pop music with growling vocals is labeled Death Metal.) Jason Netherton describes Death Metal vocals as "guttural growling, screeching, screaming, grungy sorts of manipulations

Alex Webster of Cannibal Corpse. Photograph by Bill Zebub.

1. The Genre and Its Sub-Genres

of the throat and stomach," and comments that the lyrical "subject matter is not generally what is heard in mainstream music. There's more attention to darker themes." Although the vast majority of Death Metal bands do use very low, beast-like, almost indiscernible growls as vocals, many also have high and screechy or operatic vocals, or simply deep and forcefully sung vocals. In nearly all Death Metal, the vocals take backstage to the music. The vocals conform to the instrumental style, rather than vice-versa.

When asked what defines Death Metal, musicians and authorities responded as follows:

> I would say in the beginning of Death Metal, it was the unpronounced growling vocals. Then came the blast beats.—Paul Ryan, Origin

> To me, it was always the vocals. If it has the vocals and the aggressive music there to some extent, it's definitely metal.—Jason Netherton, Misery Index, Dying Fetus

> Death Metal is generally referred to as any music characterized by a combination of down-tuned instruments, fast drumming (and use of the so-called "blast beat"), churning riffs, and gruff vocals that can be screamed but are typically grunted in a low, guttural voice.—Matt Medeiros, Eschaton

> Because of the various substrata, the telltale sign of Death Metal is the vocals. The vocals are usually guttural and low-pitched. When you hear a Death Metal vocalist, you should be under the impression that you are hearing a demon.—Bill Zebub, The Grimoire

> The beauty of Death Metal [is that] there can be so many forms of it, that it is difficult to classify. Some of the [essential elements] would have to be fast double bass, low guttural voice, heavy sounding down-tuned guitars.—Jeremy Turner, Origin

> Metal, especially Death Metal, is whatever you want it to be. 'You can be as fast as you want, as slow as you want, as heavy or technical as you want' [according to] D. Vincent.—John Longstreth, Origin

> True Death Metal to me is metal that is played from your fuckin' soul.—Kyle Severn, Incantation, Wolfen Society, Acheron, Funerus

> True Death Metal is Death Metal where it is apparent that the band has put effort and thought into their song composition to make it heavy, captivating, and of course brutal. Good bands take elements set forth from the

I. DEFINING DEATH METAL

pioneers of the late 80s and early 90s, but find a way to make it their own.— Iris Duran, WSOU

> For me personally, Death Metal is raw, hideous, sick music with blood curdling vocals. ... I guess everyone concentrates on gore-drenched lyrics and artwork.— Killjoy, Necrophagia

Death Metal musicians often take pride in the technical nature of their music. Many affirm that it is extremely different from popular music, predominantly because it is more complicated, more difficult to play, and more technically impressive. Whether this is true is a matter much contested in the scene. Paul Ryan of Origin describes the difference between the music he performs and pop music: "The music we create is absolute chaos, a very real expression of extremity.... It's not processed. In fact, I would say it's a hard listen. Most people today have an implanted mentality on the music they listen to. They don't want to think. They are like cattle and the music is grass: easily digested, easily disposed." Countless musicians feel similarly. When asked about the relationships between pop music and Death Metal, they responded as follows:

> Traditionally pop music has used the standard 'verse, chorus, verse, chorus, bridge, solo, verse, chorus' format, which makes it predictable and stagnant. Death Metal has no standard framework. A good Death Metal song will keep the listener on the edge of his seat while the song twists and turns through numerous time changes and scale patterns.— John Gallagher, Dying Fetus

> Metal musicians actually write and perform their own music. Most pop, especially contemporary pop, is manufactured like processed fast food to be packaged nice and glossy where looks and fleeting trends are everything. Metal, on the other hand, is timeless music that comes from the soul and has little to do with the musicians' photogenic features or dance steps. Pop artists only attract trend-following fans temporarily because they are spoon-fed to the masses and because they are "in" at the moment.— Iris Duran, WSOU

> There were good pop bands, but I would say for music these days, metal is definitely the best music talentwise, in a technical sense. It's basically bastardized classical music.— Nefarious, Macabre

> In extreme metal ... it takes a lot more talent to play the instruments properly. In pop, there's a lot of very simple timing and song structures. In pop, the hard part is writing something memorable that will be catchy and

1. THE GENRE AND ITS SUB-GENRES

brain-washing to the masses. That's easier said than done.—Killjoy, Necrophagia

On the one hand, certainly playing [Death Metal with] a hundred riffs in a song, with 50 different drum beats, and 20 different time changes, certainly that's trickier than anything you're gonna hear on the dance floor. But, there are many kinds of popular music, like well-done jazz, that are every bit as complex as Death Metal and sometimes more.... I don't have some narrow-minded opinion that Death Metal is the be-all and end-all in music. I think it can be very powerful and it can be very musical but it can also be retarded.—Karl Sanders, Nile

I like a lot of pop music for the simplicity of it. A catchy song is a catchy song—gotta admire a good melody line. Being a songwriter, I can see the glory in that. Metal music can be very stunning and very intense when all cylinders are clicking. It can also sound like a true pile-of-shit noise. It's a band-to-band, case-to-case topic.—King Fowley, Deceased, October 31st, Doomstone

Death Metal bands [unlike pop bands] have artistic freedom. There is nothing that a Death Metal band can do or put into an album that will lose fans, other than weakening the music. Death Metal personalities are also not crafted by publicists. All Death Metal musicians are down-to-earth, and their lyrics and concepts stay in the realm of the listener's mind.—Bill Zebub, The Grimoire

Death Metal and Jazz are the most musically complicated things. It's really mindless—all the pop music—with electronic drums and stuff. Death Metal takes people who are really into the music and their instruments. It does require some kind of training.—Erik Sayenga, Dying Fetus, Witch-Hunt

I think that pop music is created for the simple-minded. Most of it is in simple timing, with a catchy tune that is easy on the ears. It is usually written by someone else other than the person actually performing it. Metal is harsh on the ears, often with odd time changes. It is fast, aggressive music that usually frightens those who are not used to it.—Jeremy Turner, Origin

Even some of the simplest Death Metal is higher in quality and more complex [than pop]. A lot of Death Metal is very technical in some form or another. It could be very aggressive playing or twisted technical songwriting. There is always something going on in metal. Pop music is just gay, simple-minded music.—Kyle Severn, Incantation, Wolfen Society, Acheron, Funerus

Not all metal is complex. But a lot of metal music does two things that are virtually alien to pop: it incorporates many tempo changes that can bewilder a shallow listener, and bolder bands have little or no repetition within a song, so there is no "hook" that is so precious to pop.— Bill Zebub, *The Grimoire*

Death Metal shows a lot more musical abilities than pop music. In Death Metal, you get a lot of jazzy kinds of things going on with the guitars. Classical music, all sorts of music [are] elements of Death Metal. I think anybody playing in a good, solid Death Metal band could pull off what most pop bands do, but I think a lot of pop band musicians could not pull off Death Metal. It's really easy to shove a song out in pop music. You could come up with five riffs for one song, whereas in Death Metal, you've got so many time changes.— Seth Newton, Witch-Hunt

For the most part, I would agree with the statement [that metal music is higher in quality and more musically complex than pop]. That is not to say that all Death Metal is genius and all pop is crap; in some cases, the opposite is true. Bands like Death, Morbid Angel, or Cannibal Corpse represent a type of Death Metal that is much more musically complex than most pop. Pop tends to contain more formulaic song structures, which (obviously) give it structure. Death Metal needn't, but often does, lack this structure, which, for its fans, adds a level of complexity and intricacy, and for its non-fans, adds another layer of confusion. Death Metal is complicated, but not always in a structured way.— Matt Medeiros, Eschaton

These comments appear to be representative of a great many metal musicians. They are frequently very proud of the complex, highly technical nature of their art form. As Killjoy from Necrophagia has written, "I get bored easily with one-dimensional low guttural vocals and an album full of blast beats. I need variety and actual songwriting to keep my interest." This is not to affirm that all metal music fits this description. It is the case, however, that metal music is truly music, not mere noise as its critics declare.

Death Metal fans often reject the mainstream hard rock that is labeled metal because they do not feel it is as musically worthwhile. Record companies and popular music commentators have been announcing the return of metal with the recent popularity of bands such as Slipknot and Limp Bizkit: "It's back, big time!" announces *Billboard* magazine (Flick 4). For *Billboard* magazine, Bryan Reesman writes: "Thundering into the millennium — the class of 2000 will rise" (Reesman 32). Many Death Metal fans do not consider such mainstream music to have anything in common with their music, which they hold to be much more complex and difficult to play and compose. When asked what they thought of the metal on MTV, most interviewees responded by denying that there was any real metal on MTV. Others take a far more benign view of New Metal. Erik Sayenga thinks "it's cool what bands like Slipknot are doing. They're bringing In Flames [a melodic Death Metal band] on tour. They're making people realize there's a more extreme side of music that is accessible. It makes kids look into things at Best Buy, wondering, 'Is there anything like Slipknot?' And then they start getting into other bands."

Many musicians and fans of Death Metal are more hesitant in singing the praises of mainstream metal. These reasons often go far deeper than simple distaste for the simplistic nature of mainstream music. Whether Death Metal music could ever go mainstream and still be Death Metal is a matter much contested. Jason Netherton has suggested that "to commercialize [Death Metal] would mean it would have to be packaged and diluted to the point where it would be acceptable to a larger audience. It would have to cross genres to be acceptable to a variety of people." Many noteworthy musicians like Killjoy of Necrophagia, Nefarious of Macabre, and Erik Sayenga of Dying Fetus have declared that they would not mind the mainstreaming of Death Metal, if it could remain unchanged and yet earn more money. Many, however, are very hesitant. Even Sayenga is concerned that, if Death Metal went mainstream, "it would just turn into another trend." Origin members Jeremy Turner and Paul Ryan also have mixed feelings on the matter. Ryan admits that "it would be great to have totally sold-out shows and money, but are the people really into the music? I admire the fact that the people who come to the shows are really into Death Metal ... live it, love it." Turner is more concerned with the inevitable watering-down of the music that he feels would occur if Death Metal went mainstream, but he believes that greater publicity would be good for the music because "there are definitely people who haven't heard this style of music who would like it if exposed to it."

Perhaps these mixed feelings result from some fundamental incongruity between subculture and mainstream culture. Karl Sanders emphatically states that "part of Death Metal is that it's anti-commercial." He goes onto explain that, even when Death Metal has come ominously near to mainstream culture — such as the infamous Cannibal Corpse performance in *Ace Ventura: Pet Detective* — it has done so "in defiance of every other sort of music. ... That was a part of its charm: its rebellious spirit, its middle-finger in the face of the mainstream. ... If you don't have at least some of that rebellious, defiant, blasphemous spirit, it's going to be lame." Jason Netherton believes this is the case:

There's too many contradictions in the idea of Death Metal going main-

> stream. It just couldn't happen, or it wouldn't be the same anymore. It's a contradiction to say that anything that's so blatantly anti-mainstream in its character could ever be commercialized. ... I think there are a lot of reasons Death Metal fans don't like mainstream music other than they don't feel it's complex in the way it's played or composed. I think it's just a visceral rejection of mainstream culture, whether it's conscious or not. They know there's something wrong, what's going on is more than what they're spoon-fed. So they seek out other things. Some people seek out Goth music, whatever sort they fall into. And they find the new stuff more interesting. They think there's something more real about it, something that speaks to them more than the Backstreet Boys or whatever.

With these words, Jason Netherton is suggesting that that the very definition of Death Metal is tied into something greater than its musical attributes, its sound, its images, its popularity. It is difficult to define Death Metal without defining the subcultural phenomenon itself, a topic that will be taken up in later chapters. For now, let it suffice to say that Death Metal is more than a genre of music or even a number of genres. It is a "scene," a subculture, a phenomenon. Before we jump into any analysis of these abstractions, however, the concrete attributes of Death Metal music must be defined. What follows is an introduction to the musical styles of the major sub-genres in Death Metal music.

The most early and influential bands of the late 1980s and early 1990s created different forms of Death Metal music, many of which evolved into semi-independent sub-genres. Most sub-genres are only vaguely defined; there is a great deal of crossover among genres, and sometimes elements of other forms of music are incorporated into Death Metal. In any discussion of Death Metal music, one will encounter the term "brutal." Matthew Harvey has defined musical brutality as "a general lack of overtly melodic elements in the music; guttural, deep Death Metal vocals; chunky, rhythmic guitar riffs ideal for moshing; and frequent use of high speed, double-bass drumbeats." Bands are often judged in terms of brutality, drumming speed, and guitar-work complexity.

One prominent sub-genre of Death Metal is labeled "Florida Death Metal." (It is important to note that despite the geographical labels applied to classifications of Death Metal, the classes are now based more on musical style, for styles that originated in particular areas spread far and wide throughout the country.) The Floridian style is defined by a number of unique musical attributes. The guitars in Floridian Death Metal are not generally tuned as low as in other forms of Death Metal. The guitar-work is more tight, precise, and clear. Extremely fast, machine gun–like blast beats characterize the drumming in Floridian Death Metal. Of the

Erik Rutan of Hate Eternal and formerly Morbid Angel performs in 2002. Photograph by N.J. Purcell.

bands that designed and popularized the Floridian sound, Death, Morbid Angel, and Cannibal Corpse are the most successful. Other key bands in Florida Death Metal include Malevolent Creation, Deicide, Obituary, and Monstrosity.

These bands and many others worked with Scott Burns, the famous sound engineer of Florida's Morrisound studio. The high quality Morrisound production helped Florida to become the focal point of the Death Metal Scene in the early 1990s, as the popular sound spread. Even bands like Canada's Gorguts and New York's Cannibal Corpse (later relocated to Florida) would adopt the Sunshine State's style. The development of the Florida sound in the early 1990s helped to distinguish Death Metal from other popular forms of metal like Thrash Metal. Matt Medeiros writes, "By this time, producers had an idea of how to record heavy music. The primitive, raw feel of most bands prior to this would evolve into a thicker, more brutal sound," much thanks to Florida's Morrisound Studio. Many Florida bands made contributions to the development of this distinctive Death Metal style. Matt Medeiros reports that greater technical complexity was spurred by Monstrosity's "Imperial Doom," while a "groove element" was popularized by Obituary and Malevolent Creation. In terms of vocal style, the Florida sound owes a debt to Chris Barnes of early Cannibal Corpse and Glen Benton of Deicide, both of whom delivered ferociously low, indecipherable vocals.

Today, Floridian bands Morbid Angel and Cannibal Corpse remain central to the Death Metal scene. Perhaps the most influential and emulated bands in Death Metal, Morbid Angel and Cannibal Corpse have influenced the work of countless notable bands including Deeds of Flesh, Deranged, and Severe Torture. Eric Rutan of Morbid Angel created a popular spin-off band of his own called Hate Eternal. Of Morbid Angel's progenitors, Nile of South Carolina has achieved much success in recent years. Nile and Morbid Angel both feature lyrics grounded in ancient myths and utilize some similar musical tactics. The Floridian band Angelcorpse (originally from Missouri) has also found success with a style quite similar to that of early Morbid Angel. Interestingly, many of the bands emerging from Brazil in recent years have adopted sounds heavily influenced by Morbid Angel. Among these are Abhorrence, Nephasth, Rebaelliun, and Mental Horror. The European Black Metal scene owes a heavy debt to Morbid Angel as well, for the band's sound has been incorporated into the work of major European bands like Emperor, Zyklon, and Dimmu Borgir.

As important as the Florida sound has been in the global Death Metal scene, its significance is matched by the New York style of Death Metal.

Matthew Harvey writes that "the New York style of Death Metal is based around down-tuned, muscular, palm-muted 'slam' riffs that are ideal for moshing." Suffocation is generally credited with defining the New York style. Suffocation's *Human Waste* EP and *Effigy of the Forgotten* album incorporated many of the elements of the Floridian style but added an emphasis on rhythm and frequent time and tempo changes. "Suffocation created churning, crushing breakdowns which would become the mark of the New York style of Death Metal," writes Medeiros. This sound became increasingly popular in the mid–1990s. Slow "slam" riffs helped bands like Internal Bleeding and Pyrexia, inspired by Suffocation, to become successful in the mid 1990s.

Today, New York style bands like Skinless and Dying Fetus dominate the scene with "crowd-pleasing mosh riffs and complex arrangements," reports Harvey. Of the two bands, Dying Fetus is the more prominent. John Gallagher, the only founding member of Dying Fetus who remains in the band has characterized the music as "brutal Death Metal with slam sections, technical passages, and pure aggression. Our style has gotten a bit more technical in recent years, but still retains the simplistic, heavy beat-down of the early days." Jason Netherton, formerly of Dying Fetus, describes the band's music as "a mixture of Death Metal, Grindcore, and Hardcore." Dying Fetus is also known for its distinctive vocal style, which includes two vocalists. Until 2000, "longtime lead singer Jason Netherton used a more mid-range growl to offset guitarist John Gallagher's sepulchral rasp," reports Harvey.

Like Dying Fetus, Skinless has incorporated Suffocation-style mosh riffs into the band's highly entertaining performance. Skinless and other bands, including Malignancy and Fleshgrind, have united this style of music with gory Cannibal Corpse-style lyrics to create a very popular combination. Skinless's first and second albums (*Progression Toward Evil* and *Foreshadowing Our Demise*, respectively) feature blast beats, non-linear arrangements, and very humorous gore lyrics, apparently intended to delight *and* disgust.

While New York Death Metal is commonly defined by the style of the aforementioned bands, a substantially different sort of Death Metal also arose from the New York area. This style may be heard in the work of New York bands like Incantation, Immolation, and Mortician. Immolation emerged on the scene first, releasing two demos as Rigor Mortis in 1986 and 1987. In the following four years, Immolation would release two more demos and a debut album, establishing the band's name and reputation. With the first album, "Dawn of Possession," Immolation offered listeners extremely deep vocals, menacing guitar work, and anti-Christian lyrics.

Ross Dolan of Immolation. Photograph by Bill Zebub.

Immolation paid close attention to tempo, time, and pace changes. Resonating and haunting slow sections offset fast-paced menacing riffs. Immolation has remained a major force in the Death Metal Scene with the release of three more albums: "Here in After," "Failures for Gods," and "Close to a World Below."

As Immolation grew in popularity, Incantation (from New Jersey) emerged in the New York scene. Like Immolation, Incantation featured extremely deep vocals, haunting slow sections, and anti-Christian lyrics. The two bands also accented their guitar work by placing high-pitched notes within the deep, low music. Since the release of debut album *Onward to Golgotha* in 1992, Incantation has released five albums, most recently *Blasphemy*.

Mortician must be mentioned in conjunction with Immolation and Incantation. In 1990, Mortician released the *Brutally Mutilated* EP featuring singer/bassist Will Rahmer, who had done vocal session work for Incantation. Mortician shares with and even surpasses Immolation and Incantation in depth of vocals. Mortician also uses extremely low guitar-tuning and constant sound samples from horror movies. After the death of the band's drummer, Mortician released *House by the Cemetery* using the exceptionally fast and precise beats of a drum machine rather than a human drummer. Mortician would continue to use a drum machine for subsequent releases *Hacked Up for Barbecue*, *Zombie Apocalypse*, *Chainsaw Dismemberment*, and *Domain of Death*. The band can be credited with making use of a drum machine acceptable; this method has been used successfully by notable bands like Agoraphobic Nosebleed, Centinex, and Damnable.

As the American Death Metal scene developed, the Grindcore Movement was blossoming in Europe. British band Napalm Death spearheaded the movement with the debut album *Scum* and its follow-up, *From Enslavement to Obliteration*. Napalm Death featured incredibly fast and short songs, packing 27 or 28 into an album. The music featured deep and raspy vocals, extremely fast drums, unrefined and distorted bass, and simple and fast guitar work. Napalm Death's lyrics were notable for their socio-political content and critical social commentary.

Napalm Death member Bill Steer eventually devoted himself exclusively to his side project Carcass. Carcass' debut album *Reek of Putrefaction* is said to have spurred the British Grindcore movement with its precise riffs and outrageous guitar solos. *Reek of Putrefaction* featured grungy production, high and low-pitched growls, and gore-centered lyrics with elaborate medical terminology. Carcass' following album, *Symphonies of Sickness*, featured slower and catchier songs, and showed the band's movement into the Death Metal genre. The next album, *Necroticism: Descanting the Insalubrious* was pure Death Metal with intricate dynamics, complex structured songs, and refined guitar solos. After the release of *Heartwork*, Carcass moved away from the Death Metal genre. However, the complex melodic songs of the later Carcass material would influence the contemporary Swedish Death Metal movement, which features the slower and more melodious music of bands like In Flames, Dark Tranquility, and Arch Enemy.

Before this newer form of Swedish Death Metal is discussed, the early Swedish Death Metal Movement must be noted. The Swedish musical style is characterized by non-standard and low guitar tuning (resembling Carcass), more melody, and groovier or catchier songs. Many Swedish bands chose to record with the high quality production of Sunlight Studios in Stockholm. Perhaps the earliest Swedish Death Metal band of note is Nihilist. Nihilist released three demos in 1988 and 1989 (*Premature Autopsy*, *Only Shreds Remain*, and *Drowned*). These and the demos of Carnage and Dismember would influence the development of the key Swedish bands Entombed and Unleashed.

In 1990, Entombed released *Left Hand Path*, the album that, in many ways, defined Swedish Death Metal. Despite the high quality of the production, Harvey describes the guitar sound as "the aural equivalent of a chainsaw through flesh." This unique sound, which involves the use of a distortion pedal with all knobs turned to ten, would become the hallmark of Swedish Death Metal. After the release of Entombed's second album *Clandestine*, the band's sound moved closer to the Rock genre than the Death Metal genre. The second very notable Swedish band of the time was Unleashed. Unleashed combined traditional metal dynamics and riffing with Viking themes. Unleashed's material also grew more simplistic as time went on, and the band left the Death Metal genre behind. A third Swedish band that must be mentioned is Grave. Grave used very deep vocals and brutal guitar work to produce heavier music than the typical Swedish material. Grave, too, would later alter their sound, adopting a Hardcore-influenced sound.

After Entombed left the Death Metal genre, Dismember stepped forward to lead the Swedish Death Metal Movement. Dismember released the debut album *Like an Ever Flowing Stream* in 1991. The band would retain the classic Swedish sound with later albums like *Indecent and Obscene* and *Pieces*. It is this sound which would heavily influence the Finnish Death Metal movement in the early 1990s. The Swedish sound can be heard in the early work of bands like Xysma, Amorphis (previously Abhorrence), Convulse, and Demilich.

Gradually the Swedish Death Metal sound morphed into the contemporary Swedish movement with a significantly different sound. The Swedish band Hypocrisy illustrates this transformation. Hypocrisy's early albums (such as *Penetralia*) reflect the classic Swedish sound. In later albums, however, Hypocrisy incorporated sounds from different genres of music, including gothic and pop. These albums, such as *Abducted*, often featured very clean production. Melody and clean production helped to make the band's music commercially viable and even brought it into the European mainstream. Hypocrisy's later sound reflects the beginning of the contemporary Swedish Death Metal movement. This new movement emphasizes the harmonies and melodic aspects of traditional metal, rather than the chaotic and brutal sounds of much Death Metal. The only thing that might be considered "brutal" about this sort of music is the callous vocal style, which is very similar to traditional Death Metal vocals. The two most prominent bands of this sort are In Flames and Dark Tranquility.

As Sweden formed its own brand of Death Metal, yet another sub-genre of Death Metal was emerging in Britain. British bands My Dying Bride and Paradise Lost (heavily influenced by the Swedish band Celtic Frost) produced slow, deep Death Metal with simple yet gloomy songs. They often added operatic female vocals to the mix. According to Harvey, this atmospheric music "relied on slow, lurching tempos and spacious, instrumentally layered arrangements ... miles away from the Death Metal norm." My Dying Bride, Paradise Lost, and several other British bands influenced by this depressed sound developed what is known as Doom Death Metal. The Doom genre would provide a home to bands such as the British Cathedral and Anathema, Finnish Amorphis and Thergothon, Dutch The Gathering, and Australian Disembowelment. In the United States, Winter and Morgion would spread the gloom and ambience of dark Doom Death Metal.

In the late 1990s, a sub-genre now entitled "Old School" Death Metal resurged. This sub-genre is characterized by more simple and primitive music, with less speed, fewer blast beats, and less focus on musical technicality. Pioneering this resurgence is Necrophagia, a band initially formed in the 1980s and re-formed with much publicity in 1998. Other notable bands in this vein include Abscess and Nunslaughter. While in America, "Old School" Death Metal has found new champions in Abscess and The Ravenous; the forerunners in the European scene include Bloodbath, Mortem, and Pentacle.

Another sub-genre of Death Metal that cannot be geographically defined is the Gore-Grind genre. This sub-genre is heavily inspired by early Carcass material. Three Swedish bands—General Surgery, Regurgitate, and Necrony — have created music that falls into this genre and have mimicked the song titles and lyrics of Carcass with elaborate medical terminology. According to Harvey:

> Gore-Grind music is characterized by its preoccupation with pitch-shifted or extremely low vocals, use of gore and forensic pathology as its exclusive subject matter, and often very fast tempos. Grind-Gore bands also have the refreshing tendency not to take themselves or their lyrics too seriously. This is evidenced by song titles like Sanity's Dawn's "Nice to Eat You" and Hemorrhage's "Decom-posers," as well as the often intricate and disgusting yet undeniably cartoonish splatter drawings that adorn many Gore-Grind album sleeves.

The band Dead Infection provides an extreme example of this form of music. The band's *Chapter of Accidents* album is described by Harvey as "a low-end barrage of inhuman noise." The major bands of the current Gore-Grind scene are Sanity's Dawn of Germany and Last Days of Humanity from the Netherlands. In the United States, a few bands have also become well-known for Gore-Grind Death Metal in the vein of Carcass. These include California bands like Impaled, Exhumed and The Meat Shits.

The work of the The Meat Shits might be placed in another category of Death Metal, defined solely on the basis of its lyrical content and unique imagery: the Porn-Grind sub-genre. A focus on pornographic content characterizes the music of several bands, including the German bands Dead and Gut. While Dead retains a Grindcore musical style, Gut's music includes simpler, slower, and more rock-like songs. In America, pornographic imagery has been adopted with success by bands like Lividity and Waco Jesus.

Hopefully, this discussion has revealed that within a single underground music scene, which most people have never even heard of, there is complexity, variety, and specialization. The categories mentioned here are neither exhaustive nor mutually exclusive. The sub-genres continue to grow, diversify, and change as Death Metal music moves into its future.

2

Fundamental Dynamics of the Scene

This chapter will introduce the elements that together make the Death Metal scene a lively and functioning force. These include the clubs that hold shows, the labels that release the music, the fanzines that cover the scene, and the fans and musicians who both look and act the part of Death Metal enthusiasts. The scene has evolved over time: shrinking, expanding, and generally changing in various ways since its emergence in the 1980s. Throughout this period, it has survived and at times prospered through the efforts of dedicated individuals in the Death Metal community.

In the early 1980s, before labels were interested in signing Death Metal bands, tape-trading was the main means of circulating and marketing the music. Bands sent their homemade tapes to other bands all over the country (and sometimes the world). Mass mailings of flyers, demos, and ads for fanzines formed an interconnected network of bands and fans devoted to spreading their music. According to Nefarious of Macabre, being a successful Death Metal band in the early days meant "lots of writing people back, mail order stuff, a lot of interviews, trying to get into magazines, sending free tapes out to people all over the world." Keeping the infant scene alive entailed tremendous effort on the part of musicians. Explains

Seth Newton, "Before the Internet came out, we had to do ground mail, keeping in contact, passing out people's ads. That was the only way to really get your name around — pass things around, trade. You'd make ads for your band, and other bands would give you like ten ads, and each mail you sent to someone, you might put their ad into your mail." Some individuals created their own miniature distribution services, collecting and selling fairly small quantities of Death Metal albums and merchandise.

Killjoy, who was in the scene from the start, had this to say of its early days: "I formed Necrophagia in late 1983 and released our first demo, "Death is Fun," in May 1984. Tape-trading was very big, and there were lots of fanzines that would review demos. Also, trading flyers, stickers, and shirts was going on a lot." Deceased's King Fowley, another important figure in the new scene, reminisced about the early days: "We built a name by giving away over 2,000 free demos of our first tape in '86. I became a devoted 'pen-pal' to many metal friends the world over, and that never stopped! Whether by hand-written letter, phone, or e-mail, it's all communication!" This communication and cooperation brought Death Metal all over the world and laid the foundations of a thriving underground.

Fanzines quickly became an important part of the underground network. Although they were often no more than stapled stacks of copied pages, the zines informed fans about bands and music and provided contact information so fans could order otherwise unavailable albums. Sometimes mainstream metal magazines like *Metal Forces* would carry lists of fanzines to advertise the zines' existence and increase their popularity. Small though notable fanzines of the time included *Neckbrace Deathzine*, *Slayer*, *Total Thrash*, and *Violent Noize*. Later in the 1980s, the mainstream metal press took greater notice of Death Metal bands like Death, Obituary, and Morbid Angel. As Thrash Metal grew less popular, and more and more Death Metal bands sprouted up, Thrash magazines, like *Metal Maniacs*, also covered Death Metal music. Additionally, more professional Death Metal fanzines— including *Sounds of Death*, *Pit Magazine*, and *The Grimoire of Exalted Deeds*— emerged. Bill Zebub, editor-in-chief of the *Grimoire*, tells an interesting tale of the magazine's founding:

> I had a new job at a company that had computers equipped with templates for newsletters. The newsletters were already designed. All I had to do was replace the dummy text with my own material. Actually, that is the only thing I knew how to do. I didn't know how to replace the clip-art, so my first two issues had no horror themes. All the pictures were of cartoon fish, flowers, cats, etc. I became aware of the metal mail network. Bands would mail out flyers for their demos, and as a courtesy, they would include other metal flyers in the envelopes. So I pumped massive quantities of my flyers all over

the world. I had free photocopying privileges, so I started producing mass quantities of my zine and handing them out at metal shows. The fanzine evolved from a photocopied newsletter to a magazine that is full-glossy and almost 50 percent full color! I never planned for this to happen. All I wanted was something metal to do.

Because they provided means for fans to order music — often directly from bands—fanzines were an important force in the scene throughout the 1990s.

Although traditional fanzines are less prevalent today, the Internet has become host to numerous "webzines" which cover Death Metal. These include www.deathgrind.com and www.braindead.com. The Internet has enabled bands to handle publicity, spread their material, and communicate with greater ease. This added convenience has been a boon to the Death Metal scene. At the same time, however, the online culture has had some negative effects on the scene. King Fowley believes that "the Internet has slowed a lot of 'turnouts' for gigs. The whole world is losing their social skills, it seems." Jason Netheron also believes that, in some ways, the World Wide Web has had deleterious impact on the Death Metal Scene:

> The scene has gotten more global; with the advent of the Internet, things are faster in terms of communication or whatever else, but a lot of it gets trivialized. I miss writing actual letters and getting letters in the mail (meaning correspondence with other metal heads all over the world). I would not trade one long, well-written, hand-written letter for 25 half-assed e-mails full of spelling errors and empty of anything substantial to say.

Not surprisingly, early Death Metal bands were not signed to sizable labels; those that did get signed were picked up by small metal labels. Many of these labels, such as Combat, New Renaissance, Cobra, Banzai, and Megaforce, would fade from existence in the early 1990s. By this time, however, larger labels began to sign Death Metal bands that would play an important role in the scene. According to Bill Zebub, this was both a blessing and a curse: "Death Metal enjoyed a period of mass-signings from various labels, like Roadrunner. But it was not a Death Metal dream come true because many talentless bands were offered contracts, and they helped to water down the impact of true Death Metal. Record companies began cutting off the lesser bands and keeping the money-makers." Roadrunner records was among the large labels to take an interest in Death Metal at its commercial peak. Roadrunner, which had established its name through the release of more mainstream Thrash Metal albums, picked up Death Metal bands like Obituary, Deicide, Malevolent Creation, Gorguts, and

Sepultura. Roadrunner still hosts some important Death Metal bands, but in recent years has shifted its focus to more mainstream "New Metal."

Other labels that became important forces in the early 1990s Death Metal scene included Nuclear Blast, Earache, and Relapse. Nuclear Blast Records began in Germany as a predominantly punk label but later released music of Death Metal bands like Pungent Stench and Master. Today, Nuclear Blast focuses on more traditional Heavy Metal. Earache began in Britain, releasing the music of major Grindcore bands like Napalm Death and Carcass. Earache later signed more Death Metal bands and released the albums of important bands like Morbid Angel, Entombed, Bolt Thrower, Repulsion, and Carnage. Earache retains many key Death Metal bands today.

On the whole, Nuclear Blast, Earache, and other larger labels are not terribly interested in Death Metal today. This is a sore subject and a source of concern for many dedicated musicians. Nile's Karl Sanders is thoroughly disappointed with major labels and what he sees as their abandonment of Death Metal musicians:

> There's so many labels that don't actually care. I mean Metal Blade dropped Immolation. In my view, Immolation is one of the one true death metal bands that's actually doing something musically worthwhile. They got *dropped* by Metal Blade. I was talking with the president of our record company [Relapse Records], Matt Jacobson, about Krisiun [a talented Brazilian band], and he said, "You know what, Karl ... no matter how good a band they are, [their record label] doesn't care and isn't going to do what it takes to take them where they deserve to go." Krisiun has gotten what they've gotten because they've busted their ass.

At the moment, Relapse Records is perhaps the most important of the Death Metal labels. An American company, Relapse began in the early 1990s as a distribution service as well as a record label. Relapse signed mostly American Death Metal bands, many of which would become extremely influential in the scene. These early Relapse bands include Incantation, Deceased, Mortician, and Suffocation. Although Relapse uses predominantly small-scale and grass-roots marketing efforts — for instance, having bands tour relentlessly — the label is perhaps the most important force in the Death Metal scene today, featuring notable bands such as Nile, Dying Fetus, and Skinless.

To fully understand the Death Metal scene, one should be familiar with a few of the more superficial traits of Death Metal fans, such as their manner of dress. How would one recognize a metal fan? At shows, metal heads wear black more than any other color. Most of the males have long hair and wear band t-shirts adorned with gory pictures or offensive words. Black jeans are extremely common, but one also sees leather, cargo, and camouflage pants. The typical Death Metal fan wears black boots (though tennis shoes are also frequently found). Fans also commonly wear black leather or denim jackets covered in band-related patches. Some wear metal jewelry or intimidating spikes and bullet belts. Many have tattoos or piercings, although probably not a majority.

The females at Death Metal shows often dress in the same fashion as the males, but they frequently adopt a more feminine style, wearing fitted shirts and pants in dark colors. Gothic fashions, such as long black dresses, are also common among females at Death Metal shows. On the whole, Death Metal fans look very unconventional, and they can appear fairly frightening. Their intentional choice of dark colors, boots, and metal accessories only contributes to this frightening look. (More will be said later on the possible function or meaning of such attire, which will make more sense after the population is better described.) In general, metal fans are quite atypical looking, and the average person would certainly be able to spot one walking towards him on the sidewalk. He might also try to cross the street! There is nothing pretty about metal.

Despite these definite trends in appearance, the clothing and accessories of Death Metal fans have changed to some degree over the years. Iris Duran, who has been attending Death Metal shows for roughly a decade, has made note of the changes over time. According to Iris: "The fashion doesn't appear to have changed too much. It still appears to be your standard band t-shirt and black pants. One noticeable change is less men with long hair. I remember in the early 90s Death Metal explosion, the vast majority of Death Metal musicians and concert attendees had long hair. Now it is not uncommon to attend a show and see half of the men without long hair." King Fowley concurs that "people have lost the hair a lot — a lot of shaved heads ... but the brain under those skulls is pretty much the same." Jason Netherton believes that the differences run slightly deeper and are a consequence of the merging of different underground scenes. For instance, shorter hair can be partially attributed to the introduction of Hardcore fashion styles into the Death Metal genre.

Although there is great continuity in clothing and appearance trends across national boundaries, there are certain differences in the way that metal fans from different areas dress. Kyle Severn has toured all over the world with Incantation, and in his experience, "The fans in the third world countries and in Germany tend to ... wear the old-school attire (denim, leather, and bullet belts). Pretty much everywhere else, metallers are always dressed in black and have leather and spikes." Explains King Fowley, "It

Glen Benton of Deicide. Photograph by Bill Zebub.

really looks quite alike in the smaller and bigger towns—some leather, some jeans, some goth/darkwave-looking people; some shaved heads, some long hair; no real difference. Overseas, you see more of the denim and leather, a lot more of the traditional metal stylings. But ... metal is metal!"

At the heart of the Death Metal scene is the live show. Here, fans congregate, bands play and sell their merchandise, and the social atmosphere is enjoyed by all. The typical Death Metal show attracts under 100 people into a crowded, noisy, generally smoke-filled club. Shows can be held in a variety of places, from small bars to concert halls. Within both the U.S. and Europe, the size of the shows varies, for Death Metal is more popular in some regions than in others. Says Jeremy Turner of Origin, "There seems to be a bigger turnout and a racier reaction on the coasts to our style of music. Big cities usually get really good turnouts. Places like San Francisco have had some crazy, crazy shows." Larger U.S. festivals and major tours can attract several hundred (sometimes even a few thousand) fans. Major annual fests in the United States include the Milwaukee Metalfest, the New England Hardcore and Metal Fest, and the Ohio Death Fest. In Europe, shows and fests are often much larger and can attract many thousands of fans. Discussing the differences in shows between Europe and the United States, Bill Zebub writes:

> America's biggest metal event is the Milwaukee Metalfest, held every year. But metal fans from Europe find it to be a joke. A notable difference between an American metal festival and a European one is the ratio of men to women. There is a far greater number of female metal fans at shows in Europe. Also, the Milwaukee Metalfest is ridiculed worldwide because of the fans who attend—most of them do not look metal at all. Europeans have difficulty understanding the short hair and the non-metal garb.

The European scene is certainly different from the American scene, and in many cases, thrives a great deal more. Musicians claim that they are treated better in Europe by promoters and that the fans are also more appreciative. Commenting on the European scene, Dying Fetus' Erik Sayenga explains that "it is cool to be metal over there. It's crazy. Every night, there's like thousands of people going crazy, asking for autographs, everything." Karl Sanders' experience with Nile has been similar:

> When you go overseas, the kids are much more serious about the music. They know the bands. They know your songs. They come into the show because they like your work, not because you happen to be the show that's in town to save us from boredom. Kids in Europe get shows all the time. They only go to the ones they like. Whereas here, a lot of times, I'll go to a

show and people will be like, "Who're you? What's the name of your band? Never heard of you." And we'll be headlining the show! You know, I have to start to wonder, is not our American metal scene suffering from a lot of the trendy aspects as a lot of other music scenes in America? I think an MTV disease is at the root of it all. American kids are force-fed and dictated culture. And sadly enough, I think that the kids that don't necessarily fit in with the first choice of culture, you know the more popular stuff you see of MTV, those who don't fit in, who are outcasts, a lot of them just fall into these other things. This might be Hardcore, it might be New Metal, it might be Death Metal. But they still suffer from the same sheep-herded, force-fed [mentality]. You know, you tell them what to like and that's what they're gonna like. That's the mentality of America.

Jason Netherton concurs that in America "the lifestyle is mainstream while the music is not. For some of us, metal is a way of life. For others, it's just something that they play driving down the road."

In general, the relatively small size of most metal shows in the United States and the poor promotion that accompanies them reflects poorly on the producers of American shows. Some musicians are deeply appreciative of the efforts of festival promoters (like Jack Koshick, who is behind the Milwaukee fest and other major metal festivals). Other musicians are deeply disillusioned with promoters' efforts. Karl Sanders of Nile has gone so far as to attribute the diminution of the Death Metal scene to "people like Jack Koshick [who are] just siphoning the life out of metal." Sanders vented at length about the poor promotion skills of the masterminds behind today's metal festivals:

> There are times when I go to a show, and I know that show's been booked for months, our record company sent posters, flyers, bought ads, whatever. Do I see any promotion around town? No. How do they expect to make any money if they don't try? It's like they're trying to make some money while doing absolutely the least possible. Well, that's not helping anybody, it's not even helping themselves. If more people were willing to get their hands dirty, to work harder, they'd see the benefits of their hard work, and the scene would be doing better. But I think we've got kind of a lame batch of people in the business right now, who don't care, who are not willing to work hard. They're just taking what money there is and running with the money, not doing anything worthwhile with it.

Other musicians are more satisfied with the efforts of Koshick and his compatriots in the promotion business. After all, some point out, the scene is meant to be underground. Matt Medeiros is more inclined to adopt this perspective: "Turnouts for shows are usually pretty good ... if the scene was bigger, there would be a lot more crap to filter out. ... Sure, I would like metal to be profitable to bands, so I want more kids to come out to shows, but there is a fine line between extra support and saturation."

The size, format, and promotion behind shows are clearly hot topics. This is only appropriate given that shows are the heart and soul of the scene. They are often the main place (in addition to mail-services) to obtain Death Metal albums and other items which are not available at the typical music store. Shows, and particularly festivals, can become underground business extravaganzas for record labels and vendors who set up tables and hawk music and t-shirts. At the typical show, flyers advertising future shows and other bands are distributed. Fans socialize in between and sometimes during sets. Jason Netherton believes that, as the years have progressed, the format of Death Metal shows has remained "essentially just the same. You go to the shows and the fans and Death Metal people are there, and it's sort of like a little cultural gathering."

When the bands are playing, it is often too loud to talk, and most people simply stand and listen, tapping their feet, singing along, or shaking their heads to the beat of the music. While popular bands are playing, fans show their appreciation by "getting into" the music in various ways. According to Iris Duran, the show atmosphere entails "socializing around the borders of the club, people in the pit, people in the front head-banging, people by the merchants, and people at the bar." Metal heads are famous for fist-shaking, head-banging, stage-diving, and moshing. Moshing involves a kind of rough play where fans push and jostle one another in a sometimes harsh, though rarely hostile, manner. Generally, if someone falls down in the mosh pit, those nearby will help him to his feet. Mosh pits are predominantly male phenomena, perhaps because most males are better suited to endure the rough physicality of the pit. Occasionally, however, there are females who participate in moshing activities like their male counterparts.

There are regional differences in the behavior of fans. In the Northeast, mosh pits can look like frenzied kung-fu matches, and many fans engage in slam dancing, which involves slamming their feet on the ground in rhythm with the music. The rest of the U.S. is home to the more traditional mosh pit activities of simple pushing and shoving. Often, in Europe, fans simply head-bang and wave their fists rather than moshing. Writes Incantation's Kyle Severn: "In the past, there seemed to be a lot of head- and fist-banging maniacs. I think nowadays, there's a lot more physical action going on from the fans. You get a lot of slam dancing and even 'fighting' for some of the more brutal and faster bands, especially in the U.S."

Nile show in 2002. Photograph by N.J. Purcell.

Are mosh-pits dangerous? For someone unaccustomed to moshing, they might be. However, no matter how novice the mosher, it is rare for anyone to incur injuries that could be considered serious. In fact, at metal shows, one will almost always find photographers with expensive camera equipment standing confidently and safely very close to the center of the action. Years of field research for this study revealed no casualties suffering more than a scrape or bruise. Interestingly, nearly everyone specifically avoids colliding with females and sometimes males attempt to shield the females. Additionally, metal shows are not dangerous to the by-standing attendee. This is not a situation in which anyone can be randomly drawn or deliberately pulled into the pit. There is no danger save that which fans deliberately and knowingly invite to themselves.

In general, no intentional hurting takes place at Death Metal shows. Therefore, those who describe mosh pits as free-for-all fights are grossly mistaken. Granted, pits are wild and violent and can be dangerous. Typically, however, they are *not* hostile and no one is fighting against his or her fellow dancers. Mosh pits most certainly involve a release of emotion, of passion, and perhaps even of hostility, but, as a general rule, this release is geared towards no one. Instead, such dancing is a shared experience among moshers who envision one another as friends or brothers more than enemies or opponents.

There can certainly be hostile violence at shows, but it is usually not related to the dancing. When mosh pits do provoke violence, it is usually because someone came to the show in search of a violent encounter, which happens in the Death Metal scene and most other scenes as well. There are certainly some people who, like many Americans, assume metal shows are violent, and therefore attend shows out of a desire to begin a fight. This is relatively rare. More often, violence takes place when shows are held at bars and many of the persons in attendance are intoxicated. The music alone does not provoke violence, but the alcohol seems to. Although drunken bar room brawls do occur at shows, most fans seem disgusted with them. Death Metal shows are rare enough and violence would discourage club owners from booking Death Metal acts. This alone can make Death Metal fans quite averse to violent encounters.

This aversion was revealed in a number of the interviews. When interviewees were asked what they disliked most about the scene, a large number of them mentioned the violent individuals who can ruin the fun for everyone else. Metal fan Rob George stated that he hates most "the people who drink too much at shows and get into stupid fights." Adrianne Buchta agreed, stating that the thing she dislikes most about metal shows is "stupid people who get into asinine fights." John Dreisbach cited disgust with occasional fighting as the reason why he does not go to more shows. Musician Matthew Medeiros, formerly of the band Eschaton, elaborates on this problem:

> Granted, this violence [in the metal scene] is not nearly as pervasive as non-members of the scene would have you believe, but there have been instances of hostility in the past. When this happens [at shows], people don't look at it in terms of the scene. They look at it in terms of two people who have a problem with each other which may actually have nothing to do with the music or the culture in any way. ... People get drunk and do stupid shit. They throw shit or start fights. It's ridiculous ... For me, the good of the scene outweighs the bad, but there is plenty of bad.

In general, all of those metal fans interviewed indicated that violence was no more likely at a Death Metal show than at a bar where some other sort of music is played. Research by Matt Medeiros found that bouncers working at shows overwhelmingly affirmed that they would prefer to work at a metal show than any pop show because there were fewer fights and less violence in the metal scene.

A primary aspect of a Death Metal show, namely the social interaction between songs and sets, is friendly and nonviolent. Many attendees report this to be a main attraction at shows. It is a chance to meet people who share similar interests, to hang out, and to interact socially. Several of those interviewed indicated that social interaction was their primary reason for going to shows rather than just listening to music at home. When asked why they attend shows, interviewees brought up the better quality and intensity of the music, the chance to see one's idols in person, and most of all, the social atmosphere. Matthew Medeiros claims that social interaction is the aim of shows: "When there's a show and people are antisocial, I complain that they should just stand around at home." It seems that for most metal fans, concerts are a fun, social experience more than anything else.

The performers often feel similarly. While in most genres of music, there is a sharp division between the idols upon the stage and the screaming fans below, in Death Metal there is more of a partnership or brotherhood between performers and listeners. Band members frequently find their way into the audience when they are not on the stage. Fans are often able to converse with the very musicians they came to watch. Band members themselves find this to be a rewarding experience. Says John Longstreth of Origin, "As far as the members of the band and the fans go, it's one and the same. We are the same people—just metal heads, just fans."

Of course, musicians have the added responsibility of stepping on stage and providing the audience with sometimes remarkable and often wild performances. In a purely physical sense, Death Metal music is demanding upon musicians. Arguably, the average Death Metal drummer must pull off an act more aerobically taxing than any 'NSYNC routine. Every band member is expected to put heart and soul into the performance. Of his time as the bassist and singer of Angelcorpse, Pete Helmkamp writes:

> You must have the persona on stage—the tough, fierce, brutal dictator (the General as I've been called) on stage vomiting out the lyrics, banging your head until your eyes pound, and ripping away on the bass ... but then off stage, you must be approachable, must be a man in a world of men, where folks can speak with you on an even keel, can ask your opinion (and that they'll get), can give you theirs. I'd like to think that my presence both on and offstage has made an indelible impression on those who've crossed paths with me.

Helmkamp's vision is shared by many musicians who adore the experience of thrilling the audience. Sherwood of Skinless is a notable example. An impressive vocalist, and all around "nice guy," Sherwood's stage antics have earned him a reputation for excitement and insanity. His fre-

Pete Helmkamp performs in Angelcorpse. Photograph by Robin Mazen.

quent stage dives — microphone in hand — into an audience full of screaming, moshing fans demonstrate the lengths to which Death Metal musicians will go to please and commune with an audience. Jason Netherton best expressed this sentiment: "Playing live is the best feeling in the world. It's the justification for everything you go through — just for that moment, to play your music live."

In conclusion, the Death Metal underground is a cultural environment that provides fulfilling experiences to musicians and their fans. It is a place of vital and varied activity — social, economic, and musical. It is a friendly community immeasurably different from the stereotypical vision of a depressed, antisocial, and aggressive collection of youth. The Death Metal scene has evolved substantially since its earliest stages, and it continues to change with the times and the tastes of its enthusiastic fans.

3

Lyrical Content

Given the extreme nature of Death Metal, it is no surprise that the lyrical content is equally extreme and often very offensive, disturbing, and disgusting to the average outsider. Most critics cite the lyrics of Death Metal music as their reason for condemning it. It is quite fascinating to note, however, that the lyrics in Death Metal are most frequently unintelligible, and many devoted Death Metal fans would be unable to recite the lyrics of even their favorite bands. Often, lyrics are poorly written (or even composed by foreign band members with little grasp of the language in which they write). For this reason, it is generally accepted that the lyrics in Death Metal (like album art and band photos) serve predominantly as a means for bands to promote an image that visually displays the aggression and extremity of their music.

Most of the lyrics within the Death Metal genre fall into the following general categorizations: gore/horror/porn; Satanism/occultism/anti-Christian; sociopolitical commentary; independence themes; and war/apocalypse themes.[2] Each general category can contain numerous different sub-categories and interpretations of the same general subject matter. Within each category, it is important to distinguish the real messages from the fantastic, though it is sometimes impossible to draw a firm line between the two realms. In general we can conclude that the lyrics depicting gore and psychological horror do not represent reality. They are deeply removed into the realm of fantasy and, according to all of those interviewed, are not to be taken seriously. The hostile anti-religious or anti-political themes are more difficult to classify because they often reveal a muddled mixture of fantasy and reality. Most political, social, and personal statements are more overtly reflective of and responsive to reality. Similarly, lyrics about independence and unity often appeal to reality rather than fantasy.[3]

Occult themes were present in underground music long before the dawn of Death Metal. Mysticism and the occult accented the lyrics of major 1970s bands like Black Sabbath, Led Zeppelin, Witchfynde, Iron Maiden, and others. Among the first bands actually claiming to adhere to Satanism, Venom of Britain must be mentioned. The image and lyrics of the early 1980s band glorified Satan. It was so-called "Black Metal" music that prompted the development of genre titles such as Death Metal. The anti-religious themes embraced by Venom were adopted by the Venom fans who formed the bands Hellhammer/Celtic Frost and Possessed, both of which would impact the Death Metal genre tremendously.

Possessed focused on the traditional anti–Christian words and images of metal bands like Slayer, evoking pictures of hellfire and damnation. The band also incorporated music from the film *The Exorcist* into their debut album, an early example of Death Metal's close association with the horror film genre. The lyrics of Possessed were extremely basic and simple, inverting Christian images without much creativity. Hellhammer, renamed Celtic Frost, utilized more elaborate and refined imagery to communicate visions of the occult. Although the Swiss band wrote in their non-native English, they managed to convey a tragic romantic sentiment in their mournful relations of ancient battles and apocalyptic tomorrows. Some Celtic Frost lyrics were inspired by the horror stories of H. P. Lovecraft, a 19th century author. Lovecraft spun fantastic tales of strange creatures, "Cthulu gods," and physical manifestations of destructive concepts like chaos. The imagery and ideas of Lovecraft were incorporated into the lyrics of a number of Death Metal bands. The Celtic Frost song "Morbid Tales," for instance, describes a post-nuclear world of humans worshipping the Cthulu Gods.

The Death Metal legend Morbid Angel has incorporated Lovecraft's work into many of the band's lyrics. Lovecraft's book of spells, The Necronomicon, is quoted in the song "Lord of all Fevers and Plagues": "Ninnghizhidda, open my eyes, Ninnghizhidda, hear my cries... I call forth the god Pazuzu, I call forth the lord of plague ... Ia Iak Sakkakh, Iak Sakkakth, Ia Shaxul, Ia Kingu, Ia Cthulu. Ia Azbul, Ia Azabua." Morbid Angel combines such occult lyrics with traditional anti-religious and Satanic themes in blasphemous songs like "Damnation" and "Evil Spells." Other important Death Metal bands, such as Massacre and Nile, incorporate Lovecraft's work into their repertoires. Massacre songs that exemplify this phenomenon include "From Beyond," Dawn of Eternity," "Defeat Remain," and "Symbolic Immortality." Nile's lyrics mix Lovecraft's imagery with themes from Egyptian and Sumerian mythology. The song "Die Rache Krieg Lied der Assyriche," written in the band's early years, reads "Ia Mamtaru, Ia Lammia, Ia Asaku, Ia Pazuzu, Ia Zixul zi Azkak, Ia Gula zi Pazu."

Bands more typically communicate fright and darkness through the use of standard anti-Christian images and themes, based far more in fantasy than in reality. Examples include Incantation's song "Disciples of Blasphemous Reprisal" from "Diabolical Conquest" (1998): "Catholic degeneration, unholy desolation, perversions of the trinity, the sign of unholy victory, angels falling eternally, 666 blasphemy." These lyrics generally just evoke sacrilegious imagery rather than purvey any concrete message or theme that directly relates to the world.

Often the mystical and frightening images of Satanism are replaced by more realistic attacks on Christianity as an institution and a means of mind control. Immolation has maintained an anti-organized-religion stance throughout the band's career. Immolation's lyrics express a deep distrust of Christianity as a philosophy of lies and fantasies designed to obtain power and control over the masses. In the song "No Jesus, No Beast," the band chants "Can you hear us, Death to Jesus," presenting God and Satan as fictional characters designed to suppress freedom and individualism. Immolation warns of the "second coming" in the song "Once Ordained": "You will all be fooled, when he reveals himself... He'll rise, We'll fall, His rule, Our end."

The lyrical style of Immolation may also be found in the work of Entombed, the Swedish creators of the album "Left Hand Path." Entombed's song "The Truth Beyond" mourns "People put to death in the name of God, And blood run red in eternal flood, The word has been spread throughout the centuries, Millions of corpses lying in the cemeteries, Reek of Christianity, Down of obscuration, The birth of insanity, And death to liberation ... Discover the lies; There is no resurrection, Get your eyes open wide, And discover the lies, See the truth beyond, The shadows of a Fool's paradise." The Swedish band Grave takes a similar stance in songs like "Christinsanity." Many other Death Metal acts have used their lyrics to bitterly criticize the Church as a money-grabbing and politically manipulative organization. Dying Fetus' "Praise the Lord (Opiate of the Masses)," Death's "Spiritual Healing", and Napalm Death's "Suffer the Children" convey deep criticisms of Christianity.

Today, the forbearers of this lyrical style are Deicide and Morbid Angel. Deicide's early material displays crude and simplistic Satanism. For example, the song "Trifixion" in the Deicide debut does little more than offer praise to the Devil and condemn God and Christ, with little mention of why. The band's later lyrics are more complex and critical of Christianity. In the Deicide song "Blame It on God" from the 1997 album *Serpents of the Light*, lyricist Glen Benton presents his view of God as an uncaring father. Benton tears into God for allowing his own son, Jesus Christ, to suffer and die. He compares the fate of Christ to that of all humans, condemned to struggle through painful lives in an unjust world without help from their creator. This anti-religious sentiment almost borders on social commentary, and is a good deal less fantastic than the standard fare in the genre.

Like Deicide, Morbid Angel has evolved in its anti-Christian lyrical stance. The band's very early songs, like "Chapel of Ghouls" and "Bleed for the Devil," simply spout blasphemy without much depth (or even sense): "Bleed for the Devil, Impious mortal lives, feel the enticing power, fill the chasm of your soul." Gradually, the band's lyrics would evolve and grow in sophistication. In the song "God of Emptiness" from the 1993 album "Covenant," Morbid Angel professes anger towards a higher power: "Lies — and you fill their souls with all oppressions of this world. And all the glory you receive? So what makes you supreme? Lies." In truth, these lyrics are not evil by any definition of the word, but they are certainly not accepting of traditional religious views and values. Today, the band's lyrics are even more philosophical and thought-provoking. Current lyricist Trey Azagthoth has diagramed his personal ideology in the album "Formulas Fatal to the Flesh." His stance is blasphemous and non-traditional, but hardly evil.

A few bands have attempted to present specific philosophies or describe themselves as members of an organized occult group, like the Order of Set or the Church of Satan. The latter organization was formed in the 1960s by Anton LeVey, whose socially Darwinian views have been used to justify fascism and racism. Bands such as Acheron and Angelcorpse are thought to have adopted lyrics rooted in these visions. Acheron's lyricist was actually a "minister" in the Church of Satan. Angelcorpse has invoked fascist images in songs like "Solar Wills" and "Stormgods Unbound." Both songs include descriptions of a powerful "sun wheel," the English translation of the word "swastika." "Solar Wills" declares "The stirrings of genocide unfurl, Commanding swine to the abattoir ... Four-armed comet scrapes the earth, Solar Wills," while "Stormgods Unbound" describes "Proud-Iron youth, of the noble cultures of the past ... A volk of purity of vigor ... Sun wheels expansive, through thunder and blood bold, Weltmacht oder neidergang."

3. Lyrical Content 43

Former members of major Death Metal bands like Morbid Angel and Malevolent Creation have also been suspected of racist and right-wing leanings. David Vincent, formerly of Morbid Angel, made suspected references to Hitler and has mentioned Frederick Nietzsche, Charles Manson, and others on his thanks list for the album *Blessed Are the Sick*. Malevolent Creation's album *Eternal* caused much controversy due to usage of the word "nigger" in the concluding line of one song.[4] Although the Death Metal audience as a whole generally avows strong disapproval of white supremacy and racism, many fans and bands in the Black Metal scene have embraced such themes. Such bands include Emperor/Zyklon-B, Mayhem, Burzum, and Absurd.

Throughout Death Metal's history, the two lyrical themes that have dominated the genre are the aforementioned blasphemous tirades and pure gore. The pioneers of Death Metal gore lyrics were Death and Necrophagia. In the early years of Death, horror films inspired the band's lyrics. Films like Cannibal Ferox, Gates of Hell, and Evil Dead gave birth to the Death songs "Torn to Pieces," "Regurgitated Guts," and "Evil Dead," respectively. Lyricist Killjoy of Necrophagia was similarly inspired by horror films. The Necrophagia song "Ancient Slumber," for instance, is based on the film Evil Dead. Bands Deicide and Repulsion would bring equally gory and horror-film-inspired lyrics to the Death Metal scene. Deicide's "Dead By Dawn" song is based on *Evil Dead II*, while Repulsion songs showcase various sources of gore, death, disease, and mutilation in songs like "Radiation Sickness," "Splattered Cadavers, "Festering Boils," and "Bodily Dismemberment." Such lyrical pioneers helped to bring extreme gore into the mainstream of Death Metal.

New-York band Mortician became famous for using horror-film samples and gore lyrics. The film *Texas Chainsaw Massacre* inspired the covers of the albums *Chainsaw Dismemberment* and *Hacked Up for Barbecue*. Mortician embodies the most simplistic and primitive approach to gore lyrics. The band's song "Stab" from the album *Chainsaw Dismemberment* (1999), best exemplifies the gratuitous scenes of violence presented in Mortician songs: "Psycho killers, endless slaughter, eviscerated, throats will be slit, cut, chopped, hacked, stabbed in the back, calls of terror, game of horror, fuck up, you die, gutted alive."

Cannibal Corpse, most infamous for the lyrics written by former front-man Chris Barnes (who has been quoted in dismay by such powerful politicians as Bob Dole and John McCain), would explore psychological themes in its presentation of gory images. From the 1992 album *Tomb of the Mutilated*, the song "Necropedophile" offers Barnes' speculation on the inner workings of the deranged mind driven to murder children and rape their dead bodies. Lyrics such as these not only touch on the physical effects of depravity, but contemplate the psychological state of a person suffering from this derangement. Cryptopsy, in the song "Phobophile" from the 1996 album *None So Vile*, presents an equally chilling interpretation of the mental state of a very sick human being: "Said amputee's stumps are my way of saying 'thank you for just being you.' Its fear tastes better than its limbs. Terror of mortality I draw from the slowly dying damned." These lyrics not only describe gruesome acts, but also offer speculation as to the feelings, drives, and desires that would motivate a person to commit such acts.

Some gory and violent lyrics describe the execution of disturbing vengeful and sexual fantasies. Hatred toward enemies or females has also been expressed in many lyrics. Such themes abound in the lyrics of Cannibal Corpse. Desires are indulged and anger explodes in songs like "Stripped, Raped, and Strangled," "Fucked with a Knife," "Pulverized," and "Hammer-Smashed Face." The lyrics of these songs contain terrifying lines describing morbid urges to slaughter and sexually exploit others, particularly the weak. Perhaps these songs are especially disturbing because they relate such tales of horror from the perspective of the perpetrator.

A significant variation on gore lyrics may be found in the work of bands inspired by Carcass. Carcass is known for introducing complicated medical terminology into the lyrical descriptions of gore and death. This style is typified by song titles like "Pyosisfied," "Excoriating Abdominal Emanation," and "Mucupurulence Excretor." This elaborately putrid vocabulary runs throughout the band's lyrics, as in the line "I rip open pectoral cavities to devour my still-steaming grub, Drinking adeps and effluence, smearing myself in congealing blood, I tear at sautéd crackling to guzzle on fetid swag, Butchered remains are carved and collected in a doggy-bag." The acts of demented pathologists are described in songs like "Psychopathologist" and "Reek of Putrefaction." In Carcass's material, the dead human body becomes a theater for disgusting and perverse entertainment. There is a certain irony in the lyrics of bands like Carcass, for they describe absurdly revolting ideas in the most medically appropriate terminology. This result is something bizarrely comical.

Gore lyrics of other bands would become similarly humorous. Impetigo from Illinois adopted this less serious approach with songs like "Dis-organ-ized," "Jane Fonda Sucks," and "Teenage Bitch Death Mucus Monster from Hell." Many of the band's song and album titles were taken directly from B-grade horror films. Other bands would find humor in the gruesome acts of serial killers. Chicago band Macabre bases each song on the life or actions of a different serial killer, from the most infamous killers to more low profile psychopaths. "The Ted Bundy Song" lightheartedly relates "a story of Ted Bundy, murdered young girls, Monday through Sunday." Perhaps the humor is more overt in the song "McDahmers" from the 2000 album *Dahmer*: "The ketchup was blood, the mustard was pus, inside the closet was pickled private parts." We need not continue on to the description of the Chicken McNuggets.

Puns on words and bastardizations of sanctified songs and phrases often adorn the lyrics of gore bands, adding an extra layer of humor. Macabre has usurped tunes from folk favorites, like "When Johnny Comes Marching Home Again" and "She'll Be Comin' 'Round the Mountain When She Comes," adding perverse lyrics in a display of utter irreverence. Impaled defiles the prayers "Hail Mary" and "Our Father" in the song "Fecal Rites": "Holy anus full of shit, the corn is with me, Blessed be the copraphagious, messed be the fruit of thy feast ... Thy kingdom bung, Thy will be dung."

As in low-budget gore films, misogyny is a common theme in the gore lyrics of many Death Metal bands. Pornographic gore lyrics are common in the work of bands like Cannibal Corpse, Gut, Dead, and Lividity. In fact, the members of the band Gut have elected to label themselves "Spermsoaked Consumers of Pussy Barbecue," "Masturbators of 1,000 Splatter Whores," and "Commander of the Anti-Whore Gestapo." Gut's songs, often intended to be humorous, are grossly misogynistic, boasting titles such as "Defaced Slut," "Anal Sushi," "She Died with Her Legs Spread," "Dead Girls Don't Say No," and "Spermatic Suffocation." Sarcastically exploring fetishism, lyricists find humor in concepts like "Raping the Elderly" by Blood Duster or "MS Rape-a-thon" by Undinism. Songs like Cannibal Corpse's "Meathook Sodomy," "I Come Blood," "Fucked with a Knife," "She Was Asking for it," and "Addicted to Vaginal Skin," as well as Lividity's "Randomly Raped Rectum" and "Rectal Wench," indicate that pornographic gore lyrics are prominent and recurrent elements in Death Metal.

Carnage is sometimes presented less graphically and more realistically by Death Metal bands exploring themes of war and apocalypse. Angelcorpse has created images of the apocalypse on the album *Exterminate*, and one will find apocalyptic song themes scattered through Mortician's work, featuring song titles like "Extinction of Mankind," "Mutilation of the Human Race," "World Damnation," and "Apocalyptic Devastation." The English band Bolt Thrower has consistently embraced themes of war and the apocalypse, including lyrical descriptions of both mythical and actual battles. The lyrics that focus on war and apocalypse are significantly different from most gore lyrics in that they describe events, images, and even characters based in reality rather than fantasy. As evidenced in the humorous approaches of most gore bands, the lyrics are not to be taken seriously and the actions described are not endorsed.

Congressmen seem to believe that gore-oriented songs are serious and that those who listen to them are likely to take part in the vile behavior described within the songs. They do not discern the difference between fantasy and reality in these lyrics, yet most metal fans feel themselves capable of recognizing this distinction. One of the youngest pre-teenage survey participants took a moment to write in defense of his favorite music: "Death Metal just talks about crazy slaughter that you know never happens, but [it] is just making fun of it all. ...Death Metal fans don't go out and slaughter people and eat them because Death Metal lyrics shouldn't be taken seriously. They should be laughed at." Nearly every interviewee agreed with this fan on the topic of Death Metal's gore lyrics. Often Death Metal albums give the reader a taste of the purely outlandish and bizarre nature of gore lyrics, which are thrilling and chilling. Fans seem convinced that the actual scenes and activities depicted in such lyrics are not at all connected to reality, but politicians do not agree. It can be objectively stated that most of what is depicted in such lyrics does not occur in reality, and never has. In many instances, there is no purpose in trying to discern a meaningful theme beyond the violent, shocking, and aggressive nature of many of the gore lyrics in Death Metal.

Many of the musicians interviewed assert that the lyrics are not meant to have meaning, much less are they meant to be translated into reality or taken as an impetus to act on violent impulses. Matthew Harvey has suggested that, at most, gore lyrics represent a rejection of conventional aesthetic and sexual values. He believes that by inverting the normal and natural perception of what is attractive and what is repulsive, gore lyrics essentially provide the same opportunity for questioning accepted norms and mores as anti-religious themes. In short, they prompt a questioning of pre-prescribed notions of what people should and should not accept or do. There is still no literal relationship between the gore images and reality.

On the contrary, Death Metal bands with sociopolitical lyrics often describe reality and use their lyrics to offer critical, if not always prescriptive, commentary. Still, the lyrics are not always literal. Such bands often adopt a strange mixture of violent imagery and genuine sociopolitical commentary. Dying Fetus provides an apt example of lyrics that deliver a message about reality meshed with images of violence and expressions of hostility. Dying Fetus' 1998 album *Killing on Adrenaline* demonstrates this lyrical phenomenon in the song "Procreate the Malformed": "Corporation nations start the game, Persist exploit, rip-off, defame, Put one against the other till they're dead, beat them, face down make them eat shit, burn the fucking global village down ... UN, IMF, they're all the same, nations all enslaved ... A lack of total vision, it's social amputation, they're locked inside a world apart from reality." Many find this particularly disturbing because of the presentation of real issues combined with the advocacy of violent reprisals. It is important to note, however, just how outlandish and unrealistic the actual descriptions of violence are. They utilize completely fantastic imagery: there is analogical symbolism rather than real advocacy of terrorism in a phrase like "burn the global village down." Anger without direction is expressed toward corporations with words like "make them eat shit." Who are "they"? In truth, for many listeners, these lyrics serve merely as a release for aggression and anger at the social order. This fact should not be mistaken for a total absence of meaningful and prescriptive sociopolitical messages in such lyrics. Inherent in even the most violent imagery, one may find messages that are both critical of the status quo and prescriptive.[5]

In contrast to the light-hearted masochism of porn-gore bands, a serious criticism of sexism can be found in the deeply sarcastic lyrics of Napalm Death songs like "It's a Man's World": "God give me strength, women suck my length. ...It's a man's world, so you'd better act like one. Cunt, born some more, to be big and strong like Daddy, drill them to perpetuate into the ultimate form of stupidity." Napalm Death also criticizes sexism within the mainstream metal scene and the underground punk genre. According to the song "Cock-Rock Alienation," "Capitalism, Racism, Sexism [are] the foundations of Cock-Rocking idealism." "The Missing Link" mourns hypocrisy and misogyny: "Earnest words, calling for unity of the sexes, when she's still the chick, or stupid bitch, ridiculed for showing an interest." Napalm Death lyrics explore many other social issues, including corporate exploitation, racism, drug addiction, homophobia, and mindless conformity. "Multi-National Corporations" are criticized as the "genocide of the starving nations," while racists are challenged to "look into yourself, you'll find the real oppressor, to live a life of unchallenged hate, it's yourself who's the nigger." The song "Aryanisms" captures much of Napalm Death's philosophy stating the constructive truth that "harmony can only flourish with mutual regard."

Many Death Metal bands have tackled social issues ranging from environmental concerns to social values to drug abuse. Obituary's 1994 album *World Demise* expresses concern over the deterioration of the environment and continued pollution; the album is covered with images of oil-covered ducks, dead seals, and syringes lying on beaches. Environmental themes are rare, but the pain and hopelessness of drug addiction is a somewhat more common theme. The band Atrocity, for instance, created an anti-heroin concept album called *Hallucinations* in 1990. Social commentary has also adorned the lyric sheets of Death's later albums. Anti-abortion messages may be found in songs like "Altering the Future," and the problem of infants born with addictions is explored in "Living Monstrosity."

The theme of embracing freedom and thinking for oneself became a prominent concept emphasized in Death lyrics. Death's 1993 album *Individual Thought Patterns* contains songs like "The Philosopher" which criticize the blind acceptance of others' theories and decry thought without originality. Death lyricist Chuck Schuldiner, recently deceased, used lyrics to present his personal reflections and philosophical analyses such as those in "Individual Thought Patterns." Newer bands, like God Forbid, resuscitate such critical yet positive themes. The following lyrics are from God Forbid's 1999 album *Reject the Sickness*: "Meaningless morals of a class unlike you, a struggle of embraced words which ring untrue ... weather the storm, go your own way, for freedom against the lies told to you ... regurgitation of old becoming new, corrupting the bowels of society, values plague for dominion, lower class bent on redemption." It seems that where there is a legitimate critique of the social order, there is also some vague prescription for change or at least the plea for a new order.

The themes of individuality and freedom often emerge in lyrics with sociopolitical overtones. Even more often, individuality is endorsed in pleas to reject dominant religion and mainstream culture. Death Metal entails an irreverent rejection of cultural norms, and in any such rebellion, there lies an inherent call to individualism. Thus, themes of individuality and freedom are extremely common in Death Metal. Many of the lyrics are reminiscent of Enlightenment philosophers' calls for an end to intellectual "tutelage," as Immanuel Kant put it. The Monstrosity song "Slaves and Masters" from the 1996 album *Millennium* brings out the theme of individualism in an almost Humean criticism of organized religion: "Open your mind as it was the day you were born. Your religion is just a waste of time. Striving harder, ever harder, to please individual gods, they follow blindly, lives are wasted, slaves and masters of ourselves ... Unlock the mysteries of the soul. Drown in the essential knowledge that we're all gods on our own." Pat Robertson might not approve, but then again, such words got David Hume into some trouble, too. This does not detract from their meaning or value. Death criticizes blind adherence to the dictates of powerful forces on the *Individual Thought Patterns* album: "Like a drug it feeds the imagination of minds that go unanalyzed. Followers to the leaders of mass hypnotic corruption that live their lives only to criticize, Where is the invisible line that we must draw to create individual thought patterns?"

On this note, we conclude our summary of the sort of lyrics found in Death Metal music. The primary themes have been sketched out and their meanings have been touched upon. This brief description, however, has offered a glance at the lyrics themselves, which are not necessarily tied in with motivations for listening to Death Metal music. It cannot yet be said whether metal fans identify with the lyrics that are prevalent in the music that they listen to. Most importantly, it cannot be overemphasized that the material presented thus far has been but a description of the music, not of the fans themselves. The later analysis of the philosophy, behavior patterns, and attitudes of Death Metal fans will help to discern which themes in Death Metal music are truly embraced by the fans (if any), which themes are disregarded, and why we observe the patterns that we do.

Part II

The History of the Death Metal Scene

4

Origins: 1984–1988

In the 1980s, heavy music moved into the mainstream. Heavy metal mixed with hardcore and punk to create a Thrash Metal movement that featured bands like Metallica, Anthrax, Megadeth, and Slayer. In many ways, Thrash Metal and its accompanying movements gave birth to Death Metal. As several musicians see it, Death Metal was the product of Thrash bands attempting to outdo one another in terms of speed, technicality, and overall extremity. Explains Matt Medeiros, the earliest Death Metal is "characterized by many of the traits of Thrash: screamed vocals, staccato riffing and tremelo picking, screeching leads, and (due to its budget and technology) raw production. The lyrical content was often primitive but referred to general metal topics of death, destruction, and evil."

In the midst of the Thrash movement, an English band entitled Venom labeled their fast, abrasive music "Black Metal." This label prompted the development of a number of sub-genres of metal music, one of which was, of course, Death Metal. The term "Death Metal" emerged when Thomas Fischer and Martin Ain, a pair of Swiss Venom fans in the band Hellhammer (later Celtic Frost), started a fanzine called "Death Metal." Later, their record label German Noise Records used the "Death Metal" name for a compilation featuring Hellhammer. Subsequently, the Death Metal label was applied to any bands that played extremely fast and heavy music lacking any semblance of melody.

Meanwhile, in 1983, the term was co-coined by some American teens who formed the band Possessed and labeled their demo "Death Metal." After signing with Combat Records, the band released the 1985 debut album *Seven Churches*, which would prove monumental and extraordinarily influential on the development of the Death Metal genre. One of the much-imitated innovations of Possessed was the unique vocal style of Jeff Beccera, whose raw growl was far more harsh than the most extreme vocals of the Thrash genre. Nonetheless, the Thrash origins of the band were unmistakable. King Fowley summarizes the roots of Possessed's early Death Metal:

> The gloom that [bands like] Black Sabbath unleashed through their music ... did so much for metal and dark metal ... add in the "fuck the world" factor of early punk rock, the musicianship and intensity of your Iron Maidens and Judas Priests, and throw in some Venom for their complete and sheer over-the-top values, and you get a good idea of where your Possesseds, Slayers, and Kreators started.

As the 1980s matured, so did the work of Possessed. The band's 1986 release *Beyond the Gates* featured toned down and cleaner material, but the 1987 release *The Eyes of Horror* was considered as harsh in music and production as the band's original work.

Not long after the dawn of Possessed, a second monumental band was formed by a group of boys in Florida. The band Mantas, composed of Chuck Schuldiner, Kam Lee, and Rick Rozz, released a demo entitled "Death by Metal" in 1983 before breaking up. The tape was traded extensively, and the band reformed shortly thereafter under the name Death. In the two years following, Death would release two demos entitled "Reign of Terror" and "Infernal Death." Kam Lee's vocals would influence the Death Metal scene tremendously, for their low and guttural nature would become the staple of the genre. The line-up of Death would change considerably before long, and guitarist Chuck Schuldiner would adopt vocal duties. Death, however, had already made a major impact. Fast, dark riffs complimented by frenzied solos were paired with fast-paced standard drumming, creating a style that would catch on in tape-trading circles.

Within such early circles, the band Necrophagia left its mark. The Ohio band would release a series of demos with poor production and primitive music. The crude music featured slow guitars and drums to create a gloomy, frightening atmosphere complimented by horror-film-based lyrics. In far Brazil, the band Sepultura would also make its mark on the Death Metal Scene, releasing the Thrash-influenced album *Bestial Devastation* through Cogumelo Records. Throughout the 1980s, this label would helped foster a Brazilian Death Metal scene composed of bands like Chakal, Holocausto, Mutilator, and Sarcofago. Sepultura's *Bestial Devastation* included a song "Antichrist" with quadruple-time drumbeats, while Sarcofago's *INRI* album used such extreme tempos throughout.

Meanwhile, former Death members Olivo and Carlson released the debut album *Horrified* of their Michigan band Repulsion (formerly Genocide). Upon its release in 1986, *Horrified* was the fastest Death Metal album in existence, complete with extremely aggressive riffs and the quadruple-time beats of drummer Dave Grave. Although the band broke up shortly thereafter, the Midwest was graced with Chicago's Deathstrike (later Master). Deathstrike's 1985 release *Fuckin' Death* presented simple, punk-like Death Metal with sociopolitical lyrics. Later, Master would release more musically complex material and become influential in the scene.

As the 1980s wore on in Europe, Hellhammer transformed into Celtic Frost to release the 1984 album *Morbid Tales*. The album was similar to Hellhammer material except for the notable inclusion of strange instrumental tracks like "Danse Macabre" and "Nocturnal Fear," which presented strange eerie sounds and non-traditional instrumentation to create odd atmospheric music. *Morbid Tales* features simple fast guitar riffs interlaced with slow sections over double-bass drumming. Celtic Frost's 1985 album, *To Mega Therion* was similar though slower. In 1987, the band released the highly unorthodox *Into Pandemonium*, which included slow, atmospheric instrumentation and mournful moaning. Although the album would not be considered Death Metal by today's standards, it is important to note because it would prove influential to many later Death Metal bands.

Clearly, the earliest days of the genre were marked by tremendous freedom and creativity. There were essentially no boundaries and this allowed for incredible ingenuity. Karl Sanders reminisces about this freedom:

> In the early days of Death Metal, it was just wide open. You could do practically anything musically, and as long as it was heavy and extreme, well heck, there you go. If you had a band, you didn't have to be glossily presented and airbrushed or whatever. Your music could be raw and it was fine. People would accept music in demo form without it going into production and all that. Anybody could do it, and there was a lot of crap. But the good stuff had a chance to be heard that would never otherwise have been heard.

At the same time, Sanders admits that "the bands back then played pretty sloppily. ... In the mid to late 80s, the people playing underground Death Metal were in love with the music but perhaps not yet musically capable of achieving the potential of what Death Metal had to offer." Others, like King Fowley, would disagree with this observation, arguing that early Death Metal showed more in the way of musicianship than contemporary Death Metal. On whichever side of debate one falls, there is unanimous agreement that the earliest Death Metal bands offered much in the way of devotion, passion, and sheer love for the music.

Throughout the 1980s, the Death Metal scene in America was expanding. In Maryland, King Fowley's Deceased began to generate its Heavy Metal/Death Metal music, while in Ohio, Nunslaughter released a number of extremely brutal demos. Both bands still exist today. At the time, however, Florida was the heart of the Death Metal world. In 1986, Morbid Angel emerged with the album *Abominations of Desolation*, and the band quickly gained a reputation for gruesome stage antics. Before Morbid Angel released the demo "Thy Kingdom Come" in 1987, vocalist David Vincent replaced vocalist/drummer Mike Browning. Browning's band Incubus released a notable demo, but it did not gain much attention.[6]

The year 1987 also saw the release of Death's *Scream Bloody Gore*, which featured the drumming of Californian Chris Riefert. Touted as "REAL Death Metal," it was the first well-promoted Death Metal album released through Combat Records.[7] When Schuldiner returned to Florida, Riefert stayed in California to work with Autopsy, which would release *Demo 87* and *Critical Madness* soon thereafter. Also in 1987, Necrophagia released *Season of the Dead*—complete with slow, churning riffs and decent production—before the band split up.

Across the sea, in the UK, Napalm Death would release *Scum* in 1987. The two-sided album was extremely influential. Though side one featured very punk-influenced guitaring, the second side displayed the impressive Death Metal guitarwork of Bill Steer, which would spur the Grindcore movement. The tempos of the album were incredibly fast, with quadruple-time beats and extremely short songs. The album also featured deep grunted vocals advocating leftist politics. Napalm Death followed *Scum* with the equally extreme 1988 release *From Enslavement to Obliteration*. Soon, British Grindcore bands like Unseen Terror, Ripcord, Heresy, Concrete Sox, Carcass, The Electro-Hippies, and others began popping up.

Of these bands, Carcass, a project of Napalm Death guitarist Bill Steer, would become immensely influential. In 1988, Carcass released the Grindcore album *Reek of Putrefaction*. The album was adorned with images of decaying corpses and used elaborate medical terminology to describe putrid bodies and forensic procedures gone wrong. According to Harvey, Carcass "adapted the Grindcore formula to include more metallic, chugging sections ... [and] the constant juxtaposition of shrieking vocals (provided by bassist/lyricist Jeff Walker) and guttural growls (performed by

4. Origins: 1984–1988

Bill Steer)." The evolving Grindcore of Carcass and Napalm Death brought both bands closer and closer to the Death Metal genre.

The influence of Grindcore would be felt in America through the work of bands like California's Terrorizer. The band's debut, *World Downfall*, was traded throughout the underground, and members of the band would go on to make significant contributions to the Death Metal genre. While guitarist Jesse Pintado took over for Bill Steer in Napalm Death, drummer Pete Sandoval moved to Florida to develop Morbid Angel. Terrorizer's bassist David Vincent would also depart for Morbid Angel. The Grindcore and Death Metal genres remained closely linked.

In the late 1980s, the Death Metal scene of Florida continued to grow. Massacre divided, leaving the guitarist to form his own band Xecutioner (later Obituary). Other Massacre members joined Schuldiner's Death to release *Leprosy* in 1988. The album's precision and clarity set a new standard in Death Metal. The production was clear, the lyrics were enunciated, the guitarwork (solos excluded) was smooth and sophisticated, and the kick drum was replaced with drum triggers to produce an entirely uniform beat. *Leprosy* also included lyrics about real-life issues, such as the right to die, instead of gore and violence. The album was a commercial success, and Death Metal began to emerge outside the extreme underground of tape-traders and fanzines.

Soon thereafter, labels like Roadrunner and Earache began to sign Death Metal bands. Joining Roadrunner were Deicide (formerly Amon) and Obituary from Florida, as well as Immolation (formerly Rigor Mortis) from New York and Sepultura from Brazil. Morbid Angel, Swedish band Entombed (formerly Nihilist), and British band Bolt Thrower were among those Death Metal bands to sign with Earache. The music was more available and the scene grew rapidly. As Incantation's Kyle Severn remembers:

> Metal in the 80s seemed somewhat easy to get. There was a lot of tape-trading going on. Where I grew up, we had a college radio station that played metal, so I heard a lot of good shit. ... I remember when I was young, I could walk to the record store and I had such a choice of Death Metal records to buy. I usually didn't even know where to start. I would have to bring an underground zine with me, and reading the reviews would help me make my decision.

Death Metal was entering into new commercial realms, but its summit was yet to come.

5

Rise and Fall: 1989–1994

In the later 1980s, Thrash Metal toned down to move into the mainstream, leaving those in search of the most extreme music to move towards Death Metal. The genre gained more acceptance due to the marketing of labels like Roadrunner, which found commercial success in late 1980s releases like Sepultura's *Beneath the Remains* and Obituary's *Slowly We Rot*. In 1990, Roadrunner released Deicide's self-titled debut album. The Florida band sped through twisted Slayer-style riffs and solos, complemented by the "sick" multi-layered vocals of bassist Glen Benton, a maniacal Satanist who would become a major scene personality. With releases such as these, Death Metal became the dominant force in the extreme music underground.

Major UK Grindcore bands continued in their transition toward Death Metal. This was evidenced by the 1989 Earache recordings of Napalm Death and Carcass. Napalm Death released *Mentally Murdered* in 1989, featuring longer songs with more traditional Death Metal riffs. Also in 1989, Carcass released *Symphonies of Sickness*, considered to be extremely brutal yet sophisticated Death Metal. Earache Records would release several other important recordings as the 1980s closed. Bolt Thrower's fast, heavy *Realm of Chaos* included Death Metal of the lowest tuning yet. Earache also released Entombed's *Left Hand Path* in 1990. The album would help define the Swedish Death Metal sound with a down-tuned, saw-like guitar sound blasting Punk-like and groovy rhythms offset with deep, Doom-like sections. This sound would be further developed with the 1989 release of Carnage's *Dark Recollections.*

Meanwhile, the development of Death Metal in the United States continued. Autopsy released debut album *Severed Survival* in 1989 with primitive, crude sounds of ferocious speed mixed with slow, dark, and heavy passages. Other important contributions to the American Death Metal genre in the late 1980s were made by Chicago's Macabre and Illinois' Impetigo. The center of the American Death Metal scene at the time, however, remained in Florida. Florida's scene continued to grow and develop with monumental releases from Morbid Angel, Death, and Cannibal Corpse. Morbid Angel's 1989 album *Altars of Madness* was extremely well-produced by Tampa's Morrisound Studios, with the catchy yet extreme compositions of guitarist Trey Azagthoth and the much emulated speed of drummer Pete Sandoval. Death's 1990 release *Spiritual Healing* also boasted crystal clear production and sophisticated instrumental skill with the lead guitar virtuosity of James Murphy (who replaced Rick Rozz). In 1990 Florida saw the debut of the extremely influential Cannibal Corpse. With little contention, Cannibal Corpse's first album, *Eaten Back to Life*, was deemed pure, brutal Death Metal. The album (which was the first Death Metal album released by America's Metal Blade Records) included disgusting gore lyrics sung in the remarkably low and unintelligible voice of Chris Barnes.

The American Death Metal underground expanded with much help from Ohio's Seraphic Decay Records, which released the EPs of bands that would become very influential, including Mortician, Incantation, and Goreaphobia. When Seraphic Decay's disreputable practices caused the label to fade out of prominence, newly formed Relapse Records took over where Seraphic Decay left off, signing the three aforementioned bands as well as the popular Deceased and many other important acts. In Germany, important developments occurred with the formation of the labels Century Media and Nuclear Blast in the early 1990s. Century Media signed many influential European acts like Asphyx, Sweden's Grave and Unleashed, and Germany's Morgoth. Nuclear Blast signed European bands and important American groups like Macabre, Master, and Louisiana's Incubus.

In England, the Doom Death Metal movement was taking shape in the early 1990s. Bands like Celtic Frost, My Dying Bride, Cathedral, and Anathema offered slow, deep metal with a haunting and sorrowful tone. These British bands added melody and instrumental sections to their dark metal music. Significant contributions to the Doom movement were made in other countries as well. In the U.S., Winter released the extremely slow

Trey Azagthoth of Morbid Angel raises a bleeding arm onstage. Photograph by Frank White.

5. Rise and Fall: 1989–1994

Chris Barnes, lead singer for Cannibal Corpse. Photograph by Frank White.

and prodding album *Into Darkness*. In Australia, Disembowelment combined slow Doom with brutal Death on *Transcendence into the Peripheral*.

Meanwhile, more traditional Death Metal was increasing in popularity, attracting press attention, label interest, and more money for quality recordings and promotion. In 1991, Earache releases became available in the United States through Combat Records. More and more bands would enter the genre, attempting to produce increasingly extreme music. In England, Napalm Death would release the 1990 album *Harmony Corruption*, often considered the band's first purely Death Metal album, through Earache Records. *Harmony Corruption* included cleaner Morrisound production and a more intelligible guitar pitch. Carcass' *Necroticism: Decanting the Insalubrious* was also a cleanly produced Earache album. *Necroticism* was more melodious and more technically complex than the band's former work. Finally, Earache released the third album of British band Bolt Thrower, which also featured clean production and slower tempos complimented by heavy guitar distortion.

The Swedish Death Metal movement was equally active at this time. In 1991, Sweden's Dismember (made up of former Carnage members) debuted with *Like an Ever-Flowing Stream*, an album that would be important in defining the Swedish Death Metal sound. Also in Sweden, Earache band Entombed released *Clandestine* with complex guitarwork and consistent tempos. Other significant Swedish acts to emerge in the early 1990s were Unleashed and Grave. Unleashed debuted with *Where No Life Dwells* in 1991, and Grave debuted in 1991 with *Into the Grave*, followed by 1992's *You'll Never See*. The albums incorporated simple riffs, guttural grunts, and exceptionally heavy guitars.

At this time, Florida Death Metal, with its tight technicality and clean Morrisound production, rose to new heights of creativity and popularity. In 1991, Death released *Human*, a hallmark of technical prowess (though considered less "brutal" by many fans). Also in 1991, Morbid Angel released its second album, *Blessed Are the Sick*, with cleaner production but untamed, even bizarre, guitar leads and riff patterns. The early 1990s also saw the release of Cannibal Corpse's second album, *Butchered at Birth* (1991). With the album's harsh, barely-tuned guitars, most fans saw it as pure, brutal Death Metal. Deicide's second album, *Legion* (1992), was more technical than its last and even faster with additional blast beats. Other significant releases were Malevolent Creation's *The Ten Commandments,* Monstrosity's *Imperial Doom*, and Obituary's second album, *Cause of Death*.

Elsewhere in America, other Death Metal bands introduced their sounds into the genre. In Maryland, *Deceased* debuted with *Luck of the Corpse*. From the start, Deceased occupied a unique place in the Death Metal scene thanks to a strong Thrash Metal influence. As Deceased frontman and drummer King Fowley explains,

> When I was growing up in the metal scene, Death Metal was still about Heavy Metal adding lyrics of doom and despair and, well, death! It didn't have to incorporate down-tuned guitars, and the things it became today. It was about metal and the gloomy lyrics of death and despair! As it became more "extreme," bands found any way they could to be more "over the top," be it lower tuning, deeper vocals, more extreme artwork, etc. ... Deceased was never about that! Our goal was to be *us*! We wanted to have melody yet stay very aggressive and energetic in our sound, but we also wanted to include good guitar solos, memorable choruses, and *Heavy* Metal traditions as well.

Deceased released quality Death Metal albums throughout the 1990s and into the present.

Slightly to the north, New York state would prove a breeding ground for the increasingly ferocious sounds of Death Metal. In 1991, New York's Immolation debuted with *Dawn of the Possessed*, a frightening and wraithlike condemnation of Christianity. The following year marked the

5. Rise and Fall: 1989–1994   63

King Fowley of Deceased. Photography by John Yolke.

appearance of Mortician's *Mortal Massacre* EP. *Mortal Massacre* boasted some of the lowest guitar tuning and vocals imaginable, helping to establish Will Rahmer as a formidable vocalist. In 1992, Incantation released its debut album, *Onward to Golgotha* through Relapse Records. In description of the band's music, Incantation drummer Kyle Severn writes, "The style that I play with Incantation is a very blasphemous, demented, aggressive style of Death Metal. We have raw, barbaric sound on our albums. ... We incorporate a very dark, doom-feeling [with our] riffs and drums with lots of fast, twisted blast beats."

Each of these New York bands made significant contributions to the Death Metal genre. However, as the movement expanded, nearly every state could boast a quality Death Metal band. Among the most notable contributions during Death Metal's mid-90's heyday were Massacre's *From Beyond*, Repulsion's *Excruciation*, and Master's second album *On the Eighth Day, God Created Master*. By 1993, the third album of Chicago's Macabre, *Sinister Slaughter,* was released through Nuclear Blast. Macabre's music was very unique, offbeat "murder metal" with lyrics all about serial killers. By the mid–1990s, Thrash Metal had clearly given way to Death Metal. Matt Medeiros has written at length on this crucial era in the genre's development:

64   II. THE HISTORY OF THE DEATH METAL SCENE

Kyle Severn of Incantation. Photograph by Frank White.

Death Metal came to a peak in the early nineties. ... The primitive, raw feel of most bands prior to this would evolve into a thicker, more brutal sound. ... The music itself had become more complicated. ... Most Florida bands (and accordingly the "Floridian" sound) would take a vocal cue from Chris Barnes, on Cannibal Corpse's *Butchered at Birth* and Glen Benton on Deicide's *Legion*. ... Trey Azagthoth of Morbid Angel was raising the bar for lead guitarists with his insane solos and bizarre riffs. Meanwhile, in New York,

John McEntee of Incantation. Photograph by Bill Zebub.

Suffocation was incorporating "mosh" riffs, on the *Human Waste* EP and subsequent releases. ... The technical riffing of Doug Cerrito would add the complexity seen by the likes of Death and Morbid Angel. ... [also], by this point, blast beats were common amongst many bands ... .

At this time, I saw interviews with bands like Obituary in "mainstream" metal magazines like *Hit Parader*, and Cannibal Corpse CDs were accessible at most record stores. This was when the music was most popular, and everyone was looking to cash in. A million bands and a hundred labels came out of the woodwork and eventually saturated the scene. ... There was money to be made, shows were packed, and CDs were getting sold.

At this point, numerous bands had found the sounds that made them popular and they thus decided to release albums quite similar to their former releases. As "brutal" and uncompromising as these albums may have been, many Death Metal fans mourn that there was little innovation in the genre as a whole. Deicide's *Once Upon the Cross* and Incantation's *Mortal Throne of Nazarene* fall among those that successfully tread the path already established by their creators on past albums. There were, however, several bands that significantly evolved, progressed, or otherwise changed. New York's Suffocation is perhaps the most notable among these. After the less noticed *Breeding the Spawn*, Suffocation released *Pierced from Within*. *Pierced from Within* included Suffocation's trademark thick, "chunky" sound from the *Effigy* album, but also displayed more complex and technically impressive music. Suffocation's work would later prove enormously influential.

Several Florida bands continued to garner attention through the release of groundbreaking albums. Malevolent Creation's second album, *Retribution*, was considered pure Death Metal with drumming that was immediately envied. Cannibal Corpse's third album, *Tomb of the Mutilated*, was the most popular yet. The band touched mainstream culture playing *Hammer Smashed Face* in a brief appearance in *Ace Ventura: Pet Detective*, the widely successful Jim Carey comedy. Meanwhile, Morbid Angel's third album, *Covenant*, was released by a major label, and a few Morbid Angel video clips (such as "Rapture") were even displayed on MTV during the program *Headbangers' Ball*. Perhaps the increasing mainstream acceptability of Death Metal was seen most clearly in the collaboration—brief as it may have been—between Earache and Columbia Records, a major label.

As Death Metal's ferocious tunes moved nearer to the mainstream, a number of bands changed their pace and abandoned extremity, some leaving the genre behind entirely. Death, for instance, is thought to have left the Death Metal genre with the release of the band's fifth album, *Individual

Thought Patterns (1993). The album, which was more skillful and technical, offered comprehensible vocals and was not deemed "brutal" in Death Metal terms. Obituary also produced slower, catchier material with the release of *The End Complete* (1992) and *World Demise* (1994). Overseas, a similar toning down was evidenced in several albums including Carcass's 1994 album *Heartwork* (a melodic album with intricate and impressive guitarwork), Entombed's 1993 album *Wolverine Blues* (which was slow, subdued, and more like Rock than Death Metal), and even Napalm Death's 1994 album *Fear, Emptiness, and Despair* (which was noticeably slower than the band's former work).

Given these changes and the simultaneous mainstream interest in Death Metal music, it seemed that the Death Metal scene in the mid–1990s was simply unsure of where it stood. There was a constant tension between the inviting mainstream, which seemed willing to give some Death Metal a try, and the essentially anti-mainstream culture that gave birth to and nourished the genre. Could an underground movement survive above ground?

6

The Present: 1995–2002

What was the consequence of Death Metal's foray into the mainstream? After a momentous blaze of success, many of the genre's forerunners abandoned extremity, and the mainstream all but abandoned Death Metal. The movement, however, did not die, and more Death Metal bands continued to deliver their extreme tunes. The scene simply retreated back into the underground. Explains Jason Netherton, "It's a niche market, generally to be found within a certain age group and predominantly male. With no real money behind this stuff (except for a blessed few 'big' bands), it becomes mainly a word of mouth effort channeled through underground communication networks. Respect comes afterward if you have something special about your sound."

In returning to the underground, the Death Metal scene took along some added business sense and kept connected with the aid of the newly formed Internet. According to Nile's Karl Sanders, business sense is essential today:

> You've got to work at your craft but you've got work at the business. A lot of bands just forget to have manners. A lot of business opportunities come about if you are persistent, talented, and you are a human being to other human beings. ...If someone would ask me what kind of advice I'd have for a band starting up, I'd say go buy the book *How to Win Friends and Influence People*. That will take you a long way as long as you have something that's worth selling and will do what it takes to promote yourself. ...You really have

Jason Netherton of Misery Index (and formerly Dying Fetus) in 2002. Photograph by Flo Homer.

to carpet-bomb the world with your stuff unceasingly, and if it's good, perhaps people will care.

The Internet has drastically affected the scene. According to Jason Netherton, "Establishing a name was more difficult before the Internet and it took much more money just to get things going. Today you can be in a band from nowhere and have no real longevity or even a demo and get somewhere if you spread your name enough on the Internet." The Internet has also increased the availability of music in mp3 format, which is positive in that it adds convenience, but negative in that it detracts from the need for effort and passion. Says Netherton, "When we started, we did cassette demos and mailed them everywhere. This method has steadily become obsolete with CDRs and mp3s, but because it took effort then (more money up front and time), it was something really special."

Despite the added effort entailed in perpetuating a scene without the aid of the mainstream media, Death Metal has made significant advances in recent years. Some of the most significant mid–1990s releases were made by Canadian band *Cryptopsy*. Both *Blasphemy Made Flesh* (1994) and the classic *None So Vile* (1996) were remarkably technical and breathtakingly fast. Other notable releases of the mid–1990s included those of the illustrious New York trio of Death Metal: Incantation, Immolation, and Mortician. Incantation's *Mortal Throne of Nazarene* and *Upon the Throne of Apocalypse* were considered by fans to be as brutal as the band's original works. Similarly, Immolation's *Here in After* (released by Metal Blade) and Mortician's *House by the Cemetery* have been deemed among the most fierce and uncompromising Death Metal albums.

It was Florida, however, that housed the forerunners of the scene throughout the 1990s. Cannibal Corpse's 1994 album *The Bleeding* was a bit catchier and slower but as successful as the band's previous work. *The Bleeding* was followed by the infamous album *Vile* (1996). *Vile* earned the attention and fury of Senator Bob Dole, who publicly criticized the band for its vulgarity, only augmenting Cannibal Corpse's notoriety and popularity. During the recording of *Vile*, Cannibal Corpse's notorious vocalist Chris Barnes left the band to pursue his side project, Six Feet Under, which would produce groovy, catchy music, generally considered less extreme Death Metal.

In 1995, Florida's Morbid Angel released a fourth album, *Domination*, followed by *Formulas Fatal to the Flesh* (1998), typically deemed more aggressive and complex than the former. Morbid Angel grew increasingly popular with the release of these albums. Also in Florida, Deicide continued to produce its brand of deep, fast, memorable Death Metal with *Once*

Upon the Cross (1995) and *Serpents of the Light* (1997). Nonetheless, the band's popularity waned allegedly due to troubles with a record label relatively apathetic to Death Metal.

Deicide's troubles with Roadrunner Records were symptomatic of a greater phenomenon. Larger labels simply grew disinterested with Death Metal, and fewer Death Metal bands garnered attention from Nuclear Blast, Century Media, and Earache. This left America's small but tight corporation, Relapse Records, as the forerunning Death Metal label. Relapse would release several important Death Metal albums through the 1990s into the present. Among them were Incantation's *Diabolical Conquest* (1998) and *The Infernal Storm* (2000), and Mortician's relentless, drum-machine-led *Hacked Up for Barbeque* (1996), *Zombie Apocalypse* (1998), *Chainsaw Dismemberment* (1999) and *Domain of Death* (2001). Relapse Records continues to sign and support Death Metal bands from the past and the present.

All in all, to stay vital and maintain an underground network, the scene grew more tight-knit and business savvy. Bands grew accustomed to taking on promotions and business duties themselves. Says Karl Sanders, "Promoters saw that there were so many bands that were willing to work hard to promote themselves, that they were like 'Well, why should we promote the show? Let the bands do the hard work.'" And work hard they have. Writes Paul Ryan of Origin, "We just kept plugging away at it and handing out demos at national Death Metal acts' shows, and word got around that we were for real." Rather than traditional label-led promotion, constant touring helped bands to become known and respected all over the country and even the world. Constant touring is anything but effortless. Explains Origin's Jeremy Turner, "It's like being married; you have to learn how to get along, compromise, swallow egos, etc." Jason Netherton welcomes the blood and sweat entailed in the touring experience: "You travel hundreds of miles for no money in the first year or two, and it does not matter because it is all about the metal anyway. If you can get over all of the lost money and hours of practice, then you will welcome the day you get $50, a pizza, and a nice rowdy crowd ... cause it is about the music anyway."

The bands that typified this new sensible and demanding approach included California's Deeds of Flesh, New York's Skinless, and Maryland's Dying Fetus. Relapse Records signed both Skinless and Dying Fetus. Skinless would please crowds with wild live performances and slamming, heavy mosh riffs. Dying Fetus attracted the masses with a catchy and influential sound that meshed Suffocation-like Death Metal with hardcore influences. Dying Fetus' third album, *Killing on Adrenaline*, propelled the band to

Erik Sayenga of Dying Fetus and Witch-Hunt. Photograph by Kristel Ames.

prominence. The slamming musical style of Dying Fetus would catch on and bring a powerful current of crushingly heavy — though quite "groovy"— music through the underground. Among the important bands to adopt this musical style are Fleshgrind, Pyrexia, Internal Bleeding, Devourment, Waco Jesus, Lividity, and Malignancy.

Across the world in Australia, the mid–1990s saw the release of Blood Duster's *Fisting the Dead*, and releases from other significant Australian bands like Sadistik Exekution, Abominator, Bestial Warlust, and Destroyer 666. The Australian sound mimicked the music of the earliest Death Metal bands like Possessed and early Morbid Angel. Meanwhile in Europe, the Grindcore/Death Metal movement continued throughout the 1990s. Notable bands in this genre included Spain's Hemorrhage, Germany's Gut and Dead, and Sweden's Nasum and Regurgitate. As the 1990s progressed, the Swedish sound would move into its more melodic and subdued new wave with the later releases of Entombed, Hypocrisy, and At the Gates. Melody and traditional Thrash Metal tempos characterized this new movement. Swedish bands In Flames and Dark Tranquility would help the new, memorable Swedish sound spread throughout the world.

As the 1990s approached their end, some bands from the early days of Death Metal returned with ferocity after many had thought they left the genre behind. Napalm Death, for instance, released *Leaders Not Followers* and *Enemy of the Music Business*, considered a return to "extremity" by fans. A notable reunion of the era occurred when vocalist Killjoy reformed Necrophagia in 1998. Necrophagia would release *Holocausto de la Morte* and *Black Blood Vomitorium*, featuring popular Pantera singer Phil Anselmo.

Newer bands have also made very significant contributions to the genre. Among the most important bands in the Death Metal underground today is American band Nile. The band's 1998 album *Amongst the Catacombs of Nephren-Ka* and 2000's *Black Seeds of Vengeance* included atmospheric Egyptian music in a solid Death Metal framework. Says Nile frontman Karl Sanders:

> We're definitely somewhere left of center as far as Death Metal goes. While we do have all the normal elements one associates with Death Metal—fast guitars, blasting drums, growly vocals— we do a lot of other stuff ... a lot of symphonic stuff, a lot of Middle Eastern, ethnic instrumentation. What we're really trying to do is present ancient Egyptian mythologies and history in some sort of musical sense.

Nile became very prominent in the scene thanks to talent, relentless touring, and good business sense. Karl Sanders readily volunteers that this success has come with a price of "an immense pile of hard work and never letting up. In the past five or six years, I've gotten maybe two hours of sleep a night. If you want your music or art to be successful, you have to accept that there's a certain amount of business that one has to put the same sort of effort into." Nile has succeeded in expending this effort where many other talented underground bands have failed.

A second notable Death Metal band to emerge in recent years is Krisiun. This Brazilian band would stun the scene with precise and extreme Death Metal. Krisiun's work would influence countless Brazilian bands such as Abhorrence, Mental Horror, Nephasth, and Rebaelliun. Finally, a third noteworthy Death Metal band to arise in recent years is Angelcorpse of Missouri. Though no longer in existence, Angelcorpse left an indelible mark on the scene with the albums *Hammer of the Gods*, *Exterminate*, and *The Inexorable*. Pete Helmkamp, who performed bass and vocals for Angelcorpse, proudly comments on the music that the band produced:

> Concerning Angelcorpse, one can see that we had much more in common with the essence of savage ferocity that truly makes a great band than the majority of our labelmates and peers. I don't hesitate to say that in ten years,

Angelcorpse will be one of a handful of bands that stands the test of time — a band like Possessed, for instance, whose music one never tires of — and will always hold up to the new sounds and styles of the day. I attribute this to the fact that Gene and myself (the two masterminds behind Angelcorpse) came from very different musical and personal backgrounds. As much as he and I had in common, we had different, yet this was what fueled Angelcorpse: the constant struggle, strife, camaraderie, and unified will that forged the iron, blood, and blasphemy of our music and lyrics.

As these newer bands have made important contributions to the Death Metal genre in recent years, many standard bearers in the scene continue to release pure, quality Death Metal. Immolation, for instance, recently released *Failures for Gods* and *Close to a World Below*. Among Cannibal Corpse's recent albums are *Gallery of Suicide* and *Bloodthirst*, which are thought to retain "brutality" while exploring different dynamics and tempos. In addition to Cannibal Corpse, other Florida bands continue to perpetuate the famous Florida sound. Powerful releases in recent years have been made by Monstrosity and Malevolent Creation.

Interestingly enough, it seems as though Death Metal's hard-won underground success in recent years has yet again attracted the attention of larger labels. Signs of a mild resurgence in the scene include the incorporation of more Death Metal acts onto larger labels like Earache (which recently released a Hate Eternal album) and Century Media (which recruited Krisiun and released Cryptopsy's *Whisper Supremacy* and *And Then You'll Beg*). Where does this leave the scene? At this point, it is difficult to make any predictions.

Despite the strong releases made in recent years, many musicians in the genre are skeptical about the scene's capacity to produce new and influential bands. Countless interviewees expressed concern that Death Metal bands have already done everything that can be done musically. Explains Erik Sayenga, "There's only so low you can tune or so fast you can play a blast beat." Says King Fowley, "To me, the Death Metal movement is just repeating itself, and that's really all it can do." Pete Helmkamp takes an even more extreme view: "Metal has evolved to the point of its own extinction. ... We've run out of frontiers, so to speak." There is a sense in which these concerns are very legitimate, because many bands of late are simply repeating the musical stylings of older bands. There is far less creativity than there was in the earliest days of Death Metal. Moreover, because many believe the boundaries of the genre are so explicitly defined, too much musical "creativity" might produce great music but it would not necessarily be considered Death Metal.

Nonetheless, to claim that Death Metal has no more frontiers is

6. The Present: 1995–2002

John Longstreth, James Lee, Jeremy Turner, Mike Florez, and Paul Ryan of Origin. Photograph by N.J. Purcell.

probably a premature exclusion of an array of possibilities. The members of Origin are open-minded about Death Metal's future prospects as are many musicians. Says Karl Sanders:

> There's lots more to be done. The surface isn't even scratched. People who believe that it's all been done are narrow-minded and limited in their thinking. I think in the spirit of metal, there is a work ethic. The "metal gods" reward those who are willing to work hard. If bands are willing to just regurgitate all the material that's been done before without adding anything new, then that's when it suffers, it dies on the vine. I think if you're willing to work hard and you've got new ideas, what can't be done?

In truth, the Death Metal scene has witnessed ups and downs, peaks and falls over the years. There were times in the past when the press and others declared it definitively dead. Yet, the movement soon proved them wrong. As long as there are dedicated individuals with remarkable passion producing the music they love, Death Metal will survive. The scene is likely to stay underground, but it is a more sophisticated underground composed of musicians and fans truly devoted to the music irrespective of the mainstream's approval or disapproval. Whatever lies ahead for the scene, the past has proven that Death Metal is a lasting and formidable force in the underground.

Part III

Death Metal and American Politicians

7

The Skeleton in America's Closet

We cannot stop these horrific school massacres and the larger epidemic of youth violence without talking about the culture of carnage surrounding our kids [and] turning some of them into killers.—Senator Joseph I. Lieberman

We are developing a subculture within a culture, a nation within a nation. No wonder murder rates are soaring. No wonder drug abuse is rampant. No wonder that children are shooting children on the streets of this city. No wonder children twelve years of age carry guns to school. No wonder that suicides among teenagers have reached such alarming levels. ... People should become aware of what is going on. They should become aware of the lyrics in rock music.—Senator Robert Byrd

With such messages of death and degradation delivered through the media, and with our nation awash with guns easily accessible to young people, is it any surprise that troubled youths are now taking up these weapons and going on rampages, killing their classmates and teachers?—Senator Diane Feinstein

These cultural indicators have very real implications. They bespeak a breakdown in the old rules and limits which once governed our public lives and the way we raised our children. We are left with a vacuum, a values vacuum, in which our children learn that anything goes, and which I believe is at the heart of our society's worst problems.—Senator Joseph I. Lieberman

III. DEATH METAL AND AMERICAN POLITICIANS

> Young people listen to this vile trash and it puts ideas into their heads, and they think it is the in thing to do—newborns conceived out of wedlock, condemned to lives without fathers, and potentially doomed to futures of crime, confusion, and purposelessness. Day after day, young Americans are being bombarded by the entertainment industry of this country with pornography, vulgarity, tastelessness, promiscuity, violence, drug propaganda, profanity, barbarism, nihilism, and hedonism.— Senator Robert Byrd

> These songs ... are helping to create a culture of violence that is increasingly enveloping our children, desensitizing them to consequences and ultimately cheapening the value of human life.— Senator Joseph I. Lieberman

Littleton, Colorado. Paducah, Kentucky. Little Rock, Arkansas. San Diego, California. Due to the apparent surge of dramatic murders in American schools, the topic of violence in the media has exploded on the Senate floor. Hatch, Byrd, Feinstein, and Lieberman are among the dominant coalition of congressmen blaming the entertainment industry for violent behavior in society. Music has been targeted as a cause for crime and social demoralization. Senator Orrin J. Hatch headed a Senate committee on youth violence in September of 1999. The committee concluded that "modern music lyrics have become increasingly explicit concerning sex, drugs, and violence against women. A preference for heavy metal music may be a significant marker for alienation, substance abuse, psychiatric disorders, suicide risk, sex-role stereotyping, and risk-taking behaviors during adolescence" (Senate Committee of the Judiciary, 1999). Although the Senators admit that "no studies have documented a cause and effect relationship between violent lyrics and aggressive behavior," they nonetheless declare that "modern music glorifies acts of violence" and conclude that this must translate into violent behavior and unhealthy attitudes.

Former Vice-President Al Gore and Senator Joseph Lieberman went so far as to threaten the entertainment industry (as of October 2000) that it would face legislation should the Democrats win the White House. What are Gore and Lieberman aiming at? It sounds like censorship, but they deny that label, insisting that they are not attacking the First Amendment and that "it is not too much to ask that the music industry refrain from rewarding and celebrating these purveyors of violence" (Senate Committee on the Judiciary, 1999). Al Gore is following in the footsteps of his wife who, as the founder of the Parents' Music Resource Center (PMRC), advocated limiting access to music with violent lyrical content. The PMRC is the source of the parental advisory stickers that currently adorn so many rock and rap CDs (though rarely country or pop music CDs with similar themes) (Cockburn 10–11). Democrats have made concessions to big business restrictions and anti-monopoly rules in order to allow leaders from the record industries to meet and discuss a reduction of violent themes in the art that they market. Even the Republicans support their decision; Dick and Lynn Cheney of the George W. Bush camp have teamed up with Tipper Gore and Joe Lieberman in their critique of the media. The parties have found something on which to agree: music has become a threat to society and its children. As Orrin Hatch concluded, "No one can reasonably argue that the Constitution prohibits restricting such material" (www.senate.gov/~hatch/littleton.html).

The politicians are not the only ones who fear and despise such music. The American Academy of Pediatrics has recently released a statement on the potential effects that violent media may have on children. They conclude that "children who see a lot of violence are more likely to view violence as an effective way of settling conflicts. ... Viewing violence can lead to emotional desensitization to violence in real life. ... Viewing violence may lead to real life violence" (AAP 2000). No statistical evidence is cited in their report. However, it was evocative and convincing enough to persuade the unanimous passage of the Brownback Amendment in 1999, which is intended to "push the entertainment industry to self-control, to self-regulate, to acknowledge ... that they are contributing to a crisis that is killing too many of our children" (www.senate.gov/~rpc/rva/1061/1061110.htm).

Often, articles and essays describing metal only reinforce the negative impressions of most people. The *Albuquerque Journal* wrote extensively on Death Metal in May and June of 2000. The portrayal was very negative and focused on disturbing song lyrics. According to investigative reporter Thomas J. Cole, Chris Barnes, formerly of Cannibal Corpse, "seemed puzzled when asked whether there is some invisible line of bad taste which even he won't cross" (Cole 2000). The *Albuquerque Journal* jumps from a discussion of the lyrics to the presentation of two horrific cases of murder and violence. The *Journal* interviews the mothers of two girls who were murdered by males "deeply involved in death-metal music." Although there is no establishment of causation, and although these are deviant, non-representative cases, the *Journal* seems to present them as evidence that Death Metal music causes violence and even murder. Is it fair and reasonable to draw such conclusions? Certainly, one could choose any social group and uncover two members of that group who have committed atrocities, but these members cannot be taken as representative of the whole. Death Metal, however, is easy to sensationalize, and therefore the media often demonize it. This promotes fear and prejudice, and helps to explain the nearly universal condemnation of Death Metal fans.

III. DEATH METAL AND AMERICAN POLITICIANS

It is clear that music is blamed to a large extent for violence and immorality in American culture. Although no studies have been able to confirm a relationship between interest in violent media and actual violent behavior, Americans have concluded that fans of certain types of music are to be feared and scorned. If the widely accepted hypotheses of the relationship between violence and music are true, there may be grounds for such attitudes; however, these grounds have not been established and thus popular assumptions are at present no more warranted than typical prejudice.

The Politics of Censorship

Death Metal is a relatively young phenomenon, and no precedents have been set regarding its censorship. Plenty of precedents regarding censorship itself have, however, been set. To assess the likelihood that congressional efforts at censorship of Death Metal music will succeed, it useful to look at the overall history of congressional broadcast content regulation. Events throughout history suggest that political efforts at censorship will fail. Moreover, a detailed look at congressional hearings reveals some shady behavior on the part of congressmen and some doubts as to their actual motivations in advocating censorship.

The First Amendment is repeatedly invoked by opponents of broadcasting regulation who affirm that such regulation cannot succeed (Blumner A18). The evidence seems to suggest that they are correct: "Broadcast content regulation has failed miserably and will continue to fail" (Krattenmaker & Powe 2–3). Yet despite repeated failures and the potency of the First Amendment, congressmen have perennially and passionately brought the issue to the floor. What can account for this?

According to the theory of symbolic politics, the actions of congressmen with respect to the regulation of media violence have been more symbolic than substantive. In many cases, congressmen have acted in the manner which best ensures their own promotion, enrichment, or popularity, irrespective of empirical evidence or declared moral convictions. In other cases, they have addressed the topic out of sincere concern, but have stopped short of action. In nearly every instance, congressmen have embraced the symbolic power of the media violence issue and have exploited its potential to provoke feeling through highly emotional appeals. Proponents of the symbolic politics theory would argue that Congress creates issues, manufactures opposing sides, rallies public passion and support, and fights battles without accomplishing anything substantive. Such symbolic wars make the individual politician appear to be a crusader before his constituents but prevent him from actually having to pass any legislation that could harm powerful industry executives (Hoerrner *1999* 684–98).

The first well-developed theory of symbolic politics is that of Murray Edelman. For Edelman, symbolic politics take hold when groups are interested only in symbolic reassurance: it is not merely the politicians who are manufacturing symbols and manipulating the public; the public plays an important role in legitimatising and validating the symbols embraced by congressmen (Edelman *1977* 43–4, Edelman *1971* 3–4). Thus, Congress is not trying to deceive the public into believing that media violence is responsible for actual violence; instead, congressmen as well as their constituents want to believe this, and often, both groups do (Edelman *1977* 50–55). Edelman calls this phenomenon "political quiescence" (Edelman *1985* 22–23).

Some theories of symbolic politics suggest that morals are often insincere (although this suggestion is not essential to the thesis of symbolic politics). As the research within this chapter will reveal, there is a great deal of evidence for this insincerity on the part of many politicians. Nonetheless, possession of sincere moral convictions on the part of politicians and their constituents does not invalidate the theory of symbolic politics because it does not change the fact that substantive claims and actions are absent. Moral arguments against media violence attack symbols rather than tangible things.

The main signals of symbolic political behavior are unclear, emotional, or provocative arguments, which are "sociopsychological" rather than rational (Edelman *1985* 30). Such arguments show very little intellectual grasp of the situation. They are personalized, oversimplified, based on stereotypes, and rely on insecurities and uncertainties. Symbolic scapegoats serve to relieve tension; they are opiates (Edelman *1985* 31–8). In terms of the broadcast regulation issue, one might say that media violence (rather than poverty or lax gun control) serves as a scapegoat blamed for actual violence.

Fans of Death Metal tend to adhere to this view. Countless interviewees complained that the current political battles over "violent" entertainment forms that are believed to promote violent behavior are utterly non-substantive. Karl Sanders is irate at the situation:

I think that it's a smokescreen. Most every politician or political group that is campaigning against violence is not willing to take the effort to solve the real problem of violence in our country, which I think is socially and economically motivated. Like, you have a bunch of young black males committing crimes because they're the ones that are raised and bred and put in an economic position where that's how you survive, that's what you've gotta do. Instead of solving the real problems that breed that sort of hate and violence and the whole cycle, you get people campaigning against music or violent video games or whatever. The voters are supposed to believe that they're trying to do something about violence, but they're not. [Music]'s not the cause of violence; that's utter ridiculousness.

Despite vocal advocacy of censorship, symbolic political theory suggests that the threat of censorship is not very genuine. That is, if legislation curbing media violence is passed, it will be unclear and rather ineffectual because it is a manufactured solution from the start. Edelman explains that the "underlying ambivalence" of such legislation is clear in the "irresolute manner in which regulations are enforced and particularly the predictable provision of loopholes, inefficient inspection, and devices for evasion" (Edelman *1985* 62). Often, Congress has no intention to make substantive changes; its role is that of "accommodator and conservator of established features of the status quo" (Dolbeare & Edelman 296).

Congressional interest in television violence began in the 1950s (Rowland 99–100). In 1952, the House authorized an FCC Subcommittee to investigate the violent and offensive nature of broadcast programs (Hoerrner *1999*). Representative Oren Harris (D-AR), who owned shares in a television station, led the Subcommittee. The final report was a succinct statement that all findings were inconclusive (Rowland *1983* 99–100). In 1954, the Subcommittee leadership shifted to Senator Kefauver, who had his eyes on the presidential bid in the following year's election. Kefauver himself had convoluted ties to the media industry, from which he had profited immensely. (For instance, he served as the narrator of *Crime Syndicated*, which was a rather violent television program.) Despite all of these connections with the media industry, Kefauver became one of its staunchest opponents as the chair of the Subcommittee on Juvenile Violence. Kefauver's hearings featured witnesses that presented only one side of the story, that of media-violence opponents. In the end, the Subcommittee simply called for more research on the topic and asked the FCC to take content into consideration when renewing licenses (Hoerrner *1999*). Neither of the recommendations became legislation.

The hearings on media violence and juvenile delinquency in the 1950s certainly support the theory of symbolic politics. The actions of the main players appear to have been motivated by the desire for enhanced personal popularity and self-enrichment, rather than the desire to discover truth and address youth violence. Over 1,000 pages of testimony on the possible relationship between media violence and youth violence were produced; however, no conclusions were drawn and nothing was actually accomplished (Hoerrner *1999*). Moreover, the hearings were almost purely emotive and lacked all substance. Any conclusions regarding a link between media violence and actual violence that the Subcommittee may have made were not made on the basis of scientific evidence. In short, the media violence symbol became the scapegoat for an inexplicable and highly challenging social problem, juvenile delinquency, that everyone was united in despising but that no one could really explain. A pattern emerged in the 1950s that has repeated itself a number of times. First, the government criticizes the broadcasting industry for its violent program content. Second, the industry accepts this verbal criticism and promises to improve. Third, the government stays out of the industry's business until the cycle repeats itself.

The media violence issue came into the spotlight once again in 1961 with the hearings of the Dodd Subcommittee. The hearings proceeded much as the previous had, with many impassioned pleas and very little scientific evidence. Dodd needed the media violence issue because he was suffering at the polls and doing poorly politically, but he also needed money from the broadcasting industry (Rowland 110–111). No meaningful legislative action resulted from the findings of the Dodd Subcommittee. The reason given was, of course, the First Amendment. One could probably wager safely that the congressmen were aware of the First Amendment when they initiated the hearings to begin with. They may have felt shielded all along by the Amendment. Like opponents of Death Metal today, they were comfortable shouting about media violence and confident that they would not have to rub shoulders with industry executives when it finally came down to the bottom line. The public, in turn, was very content to hear Congress talk, even if no legislative action followed. For both politicians and their constituents, talk about media violence served as a mild opiate to ease feelings of responsibility and concern for the violent acts in society.

The late 1960s saw a situation of social chaos similar to the perceived moral crisis of today, spurred by school shooting. After the riots in Watts and the assassinations of Martin Luther King Jr. and the Kennedys, Americans became increasingly concerned about violence in society. When President Lyndon Johnson called for the Presidential Commission on the Causes and Prevention of Violence in 1968, the situation betrayed the search for a scapegoat. The late 1960s investigations that took place in attempts to establish a link between media violence and actual violence were highly unscientific (Rowland 121; Ramey *2001*). The nation needed someone to blame for disturbing violent incidents, and in a state of widespread emotional and psychological distress, Americans were not overly careful in assigning culpability. The hearings were laced with specific gruesome examples, and lacking in statistical or scientific proof (Rowland 122). Nonetheless, the 1970s saw the release of the Surgeon General's final report, stating that there was indeed a correlation between exposure to media violence and level of aggressiveness (UCLA *1995*). This conclusion was far from perfect. Although there were a number of studies supporting the thesis that media violence could lead to actual violence, there were just as many significant studies refuting the same thesis (UCLA *1995*). These studies were not mentioned. Congress had achieved the desired result and acquired a useful scapegoat to relieve public tension and outcry over the violent society that encroached upon American homes and families. Yet, after the production of all of this research, all of these reports, and ultimately, a "scientific" conclusion, what would happen? Nothing (Krasnow & Longley 62). In accord with the theory of symbolic politics, Congress continued to display an enthusiastic "willingness to investigate accompanied by a marked unwillingness to legislate" (Rowland 89).

In the 1980s, Americans witnessed the continuation of the pattern that had characterized the media violence debate for the past three decades and continues today. In 1986, the Senate Judiciary Committee met to discuss an anti-trust exemption for the broadcast industry so that industry representatives could meet to discuss joint reduction in violent programming. In 1989, the House passed the Television Improvement Act of 1989 (Cooper 109–110). Instead of placing restrictions on broadcasters, it removed them by permitting negotiations between marketing executives of various companies. Thus, the Television Improvement Act effectively allowed the industry more freedom and more opportunity for economic self-advancement. At the same time, the passage of the bill made it appear that legislators had done something to address media violence. In reality, however, there were no provisions that would ensure that the broadcast industry would actually use its new freedoms to discuss the media violence issue. In fact, it was under no obligation to do so (Cooper 113–114). It is the pattern of incidents such as this which convinces one that there is little imminent threat to the First Amendment.

As the pattern became slightly more visible, politicians felt the need to increase the appearance of efforts against social violence. After all, the talk in Congress had done nothing to alleviate increasing violence rates in society at large. The effect of the symbol was no longer as potent (Simon 373, McAvoy 14, Colford 6, Albiniak 13). Gang violence was a major problem in the early 1990s, and the desire to discover the cause of the increase in juvenile crime became the focus of two congressional investigations in 1992. Interestingly enough, social scientists had found an inverse relationship between media violence and youth violence in the early 1990s: as one increased, the other decreased. This did not deter congressmen from focusing on the media violence issue. During the hearings, a popular form of presentation involved showing clips from the most violent programs on TV (Cooper 117–118). This is a perfect illustration of non-substantive symbolic politics and the attempt to evoke a strong emotional reaction rather than a rational analysis of scientific evidence.

In 1993, eight bills regarding media violence were introduced into the Senate. Legal scholars agreed that none of them would survive the constitutional test, and it was likely that the creators of the proposed bills knew this as well (Cooper 127). Congressmen embraced symbolic politics at this time in order to increase their popularity while remaining fairly certain that they would not have to do anything to alienate the broadcast industry. None of the proposed media violence bills were passed (Cooper 128).

The issue arose again in 1996, a presidential election year. The source of pressure to address the media violence issue came from the White House. Because of the imminent election, the media were wary of the sincerity of these moves (Huff 4). To challenge Hollywood or the broadcast industry seemed highly out of character for the Clinton White House (Freeman E-11). Many accused the Democrats of attempting to steal the media violence issue from the Republicans, and particularly from President Bill Clinton's opponent in the presidential race, Senator Bob Dole (R-KS), who had slammed the media in 1995 and gained much publicity as a consequence of this (Rhodes 2).

Legislation was finally passed in the form of the Telecommunications Act of 1996, which required that the television industry develop a ratings system within a year and tie it to V-Chip technology for all television sets sold in the United States (Kunkel et al 157–158). At the same time, the Act "removed many of the regulatory roadblocks preventing media competition" (Cooper 132). It was thus rather satisfactory to broadcasters. Research had shown parental advisories and ratings to have been quite useless, and it did not seem likely that the V-Chip technology could change this substantially (Cantor, Harrison, & Kremar 179, *CQ Researcher 1997* 723–742). In the end, every side seemed to benefit from the congressional discussions of media violence, although no one had accomplished anything meaningful. In short, the politics of broadcast regulation have been predominantly symbolic, and history suggests that threats to the First Amendment are not as serious as they at first appear.

9

Content Regulation Today and Tomorrow

One of the central themes of the symbolic politics theory involves the importance of images that grab attention and provoke emotion. This suggests that a single gripping event will have more effect on the public and Congress than will a detailed scientific report describing quantitatively disturbing trends in society. Throughout history, the sporadic emergence of the media violence focus in Congress has not been entirely random; it has been provoked by highly publicized and gruesome events such as vicious murder stories or high profile assassinations. In recent years, congressional attention has been largely motivated by a few incidents of school shootings. The most notable of these was the Columbine high school shooting in 1999. Although there were a few other fatal school shootings similar to the one in Littleton, Colorado, none were as dramatic or highly publicized. Many have implied that the resurgence of the issue in Congress is a direct product of the school shootings (Albiniak and McConnell 20, Anonymous *1999* 34–35, Mundy *1999a* 32).

In terms of poor morality and cultural degradation, media violence was a scapegoat in every sense of the term: the low moral standards in American culture were considered the product of the low moral standards in the media. This faulty reasoning held court after Columbine. In the moral sense, media violence was a strong scapegoat and symbol. Surely, it seems rational and responsible for congressmen to address an issue as serious as an increase in youth violence, but whether such an issue really existed is questionable. All in all, from the start of 1996 through 2001, there have been 13 fatal school shootings in the United States (www.infoplease.com/spot.schoolviolence1). All of these received significant media attention, although some were certainly emphasized more than others. Thirteen seems to be a large and disturbing number of incidents, and it has prompted Lieberman and others to refer to an "epidemic of violence" and a "rash of school shootings" (Lieberman Press Office *1999*).

These highly emotional descriptions are really quite deceptive. There is no new "epidemic of violence," and recent occurrences of school shootings cannot be defined as a "rash." School violence is not a modern phenomenon. There were major problems with violent and lethal activity in the schools of 17th century France. In England, between 1775 and 1836, there were repeated student mutinies, strikes, and violent activities. School violence is not new to America either. In colonial America during the 1800s, there were approximately 300 violent school mutinies per year. Today, nothing comparable occurs. While hundreds were killed annually in the past, that number is about 20 in the present (*CQ Researcher 1998* 883–902). Today's events are idiosyncrasies that do not reveal a trend of increased violence. In reality, the number of school-associated killings dropped by almost 25 percent from 1992–1993 to 1997–1998. School violence is very low at present. While in 1965, 33 children under 12 were arrested for murder, that number dropped to 16 in 1996. Between 1994 and 1996, juvenile murder rates dropped by 30 percent, and overall juvenile violent crime rates dropped by 12 percent. Today, school shootings account for less than one percent of the 5,000 plus gun-related deaths of children under 19 in the United States every year. A child is twice as likely to be struck by lightning as to be shot at school (*CQ Researcher 1998* 883–902). Clearly, if there is a genuine desire to improve child safety, there are other much more dangerous and imminently threatening issues to address.

Why, if the statistics are as they are, is there so much emphasis on the recent school killings? First of all, the concern of the public is roughly proportional to the media coverage of the incident, and the interest of congressmen, in turn, is roughly proportional to the interest of the public. Secondly, the recent school shootings attained more attention and press coverage because they took place in rural neighborhoods. The total number slaughtered in the five recent rural school killings was only 27. Far more children killed and were killed in urban areas. In 1996, 100 murders were committed by juveniles in rural areas, while 1,868 were committed by juveniles in urban areas (*CQ Researcher 1998* 883–902). Yet all of the emphasis has been on the former. These incidents were unexpected and shocking and thus garnered much media attention. Therefore, the public and the politicians became concerned.

In 1999, Lieberman called for a White House summit with industry executives and political figures "to call a cease-fire in the virtual arms race" (Lieberman *28 Apr 1999*). He also made the request that a national commission be formed to study the causes of juvenile violence. Lieberman, John McCain (R-AZ), Edward Markey (D-MA), and Dan Burton (R-IN) introduced a joint resolution calling for a Surgeon General's report. In discussing his calls for legislation and investigation, Lieberman repeatedly brought up Littleton and stated that the media undoubtedly played a large role in creating the "culture of carnage" in which the massacre could occur (Lieberman *4 May 1999*). In May, Lieberman, Hatch (R-UT), and Brownback (R-KA) called for an FTC investigation of the broadcast industry's marketing practices during the Senate Commerce Committee hearing entitled "Marketing Violence to Children" (Mundy *1999b* 10). On May 11, McCain and Lieberman introduced legislation calling for a National Commission to investigate the so-called "epidemic of violence" (Lieberman *11 May 99*). There was strong bipartisan support behind the media violence action. Lieberman and McCain publicly criticized the absence of many show-business executives at Clinton's post-Columbine White House summit meeting, and made specific requests of the industry to tone down the violence.

These decisive actions do not seem to match the traditional behavior of a symbolic politician. As the millennium dawned, the theory of symbolic politics was no longer such a perfect fit in describing congressional behavior. It could not, however, be wholly abandoned. The behavior of congressmen was still highly emotional and quite unscientific. The two foundations upon which their entire crusade was established were largely mythical: 1) the relationship between exposure to violent behavior and aggressive tendencies, and 2) a new surge in juvenile violence and school killings. Neither point had any basis in fact. Although these foundations were substantively weak, they were symbolically strong. After the school shootings, Americans were left wondering how and why children could feel compelled to slaughter their classmates and themselves. The answer to this most profound question could not be found in something physical, like the presence of a gun. Instead, it had to arise from some deep moral depravity in American culture. From whence did this depravity spring? Of course the media would be held responsible. Omnipresent and constantly a part of life in America, television, radio, movies, and other forms of media were close enough to be targeted, and mysterious enough to take the blame. Americans needed to hold something spiritually, psychologically, and socially responsible for the inexplicable tragedies. Rather than blaming themselves and their own moral lapses, they turned to the low ethical standards displayed in the media. Media violence fulfilled the function of the spiritual scapegoat, the symbolic cause of American depravity.

Nonetheless, by the end of the first session of the 106th Congress, neither substantive nor symbolically meaningful legislation on the topic had been passed. Although none of the legislation had been successful, the issue did not die as the year 2000 opened. On February 29, a Michigan school shooting revived discussion on the topic (Palmer 442). The Senate narrowly passed Bill S876 requiring an FCC study on the effectiveness of the 1996 regulations and, if deemed necessary, the subsequent adoption of restricted hours for violent programming, but none of the proposals became law.

Things quieted down for a time, and the issue was not discussed in the media or in Congress until another publicized incident caught America's attention in January of 2001. This incident involved a young boy's imitation of a stunt seen on the MTV show *Jackass* in which someone set his legs on fire. Lieberman remained very vocal on the issue (Lieberman *29 Jan 2001*). Subsequent to the presidential election, Lieberman and Kohl introduced the Media Marketing Accountability Act of 2001 into the Senate. Cosponsored by Byrd and Clinton (D-NY), the Media Marketing Accountability Act gave the FCC the authority to legislate against companies that market adult-rated products to children.

As the new millennium dawned, there were many ways in which congressional action on the media violence issue took on a new tone. As Lieberman's case demonstrates, it became less of a game played for political advantage and more of a genuine moral crusade. Yet the sincerity, nobility, and spiritual "substance" of recent media violence legislation does not rule out the symbolic politics theory. The crucial thing to remember is that the basis for all action on the media violence issue is not ultimately rooted in fact. It is a symbol because it is purely abstract, purely normative. Concern in the wake of the recent school killings is understandable but not wholly rational. To target media violence as a cause of the "epidemic" is as irrational and irresponsible as calling the school shootings an "epidemic" at all. Focused studies of small groups have indicated a correlation between aggressive behavior and exposure to media violence, but in the big picture, rates of youth violence are not historically correlated with the amount of violence in media programming (*CQ Researcher 1997* 723–742). At times, the rates of violence in reality increased as the rates of violence in the media increased, but at other times, the reverse was true (*CQ Researcher 1998* 883–902). On the macro level, there is no evidence suggesting a correlation between media violence and violent behavior, never mind a causal relationship.

In accepting this failure to establish causation, the media violence issue was unshackled from a daunting responsibility. It became possible for politicians to attack media violence strictly because of the moral outrage it evoked. The media became not a direct force acting upon children and making them into killers, but rather a moral pollutant creating a "culture of carnage" in which kids would kill kids. No scientific evidence was required to pounce on the rural school killings (although they betrayed no real increase in youth violence) and to blame the broadcasting industry for contributing to this (although there was in fact no correlation). The only things required were moral outrage and good intentions.

Although Death Metal only emerged onto the debate floor a few decades ago, the topic will probably be tackled with the same evocative irrationality and hot air that has accompanied all attempts at broadcast content regulation in the twentieth century. Politicians are likely to vociferously label Death Metal music as a cultural pollutant, but whether any legislation will come of their emotional tirades in another matter.

The search for a scapegoat can be innocent enough when it serves as an outlet for public concern and does not result in any destructive legal action. Although one may look upon it kindly, it is necessary to remain critical. Symbolic politics and media violence are not simply issues to be debated in academic circles; they have a direct impact on the operation of representative government and the health of society. Americans may recognize and respect the value of symbols and the need for psychologically satisfying — not merely tangibly productive — actions on the part of politicians. At the same time, they must allow neither themselves nor their representatives to fall into "political quiescence." While symbolic political behavior on non-substantive issues like media violence may serve an important function, it cannot be allowed to interfere with or disrupt action on real social issues with a tangible impact on American society.

For this reason, even if it is unlikely that censorship will become a reality, it remains important to stand against it by protesting the irrationality (and often insincerity) of politicians seeking to blame the media for violence. Although the eradication of Death Metal music is a highly unlikely scenario, it is irresponsible of politicians to use it as a scapegoat for actual violence. It not only makes a mockery of the American system of representative government, but also prevents politicians from addressing significant social factors that might actually cause violent behavior. The prospect of actual censorship may be an illegitimate threat used merely as a political tool, but the threat to the American government and society posed by irrational symbolic politics is very real.

Part IV

Confronting the Consumers of Carnage

10

Facing the Demon

One way to question whether there is any validity to political arguments for censorship of entertainment forms such as Death Metal is to look at the supposed psychological "victims" of such music: its fans. Part IV will attempt to analyze the fans of Death Metal in order to examine possible patterns in their attitudes, philosophy, and behavior. The research will focus on the controversial topic of media violence, seeking to discern whether "violent" music fans are particularly apt to engage in violent behavior. Fans of Death Metal music form the sample population.

Hopefully, the suggestions made in this book are more scientific than the generalizations already drawn by many politicians and regular Americans. Although it was beyond the scope of this project to draw a truly representative sample of fans, it should at least transcend the level of common bias and assumption. The descriptive goals of this section include the identification of demographic norms in the Death Metal population, such as race, gender, income level, education level, and employment status. At a deeper level, this research assesses familial closeness, sociability, political knowledge, and apathy. Motivations for listening to Death Metal music, reasons for attending shows, and attitudes toward the Death Metal scene will be reviewed in order to create a descriptive portrait of the population. The discernment of norms in the philosophical and ideological makeup of the population is a major aim. This final element of description ties in with the potentially explanatory element of the project, which will assess behavioral norms and tendencies toward violence in an attempt to correlate these with demographic statistics and philosophical/ethical attitudes.

Ultimately, violent and criminal behavior rates within the Death Metal scene will be compared with rates for the general population (with certain demographic traits held constant, where possible). This explanatory aspect of the research will attempt to cast down on the hypothesis that fans of "violent" music are more likely than non-fans to engage in violence as a result of the music which they listen to.

In short, Part IV allows opponents of metal to take a true look into the scene about which they may have already drawn a number of conclusions. Those who fear and despise Death Metal are thus invited to face the demon. Together, we shall embrace the "evil" to see if it indeed exists. If "those" kids who listen to "that type" of music are not bad kids at all, one must conclude that music is not a bad influence — for this is, quite frankly, as vile as it gets.

11

Demographics

There exists a small number of sources on the demographic data of the population of Heavy Metal fans. Jeffrey Arnett, Peter Christenson, and Donald Roberts offer information about metal heads in their books *It's Not Only Rock & Roll* and *Metal Heads: Heavy Metal Music and Adolescent Alienation*, respectively. According to the existing data, fans of Heavy Metal tend to be white, male, middle class, and adolescent (Christenson & Roberts 103). This information about the basic demographic data of metal fans was roughly paralleled by the findings of this study.

Death Metal fans tend to be young; however, a description of them as "adolescent" may not be in order. About 58 percent of those surveyed were teenagers, and the remainder were twenty years of age or older. Thus, 42 percent of the population really cannot be considered adolescent. The age range extended from 13 to 33, with median 19 and mode 19. The average age of fans was 20.2. (It should be noted that the research assistants were age 18–21, so it is possible that they were more likely to approach persons closer in age to themselves. However, the research assistants were cautioned against this, so it likely that the average age of about 20 is fairly representative and accurate.)

What accounts for the youthfulness of the population? As a socially unacceptable form of entertainment, Death Metal is a form of rebellion. Rebellious activities have traditionally attracted the young, for they are means of asserting uniqueness and independence from the previous generation and particularly from parents. The interviews yielded some information that might be pertinent. Death Metal is a form of entertainment, of fun. Those interviewed seem to believe that it is something to be enjoyed while there is still time to enjoy it, before entry into the "real world" usurps a great deal of time and freedom. It is considered acceptable for youths to partake in some outlandish behavior, but society would be far less tolerant of the middle-aged man who goes to rock concerts on the weekends. Older persons seem rather isolated at shows, and youth do not interact with them unless the older person is a band member or some other respected icon of the scene. One college student who was no longer a part of the Death Metal scene, although he still thoroughly enjoyed the music, succinctly expressed a view that is probably shared by many others in the scene. "I love it," he said, "but you have to grow up sometime, right?" His words were representative of most of those interviewed. Drummer Brian Jimenez evoked this sentiment while explaining to a disappointed friend why he would prefer to go on tour with the band Mortician than stay in the United States to work on a project with his local friends. Twenty-one-year-old Brian immediately brought up his age, saying that this was his last chance to really live and be adventurous because, in a few years, it would be time to start a family and to find a steady, paying job outside of the non-lucrative field of Death Metal. Responsibility, schedules, and pay do not seem compatible with Death Metal, and therefore, older persons find it difficult to remain a part of the scene. Death Metal fans themselves seem to recognize and accept the transient nature of their lifestyle. This could account for the youth of the majority of fans.

Death Metal fans are not only young, but also disproportionately male. As previously mentioned, most existing demographic data classify the population as overwhelmingly male. This study did not confirm this statement. Indeed, the majority of fans, 65.7 percent, were male. However, 34.3 percent is certainly a considerable portion of females. The surveys thus indicated that males outnumber females by about two to one, and the observations at Death Metal shows conducted in this study suggest that this statistic is quite accurate. Many of the books written on metal were written a few years ago, and this may be an explanation for the lesser number of females in attendance. One who has attended shows for years might observe the entry of more and more females into the scene. As it grows increasingly acceptable and common for females to take on the same activities as males, perhaps the gender gap will continue to close.

Nonetheless, there are significantly more males than females involved in the Death Metal scene, and possible reasons for this should be examined. Once again, one cannot ignore the factor of cultural acceptability. Although Death Metal music in general is not deemed socially acceptable, it nonetheless seems that females involved in the scene would be looked

Some females, such as Angela Gossow of Arch Enemy, have become successful musicians in the scene. Photograph by Bill Zebub.

upon in an even harsher light than males. Males in general are expected to enjoy more aggressive forms of entertainment. Perhaps they are also less likely to be turned off by violence and physicality. Girls would be judged more for their involvement in such a scene.

Martha Bayles hypothesizes at length about the reasons why more males than females are involved in the scene. She claims that many of the lyrics are misogynistic or expressive of violence against women. In truth, although there are references to violence against women, it seems that there are references to violence against *everyone*. Bayles believes that metal appeals to a masculine obsession with "hardness" and describes mosh pits as "all-male workouts" (255). Males definitely do outnumber females in the mosh pits, but it is simply not accurate to describe mosh pits as "all-male." Frequent show attendees observe many females in mosh pits. Of course, mosh pits are very physical, and naturally larger persons would feel safer in pits. Most males are larger than most females, and therefore they would feel more secure in the mosh pits and are more likely to enter them. Still, females are represented in mosh pits and their behavior within those pits is not different from the behavior of the males. It thus seems that Bayles' hypothesis about mosh pits does not have the firmest foundations.

Bayles goes on to explore what she perceives to be the masculine nature of metal. She suggests that metal is a way for males to release anger at their fathers who do not accept them and to defy their fathers by defying cultural norms. This is psychological speculation and is not backed up by any evidence. Bayles' theory is in no way confirmed by the data collected in this study from interviews and observations. In fact, over 70 percent of those surveyed described their attitude towards their parents as loving or appreciative. Bayles is convinced, however, that Heavy Metal music is "a ritual venting of hostility against all of society, not just women, for blocking the natural aggressive instincts of young males" (254).

Aggression and physicality does play a part in metal music, but it seems short-sighted to attribute this to males alone. Those females interviewed cited similar reasons for enjoying metal shows and mosh pits. Many referred to an adrenaline rush or a very intense and alive experience. Such experiences may appeal to more males than females, but those females who are involved in the scene crave the experience as much as the males. Moreover, Bayles seems to make a major assumption when she jumps from expression of aggression and physicality to "venting of hostility." Those interviewed indicate that the experience of metal shows and metal music is not hostile. Observations of shows confirm this. If someone falls while dancing, everyone nearby tries immediately to help that person up.[8]

Moshers' behavior within the pit is very physical, but there is rarely anything hostile about it. Bayles does not seem justified in her description of metal music and metal fans, nor does her theory on masculinity seem accurate.

Are there any differences between male fans and female fans? Christenson and Roberts assert that female fans seem "more disturbed" than males (107–108). They cite their reason for this to be a study in which 60 percent of female fans compared to 20 percent of male fans admitted having feelings of hopelessness (107–108). The survey results of this study noticed a similar pattern, but the distinction between males and females was not as pronounced. Approximately 65 percent of females and 41 percent of males admitted to feeling depressed often. About 35 percent of females and 54.5 percent of males claimed that they felt depressed sometimes or rarely. None of the females and 4.5 percent of males reported never feeling depressed. Of course, it does seem likely, given cultural conditions, that females could be quite a bit more willing to discuss their feelings honestly and openly because, even in modern society, this is considered more acceptable for females than for males. Moreover, the differences between male depression levels and female depression levels in the metal population do not deviate considerably from the gender differences noted in the depressed population at large, and thus it does not seem fair to label metal females "more disturbed."

In other areas, the data did not display significant differences between female fans and male fans. Females were very slightly less likely to react violently in different situations, and they were less likely to see real violence as entertaining or as a means to solve problems between individuals (29.5 percent of males compared to 18.2 percent of females). Patterns in ethical beliefs were nearly parallel for males and females in all areas, except males were slightly more likely to accept subjectivist moral reasoning (31.8 percent of females compared to 44.2 percent of males). Females did not show more deviant behavior patterns than males. For average illegal drug use rate, the groups differed by less than one half of one percent. Similarly, for average number of sexual partners in the past twelve months, males and females differed by less than one half of one percent. Male fans and female fans do not appear significantly different in terms of attitude or behavior.

The interview data do suggest that females have one motive for attending shows that is not shared by males. For females, shows offer a great opportunity to meet a potential boyfriend because males outnumber females two to one. No males cited meeting girls as a reason to attend shows, but a few girls did indicate that meeting males was a good reason

Girls in the Death Metal scene often adopt feminine gothic style of dress as shown. Photograph by N.J. Purcell

to attend shows. When asked what she liked most about metal shows, metal girl Adrianne Buchta stated that besides the music, she loves the fact that "the guys are hot, especially those Swedish men!" (There are a number of Swedish metal bands that play in the United States.)

Jeffrey Arnett found similar results in his study of female fans of metal. He describes both male and female fans as "high sensation-seeking" and affirms that most females cite similar reasons as males for enjoying the music (140). He also points out the romantic element that appeals to females more than males. Many females are attracted to or are in awe of the performers; they also see concerts as a great place for meeting guys with similar interests (140–141). Arnett points out that there is a tension between the females who come to meet boys and others who come exclusively for the music (141). The findings of this particular study seem to substantiate some of Arnett's findings. None of the girls interviewed had any problem with the idea of meeting males at shows. They did, however, express annoyance at the fact that some girls dress especially provocatively and seem to come to shows exclusively to meet males rather than to hear the music. This is a very rare phenomenon; at the typical metal show, one does not find a number of scantily clad females. Although they do occasionally appear, it is rather rare to encounter such girls at shows. In general, females have similar motivations as males for becoming fans of Death Metal, yet for them, metal possesses the added attraction of a milieu of romantic possibilities.

The topic of race in metal is as fascinating as the topic of gender. Previous studies have found that metal heads are disproportionately white, and the survey results of this study confirmed these findings. Of those surveyed, 91.1 percent were white, 1.5 percent were black, 3 percent were Hispanic, and 4.5 percent fit into none of these categories. Thus, overall, less than 10 percent of those surveyed were not white. What can account for this? It is possible that methods of data collection affected the results of the study to some degree. A number of participants were recruited online, and Internet access is greater for whites than for minorities. However, it is unlikely that that would account for much of the variation, and, in general, it seems justified to state that the metal scene possesses a disproportionate percentage of whites. Location may account for some of the variation. Much of the data was collected from persons living in suburban environments, and in such locations, there are fewer minorities than in urban environments. Research observations at metal shows in diverse New York City, as opposed to predominantly white northwestern New Jersey, seem to suggest this. In this area of New Jersey, it is quite rare to see a black person at a metal show, although there are usually at least a few non-whites. On the contrary, in New York City, the proportion of white to non-whites appears to be about even. That is, there are about as many persons from all of the minority groups combined (especially African American, Asian, and Hispanic) as there are white persons. Therefore, the location of the metal show itself will significantly affect the racial breakdown of the attendees.

Minorities who do attend shows do not seem to feel out of place. They do not stick together, nor do they keep separate from white people. Race relations seem perfectly normal and friendly. Yet why are there so many more white persons involved in the metal scene? This is a complicated question that has much to do with the role of metal in providing a community or a family. Metal may serve the same function for white youth that rap serves for blacks. In metal music, this crucial function of shared community and identity is not overtly related to race, but in rap music, it often is. For instance, lyrics in Death Metal do not address the white race specifically; however, lyrics in rap often do address themselves to minorities by directly referring to race and to the plight of minorities. Therefore, it is much easier for a black person to become a part of the metal community than for a white person to become a part of the rap scene. Still, there will be more whites than minorities involved in metal perhaps because many minorities already have a scene and a community which appeals to their need for brotherhood and shared identity. They possess this through the rap scene, which has been in existence longer than the metal scene.

Publishers Weekly magazine directly refers to metal music as "Gangsta Rap's white-kid counterpart" (Simson 62). The parallels are strong. Metal and rap are both targeted by politicians and conservative groups as sources of cultural decay, and their lyrics are condemned as extremely violent (Ballard 476–487). A study in the *Journal of Genetic Psychology* found that the very same lyrics were more likely to be perceived as antisocial and detrimental when they were presented as rap or metal than when they were presented as popular or country lyrics (Ballard 476–487). Metal and rap are thus similarly despised.

Because the metal scene and the rap scene are both communities serving the same function in very different forms, does it follow that they will oppose one another or complement one another? This is a complex topic that requires a great deal more research. However, the interviews conducted in this study provided some very valuable insights into attitudes of metal persons toward rap. Interestingly, there was a dichotomous reaction to rap. Some of the younger interviewees perceive their own scene to be more noble than the rap scene. Because they are not a part of the rap scene, they view rap through the same cultural window that mainstream Americans do. Some metal heads thus feel that rap, not metal, is the truly dangerous music form. Some cite reasons for this, but it could be argued that this reasoning often belies misinformation or cultural bias. One very young metal head stated, "If you ask me, rap is more hazardous than Death Metal. Rap deals with real life incidents like drive bys and murder ... Death Metal just talks about crazy stuff that you know never happens, but it is just making fun of it all. People who listen to rap are the ones in gangs doing drugs and committing crimes like their music advertises." This view is quite representative of the view of a number of young metal heads who have not yet recognized the parallels between their own scene and the rap scene. Such assertions about rap probably have no more foundations than common assumptions about metal music and metal fans. Both types of music address the real and the fantastic, and both types of music sensationalize and exaggerate violence. There are probably some very disturbed metal fans who take the lyrics seriously just as there are probably some rap fans who do the same things.

Other metal fans expressly dislike rap music, although they do not have a problem with rap fans. Metal heads, who value the technical complexity of metal and the instrumental prowess required to play metal music, often scoff at a music form which uses sampling of existing music instead of using instruments. Drummer John Dreisbach expresses this view: "To be honest, I listen to anything except for country and rap. I can't get into it at all, though I try to listen to as much music as possible. ... I have a tendency of getting into 'technical' music and keeping away from the basic trendy stuff."

Interviews with older members of the scene revealed more positive attitudes toward rap and more understanding of the parallels between the scenes and the similar plights shared by rap fans and metal fans. (Both feel that they are scapegoats for violence.) A few of these interviewees were familiar with the work of infamous rapper Ice-T who did much to bridge the divide between the rap and metal communities. (Ice-T was a rapper who started a metal band called Body Count.) Ice-T is considered first and foremost a rapper. He is African American and he began a record label for rap and hip-hop; his involvement in metal did not extend beyond a transient side project. Yet that side project caught the attention of some metal heads in the early nineties who came to recognize the parallels between rap and metal. These individuals view fans of rap as being much like themselves, although they hail from different cultures and produce very different art forms. Matt Medeiros, who wished to be quoted as saying, "Ice-T is my hero," had much to say on the topic:

Rap and metal have a lot in common as subcultures (not musically), though historically, they have been divided racially. Both subcultures reject mainstream pop culture. Both cultures have a sense of unity. Both cultures are elite and exclusive. Both cultures are hated by mainstream America and mainstream media, including politicians who blame the violent lyrical content of gangsta rap and Death Metal for every conceivable social atrocity.

It thus seems that there is much validity to the claim that metal is the white kid's rap.

Demographic trends among metal fans extend beyond the basic traits of age, gender, and race to encompass such factors as economics, education level, and employment status. Christenson and Roberts found that metal heads tend to be middle class, relatively uneducated, and poor performers in school (103). Some negative impressions of Death Metal fans which one would draw from Christenson and Roberts' socioeconomic data are supported by this study. Based on the survey data, it seems that the unemployment rate among metal fans is very high. Approximately 20 percent of those surveyed were neither employed nor in school. The national average rate of unemployment is 5.6 percent, so employment rate among Death Metal fans is disturbingly low. One possible explanation is that a vast number of fans are also musicians and they attempt while they are young and single to make a living from producing music and playing shows. Of course, this is not considered employment *per se*, and therefore, these individuals could significantly inflate the unemployment rate (although it is likely that the rate is still higher for Death Metal fans than for the population at large because there is such a disparity between 5.6 percent and 20 percent).

On a more positive note, the claim that metal heads are uneducated and poor students does not seem to be founded. Surprisingly, not even 1 percent of those surveyed dropped out of high school. 44.8 percent were either still in high school or finished high school and did not continue their education beyond the high school level. 6 percent attended technical school, and a full 47.8 percent either finished college or were currently enrolled in college. This is very close to the national percentages for educational attainment according to 1997 General Social Survey data. If anything, the educational attainment rates for metal fans are high rather than low. The results regarding grades were even more surprising. The average GPA of those surveyed was 3.186 (out of a possible 4.0). This is very high, and indicates that the stereotype of the uneducated, ignorant, burnt-out metal head is quite unwarranted.

In terms of income level, the majority of respondents were middle class, earning $15,000 to $39,999 annually or coming from families with an income in this category. Of those surveyed, 19.4 percent earned under $15,000, 25.4 percent earned $15,000 to $39,999, and only 4.5 percent earned over $40,000. About half, 50.7 percent, were still in school being supported by their families. Independent metal fans seem disproportionately lower class. However, of those still dependent upon their families, only 11.8 percent were lower class, 52.9 percent were middle class, and 35.2 percent were upper class. This is very reflective of social norms in the population at large. Therefore, dependent metal fans do not come from one social class disproportionately more than from any other.

However, those who are employed *and* independent are disproportionately lower class. What could account for this? First of all, metal culture is a youth-dominated culture, and younger persons just beginning their careers will not earn as much as older, more established workers. Also, the richer person, of higher socioeconomic level and thus of higher class, has something to lose in terms of reputation if he or she attends a metal show. The lower down the socioeconomic ladder we go, the less one has to lose by embracing something that is not socially acceptable. If a person already feels outcast as a result of his or her socioeconomic status, he or she will not worry about accepting something that defies cultural acceptability. In fact, he or she is more likely to be attracted to such a thing because it provides a group, an identity, a place to belong.

That brings us to a crucial conclusion about metal, for it offers a possible reason for the exclusivity of metal that is achieved through vulgarity. Metal heads often have no social status in the outside world, but they do have it in the scene. They generally cannot compete with the financially successful or "the beautiful people" glorified by the mainstream media. Thus, they probably do not want those who classify them as "substandard" or "rejects" to invade their scene and take it over. The outside world of the socially respectable can be extremely threatening. There is support for this idea based on the responses of interviewees to the question, "Would you want metal to go mainstream?" The following were some of the varied responses to this question:

> No, anything that seems to go mainstream just goes gay. If you try hard enough, you'll find [the music] you're looking for [even if it's underground]. If not, then try harder.— Kyle Severn, Incantation, Wolfen Society, Acheron, Funerus

> I am going to truthfully answer and say that if metal went mainstream I would not like it. One of the beauties of listening to metal is being able to be elitist and you can't be elitist if the masses are singing along. I guess I'll just have to keep paying 30 bucks for a t-shirt and getting my CDs as third

generation burns from other acquaintances in exchange for other equally obscure third generation burns.— Nicole Zaretski

Of course, as long as the music or content didn't change. I don't think that metal needs to be exclusive to a certain few. But don't expect me to change or conform to fit the mainstream.— Killjoy, Necrophagia

Not really, because there are already enough clowns who don't belong ... if it went mainstream, [the music] would be bad.— Bill Zebub, The Grimoire

No way.— Rob George and Adrianne Buchta, WSOU

I don't see it getting any bigger with people being so close-minded and stupid.— Paul Ryan, Origin

On the one hand, it would be nice to have Death Metal be bigger so we can see more videos on television, hear it more often on the radio, have more options for purchasing harder to find items, and have more opportunities for good tours. If Death Metal were more mainstream, bands from all over the world could afford to tour. The way things are now, many bands from Europe don't want to tour the U.S. because they fear that their tour won't be successful since metal is much less popular here. In 1994, I saw Grave (who came all the way from Sweden) play for 11 or 12 people! No wonder European bands don't necessarily jump at the opportunity to tour here. It would also be great to see Death Metal bands in bigger venues with better sound quality, as opposed to the standard Death Metal club with average or poor sound quality. On the other hand, I would hate to see the mindless trend followers lower the respectability and credibility of Death Metal by leeching onto it just because it's the new big thing.— Iris Duran, WSOU

No, not really! All I've ever asked is a fair shake at having the genre's fair time on TV, fair time with booking clubs, fair time in magazine coverage. It's all about respect.— King Fowley, Deceased, October 31st, Doomstone

Sure, why not let all of our "berzerker legions" of metal heads into the Virgin Superstore in Times Square, NY, across from that insufferable MTV building. Let us climb it like a bunch of miniature King Kongs and assassinate Carson Daly and his band of minions.— John Longstreth, Origin, Angelcorpse

Please, God, no! I love metal and all, but I wouldn't want to turn on the TV and see a Cryptopsy video on my screen. I'm sure that the video would be awesome, but I would probably cry if I saw Carson Daly saying, "Here's the new Cryptopsy video" with a stupid boy band applauding in the background. I wouldn't want metal to become mainstream because then it would

11. Demographics

Iris Duran, beautiful and glamorous, nonetheless fits into the crowd at a show. Also shown are Mike Hussey, Matt Medeiros and Steve Horvath. Photograph by N. J. Purcell.

be like everything else in the world. I love individualism! I always have and will. That's why I love the metal scene so much, because it's practically giving the finger to the trends.—John Dreisbach, With Immortality

> I personally believe that I would not like three-quarters of the stuff I do if everyone listened to it. For me at least, a part of listening to metal and industrial is being able to think and say, "Look at that girl. She is wearing a Dimmu Borgir shirt. Maybe out of 100 people, 10 at most listen to that band. Therefore she is cool." It's a sort of exercise in being elitist. There is also a kind of pride to listening to music that not many people have heard of, making you distinct and separate from the crowd merely by silently dissenting.—Nicole Zaretski

Metal fans clearly want to preserve the exclusivity of their culture. They fear the introduction of the standards and values of mainstream America. In many respects, they feel as though society rejects or excludes them because they do not possess that same appeal that polished, perfect boy bands have. In describing some of the factors of the scene which he loves most, Jason Netherton (currently of Misery Index, formerly of Dying Fetus) wrote: "You look around at a show and you see people (for the most part) who know that there is something wrong with the culture we live in, and want to live and breathe outside of it as much as possible, and see metal as standing in opposition to that plastic and candy-coated world painted by the likes of corporate music companies." The introduction of such persons and such values into the metal culture would be quite threatening. That is one of the main reasons why metal must present an ugly and frightening image. Musician Matthew Medeiros has much to say on exclusivity of metal:

> It has to be brutal and mean. Death Metal is not an inclusive subculture. In general, the metal subculture is able to drive away most of the mainstream audience just with heavy guitars and yelling. The Death Metal subculture seeks to take this "filtering" even further by tuning low, playing fast, and singing in a virtually indecipherable growl. The Death Metal subculture is dedicated and elite more so than any mainstream culture in the world. It is only the interest and dedication of a select few worldwide that allows this music to survive and thrive. A good part of the Death Metal culture is anti-mainstream values because a majority of mainstream culture has historically been anti-metal.

These words reveal much about the metal culture and provide some insight into the purpose of frightening and offensive lyrics, clothing, and other aspects of the Death Metal scene. There is a certain threat that Death Metal attempts to ward off through its vulgarity. Metal is exclusive; it is about effort and enthusiasm, not inherent talent, charm, beauty or intelligence. Anyone can be metal if he or she feels metal; that is the sole criterion, and it keeps the scene pure, protecting the solidarity, identity, and subculture status of scene members. Ironically, in being exclusive, the metal scene is not trying to be elitist in the traditional sense of the term. Metal heads are trying to keep the typical elitists out. They want to exclude from their scene those who might judge and rate them. Metal is not about classes and status. It is a non-status, if you will (just as Pariahs of the Indian caste system were not a class *per se* but were classified as being classless).[9] If those who believe in the class system and have elitist ideas were to enter the scene, what would happen to it? There could occur the introduction of a class system based on competition for inherent qualities. This is what metal heads reject because they do not want to be subject to and defined by such judgments. Metal heads themselves feel uncomfortable when elitism in a judgmental form enters their scene. Matt Medeiros comments on this:

> The problems with the metal scene are paradoxical. It is an elite subculture,

yet there are people who take this elitism to the ultimate extreme. These people are not even an active part of the greater extreme metal culture. They remain exclusively in their very tiny niche, dealing only with people who are into the same thing and admonishing people who are into other things. Due to the [small] size of the extreme metal scene, it is damaging to have this sort of intolerance and non-support. The scene will only survive if the members are working together.

In short, there can be no classes in metal. A fan is not metal based on how scary he looks or how many metal T-shirts he owns; he is metal depending on how metal he feels, how enthusiastic and passionate about the music he is. Thus, ironically, to keep judgments and classifications out, there must be exclusivity. That exclusivity is established through vulgarity. The judgmental "perfect" people will not invade and divide the scene into a hierarchy because they are repulsed by it. Better yet, metal people cannot be considered inferior to those status symbols in American society because metal heads are completely outside of the social class system and are inside their own classless system. The competition is eliminated because the opponents are no longer playing the same game.[10]

The demographic data presented thus far has aided us in our discussion of what metal is not: hierarchical, judgmental, or based on inherent qualities like beauty and intelligence. The lack of these features is what seems to attract people of a certain lower economic status. However, what Death Metal is, rather than what it is not, may be a major factor in discerning what attracts people in certain familial situations or people who are depressed to metal.

This study used several indicators to gather data about fans' familial situations, including questions about one's relationship with one's siblings, attitude toward parents, contact with extended family, and parents' relationships with one another. The results indicate that metal fans do not necessarily come from dysfunctional families, counter to many popular assumptions. Christenson and Roberts, for instance, report that metal heads are more likely to have bad relationships with their parents (103). The survey data did not confirm this, as 62.7 percent of respondents reported that they felt close to their parents while growing up and 71.6 percent described their current attitude toward their parents as loving or appreciative. This is not at all indicative of the strained familial relations that Christenson and Roberts report. Only 7.5 percent of respondents reported that they felt angry or bitter towards their parents. A majority of respondents (65.7 percent) even replied that they felt close to their siblings while growing up. More than half (69.7 percent) reported seeing extended family members frequently (more than once per month.) Nearly half of the survey participants (47.6 percent) felt that their parents' marriage was happy and stable. 16.4 percent said it was stable but unhappy, and only 7.5 percent described their parents' relationship as unstable. A large percentage of metal fans, 28.4 percent, came from families with divorced parents. This is high, but not extremely high considering the high divorce rates in the population at large. Overall, it is not fair to say that metal heads come from homes that are especially unstable, and it is not appropriate to claim that they feel hostile or bitter towards their parents. (This helps to counter Bayles' earlier definition of metal heads as young boys seeking to defy their fathers.)

In other studies, however, the percentage of metal fans coming from broken or unstable families was found to be higher. It seems very logical that people in difficult or unstable family situations would be attracted to the metal scene. Death Metal provides a family, an identity group, a place to fit in without having to conform to standards of perfection or ideal beauty/intelligence. Those interviewed who came from broken families supported this hypothesis. Drummer Brian Jimenez said metal helps him cope with the turbulent times and the vast responsibilities that come from supporting a fatherless family: "Anyone into metal isn't normal, but I'm not going to sit here and be one of those distraught souls—you're normal in that you're not normal. We've all got problems—mostly familial, some goal-seeking problems, problems with the general public through shit-core jobs. How many hard as fuck times have I been able to squeeze on through with the help of Death Metal music?" Several other interviewees who did not wish to be identified found themselves in similar familial situations and expressed similar beliefs.

Death Metal does provide a non-competitive, family-like identity group. For this reason, it may appeal to those who are depressed or alienated. Christenson states that fans of metal tend to be depressive, but he admits that they do not feel isolated and instead possess a strong identification with their peer group of fellow fans (103–105). The survey results for this study indicated a high rate of depression among metal fans. A full 49.3 percent of those interviewed admitted to feeling depressed often, although only one third of those respondents have been treated for depression. In addition, 38.8 percent felt depressed sometimes, 9 percent felt depressed rarely, and only 3 percent never felt depressed. Depression is often tied into social alienation, which may be assuaged by identification with a peer group such as the Death Metal community. It seems quite possible that the scene draws people who are depressed (and seeking relief for their feelings of alienation), rather than causing depression in its members.

Contrary to popular belief, Death Metal music does more than provide lyrics with which depressed individuals can identify. Some of those interviewed stated that the metal scene itself provided them with hope and images of success or positivity. As mentioned before, to be accepted in the metal community, one only has to be *real*, to be passionate and enthusiastic about the music. To be truly respected as a musician in the scene, one need not possess the traits that Britney Spears and the Back Street Boys possess; metal is not about qualities that one is born with (like a beautiful voice and a beautiful face). Instead, it is about qualities that one controls and is able to develop in oneself; even the harsh vocals attest to this. A few of the musicians interviewed affirmed that metal offers something that one can succeed at if only he or she exerts enough effort. The focus is on how much effort and skill one acquires, not the innate talents and traits with which one is born. This is a very positive message, a message that offers hope to those who accept it.

12

Attitudes

An analysis of the attitudes of Death Metal fans is very important because it is related to a number of common assumptions that Americans have about Death Metal fans. For instance, most of the sources on metal cited thus far have classified metal heads as hopeless, hostile, and antisocial. Christenson and Roberts describe the attitudes of metal heads as cynical, libertarian, defiant, and fanatical (103–107). Martha Bayles presents an even more frightening portrait of metal as "arousing many of the troubling passions and treacherous currents of contemporary life, with the sole aim of immunizing the young against shared values—that is, of preventing socialization" (261). This chapter tests these hypotheses by analyzing attitudes toward various social institutions like religion, marriage, and capitalism. We shall also look at attitudes toward the future and political ideology, awareness, and apathy.

One of the primary reasons why popular culture despises metal heads is related to their perceived hostility toward religion. As the earlier analysis of the lyrics in Death Metal indicated, there can be some very anti-religious themes in metal music. But are these representative of the fans' attitudes? Christenson and Roberts say that more metal heads identify themselves as Satanic than do non-metal fans, and Satanism is certainly indicative of hostility towards religion. Did the survey results in this study support the idea that metal heads are anti-religious? Not at all. Among the respondents, 14.9 percent felt organized religion is a very positive institution and stated that they are themselves religious; 14.9 percent felt that organized religion is a very positive institution, but stated that they themselves are not religious. Another 17.9 percent felt indifferently toward religion, and the largest percentage, 37.3 percent, stated that organized religion was not a good idea and that they would not become religious. Only 14.9 percent agreed with the statement, "Religion is stupid, and no one should be religious." Note that twice this number felt religion to be a very positive institution. In general, these results are certainly not indicative of hostility towards religion. Nonetheless, religious involvement and activity is quite low for metal fans. On a scale of 1.0 to 3.0 for religious involvement, where 1.0 is least involved and 3.0 is most involved, survey respondents showed very low involvement. The mean was 1.364, the median was 1.0, and the mode was 1.0. These rates are atypical and show very little religious involvement compared with the norms attained from the 1997 General Social Survey. Thus, although metal fans are generally not religious, they are not necessarily anti-religious either.

This is consistent with the idea that metal does not turn people away from religion or make them hostile to it. It is simply the case that non-religious people will be less likely to be turned off or repelled by something that most religions condemn. It is not that metal makes people non-religious; instead, religious persons will probably not seek entertainment which is considered hostile to their belief systems, whereas the non-religious will be more open to it. Note the frequently positive views on religion, but the extremely low involvement in religious activities or identification with a religion. The non-religious or anti-religious themes within the music itself could be a further attempt at enforcing the aforementioned exclusivity. (For a deeper analysis of the possible significance of anti-religious lyrics themselves, see the chapter *Rebellion and Religion*.)

Disassociation with organized religion is often viewed as a negative thing. However, it is not fair to judge the non-religious before one understands their motives for rejecting organized religion. Matthew Medeiros feels that low religiosity is a sign of strength and positivity:

> I am not anti–Christian, although I am not Christian either. I do think that organized religion is a bad idea and I think that, given my frame of experience, religion has done damage to many individuals and to some aspects of American culture as a whole. Religion to a lot of people is something that dictates a way of life. This way of life is often forced on many people at a very early age. They are not given an opportunity to make their own informed and educated decisions about it. There are people who are going to live their whole lives in accordance with a set of rules dictated by an establishment whose values come from a source whose existence cannot be confirmed. People should be intelligent and strong-willed enough to form their own beliefs and value systems.

Reasons for rejecting religion are thus rational and are tied into a strong sense of individualism, already seen in the analysis of lyrics.

Surprisingly, attitudes towards other social institutions were at least as positive. Nearly half of those surveyed (48.5 percent) affirmed that marriage is a good institution and that they either are married or plan to get married some day. Another 12.1 percent shared this positive view of marriage, and stated that they would like to get married although they doubted that they would. 28.8 percent felt indifferently towards marriage and 7.6 percent said they would not want to get married. Only 3.0 percent stated that marriage is bad institution and that no one should get married. Thus only a very small percentage of persons feel hostile toward the institution of marriage. The majority feel that it is a positive institution.

There are, however, an inordinate number of persons who do not feel that they will get married or who feel indifferently toward marriage. This seems to support the idea that metal fans do not entertain the idea of marriage right now because metal itself is largely about youth and freedom. Marriage is not very compatible with the metal lifestyle; however, this is not evidence that later on in life, these individuals will not change their opinions about marriage. In general, it seems that metal fans do not stand against social norms, although they typically do not feel ready to accept them at the moment. They are not anti-anything; they are just wary of such things and do not partake in traditional lifestyles at present. Brian Jimenez seemed to typify this attitude with his statement: "I live my life very indifferently. ...I don't go out of my way to destroy or oppose. Everyone should be like the water — malleable, free-flowing, never hindered by anything." Perhaps metal fans prefer the freedom of the metal lifestyle, although they may come to recognize that social institutions like marriage are functional and necessary at some point. Jimenez spoke about marriage during an interview: "Life ain't like Burger King. You're not gonna have it your way. You've got to make sacrifices. No one wants to be alone in this world. If you've got to lose face and get married, oh well. I'm not trying to be different. If [marriage] is what brings happiness, then so be it. Besides, it's just plain cool to see what your kid would be like." This is not an overly positive vision of marriage, but it is a very realistic one. And after all, not many twenty-year-old males would be overjoyed at the prospect of such a commitment.

Based on the results of the surveys completed in this study, it does not seem accurate to label metal fans as anti-social. This study used different questions about social interaction to develop a scale of sociability, where 1.0 is non-sociable and 3.0 is extremely sociable. The resultant scores ranged all of the way from 1.0 to 3.0, with a mean of 2.041, a median of 2.0, and a mode of 2.0. While a number of metal fans are anti-social, the majority are not. Thus, anti-social attitudes might be correlated with interest in metal music, but it is certainly not appropriate to label someone anti-social simply based on the knowledge that he or she has a preference for metal music. Overall, the results revealed that metal fans are moderately sociable on the whole, leaning neither in the direction of high sociability levels nor anti-social attitudes.

The trend of positive rather than anti-social attitudes was not refuted by data regarding attitudes towards the economically successful. Attitudes toward big business and major figures in the capitalist system were measured on a scale of 1 to 5, where 1 is the most positive and 5 is the most negative. The mean was very close to the center, 2.314, and the median was 2.000. The mode was 1.0. This is indicative of rather positive attitudes towards the economically successful. Perhaps Death Metal fans are not as dissatisfied with the status quo as they are perceived to be. Misery Index's Jason Netherton sees acceptance of the economic status quo as an unfortunate new trend for metal fans:

> The stereotypical long-haired metal freak is not very prevalent these days. (I miss the back patches and denim.) Now it's Nike and sportswear (not saying that appearance means anything, just saying that it reflects a change in values; metal heads are more accepting today of the mainstream culture and its idiosyncrasies, where before the "metal head" would go out of his/her way *not* to look like the average consumer puppet). The lifestyle is mainstream, but the music is not.

Jason Netherton is not the only important scene personality to interpret this subtle contentment with the economic status quo as an unfortunate consequence of apathy and its companion ignorance. Karl Sanders of Nile mourns a "Coca Cola culture" which has partially usurped the Death Metal scene. Actual attitudes toward capitalism itself could not be measured because not enough survey respondents could demonstrate sufficient knowledge of how the economic system operates. (This was indicated by their inability to respond correctly to certain objective questions about the economic system. See survey questions 38 and 39 in the Appendix.) Overall, the results of the analysis of attitudes toward the American economic system indicates that, although metal people might separate themselves off from most cultural norms and standards, they are not necessarily hostile towards those who are successful within the system in which they themselves choose not to compete. This is not a universal rule, for there is high variation in the survey results ($s = 1.26$), and on the scale of attitudes, values ranged all the way from 1.0 to 5.0. There are some who view the economically successful in an entirely positive light, and others who view them very negatively. In general, however, there is a slightly positive trend. Thus metal fans are certainly not all hostile toward the economically successful even if they are currently "apart" from the system.

Death Metal fans' perceived chances of achieving economic success in the future were measured on a scale of 1 to 4, where 1 is least successful and 4 is most successful. The mean was 3.39, the median was 3.50, and the mode was 3.70. So much for claims that metal fans are hopeless and cynical! Martha Bayles does not agree with the positive impression offered by this data. Bayles claims that metal heads "display a grotesque combination of vaunting ambition and drooping despair, based on the conviction that the only alternative to rock stardom is death in the gutter" (261). This study definitely poses a challenge to the words of Martha Bayles. Rock stardom is never an option for metal musicians. If one wishes to make money and achieve fame, metal music is certainly not the career of choice. Even those highly successful musicians interviewed in this study either have day jobs or find themselves in an extraordinarily precarious financial situation. Also, all of those interviewed seem quite aware of the fact that metal is not life, nor can one expect to make a living through it. Thus, the highly optimistic scores for perceived chances of economic success are not based on some misguided delusion of future rock stardom; they must be grounded in something more real.

The surveys also attempted to measure degree of contentment and view of life in general on a scale of 1 to 5, where 1 is the most pessimistic and discontent, and 5 is the most optimistic and content. Death Metal fans scored just about average, with a slightly positive trend. The range extended from 1.5 to 5.0, with a mean of 3.502 and median of 3.500. This does not support the generalization that metal heads feel "complete hopelessness" (Christenson & Roberts 107–108). Life view for Death Metal fans is not particularly positive or negative. Many do believe that they will have lives full of contact with friends and family, and this is significant because it points to a potentially positive value of metal. Although many metal fans are depressive individuals or have been treated for depression, many believe that they have found close, supportive groups of friends. According to the interviews, these friends are usually friends within the metal scene. Thus a positive outlook and life-view may be in part a product of involvement with the metal scene and of the sense of identification that it provides.

No discussion of social attitudes is complete without an analysis of political ideology, awareness, and apathy. Political knowledge was measured on a scale of 0 to 8, where 0 was least knowledgeable and 8 was most

12. Attitudes

knowledgeable. Scores ranged all the way from 0.0 to 8.0, with a mean of 4.731, median of 5.000, and mode of 5.0. This seems quite low initially, but when compared with results from the 1997 National Election Survey's measure of political knowledge, it does not seem atypical. NES measures political knowledge on a scale of 0 to 4. The mean estimated for the general population was 2.224, the median was 2.00, and the mode was 3.00. Although it is ridiculous to claim accuracy in comparing results based upon different indicators of political knowledge, it does not seem too farfetched to state that the disappointing level of political knowledge displayed by Death Metal fans is fairly typical of the general population.

Although level of political knowledge is not impressive, Death Metal fans do not seem to be atypically apathetic. Degree of political apathy was measured on a scale of 1 to 2, where 1 is the least apathetic and 2 is the most apathetic. The results placed respondents squarely in the middle: the mean was 1.51, the median was 1.50, and the mode was 1.50. This is not indicative of high levels of apathy. Some respondents would be willing to work on a candidate's campaign, and most would be willing to sign a petition or work on a protest. Nationalism was measured on the same 1 to 2 scale, and the results were similarly concentrated in the center with the mean, median, and mode at or around 1.5. Fans of metal are not particularly proud to be American, nor are they discontented with their national identity.

One notable example of political involvement within the Death Metal scene involves the work of Jason Netherton. The lyrics that Netherton created for Dying Fetus' 2000 release *Destroy the Opposition* contain intelligent comments on the ills of capitalism and globalization. Although Netherton's departure from Dying Fetus suggests that the band will no longer pursue political commentary, a continuation of this material may be found in the work of Netherton's current project, Misery Index. Netherton also created a website to express his political views and to pose a general challenge to the extreme economic injustices that characterize the global political and economic order. The site, Demockery, may be viewed at www.demockery.org. Netherton's discontent with the status quo clearly results in positive efforts to effect progressive change and to educate others about socially liberal ideology.[11]

The surveys indicate that Death Metal fans are ideologically quite liberal. Ideology was measured on a scale of 1 to 3, where 1 is the most liberal and 3 is the most conservative. The scores ranged all of the way from 1.0 to 3.0, with mean of 1.574, median of 1.300, and mode of 1.20. This is indicative of strong liberality if compared to national averages. For instance, the 1997 General Social Survey found only 25.4 percent with a liberal ideology, 38.1 percent moderate, and 36.5 percent conservative. Fans of Death Metal clearly lean left. However, a surprisingly low percentage identify with a political party. Of those who are registered to vote, 40 percent do not identify with a political party, 36 percent identify themselves as Democrats, 16 percent as Republicans, and 8 percent as some other political party. Extremely few respondents identify with a political party, and of those who do, there are more Democrats than Republicans, which is probably reflective of liberal ideology.

Given the high liberality of Death Metal fans, it seems strange that more do not identify with the Democratic party. The low party identification (in spite of willingness to get politically involved on the part of many) may be indicative of dissatisfaction with the current political system. On the surveys themselves, a number of individuals wrote comments in the margins of the page measuring political knowledge and involvement. Many expressed dissatisfaction with the Republican and Democratic candidates in election year 2000, who appeared virtually indistinguishable through their attempts to offend no one. This naturally would not please metal heads who are evidently not afraid of offending people in order to stand up for something. There were a few comments written next to the question about the Democratic candidate, which leads one to believe that there may have been higher Democratic identification if the Presidential candidate had not been Al Gore (whose wife, Tipper, is head of the PMRC), and if the vice presidential candidate had not been Joseph Lieberman, who headed many of the talks in Congress against violent entertainment forms. One participant complained about Gore's "bitch wife" and another more creative soul called Gore a "poopy-head," expressing fears of Tipper Gore, Joe Lieberman, and the general tendency of the Democratic team to advocate censorship.

In summary, fans of metal do not seem especially content with the two-party system, but they are not overly apathetic and many are willing to get involved in political activities. All of the information about attitudes collected in this study challenges existing notions of metal heads as antisocial, pessimistic malcontents. In general, there is great variation in attitudes about life-view, American economics, and cultural institutions like marriage and religion. There are no trends of negativity, and the attitudes of Death Metal fans do not seem very atypical at all.

13

Philosophy and Ethics

A number of generalizations have been drawn about the philosophical and ethical tendencies of Death Metal fans, but very little research has been done on the topic. Most of those who attempt to define the philosophy of metal look at the lyrics, but lyrical content should not be assumed to correlate with the beliefs of fans. Because of the focus on lyrical perversity, existing theories of Death Metal philosophy are quite grim and negative. This study will analyze the beliefs of the fans themselves rather than the lyrical content of Death Metal songs. (The significance of the lyrical content itself is discussed the chapters *Rebellion & Religion* and *Horror, Gore, Porn, & the American Mind*.) Analysis of philosophical and ethical systems yields extremely valuable information into the motivations for choosing certain actions. It also lends insight into the link between ethical socialization and behavior. This chapter will thus attempt an in-depth look at metaphysics, faith, ethics, and life philosophy.

As mentioned, most existing sources on metal music emphasize the negative and extremist philosophical views expressed in the lyrics. Martha Bayles, for instance, believes that the musicians of metal are nihilistic and that they are "rewarded" for their "self-destructive behavior" (261). Christenson sees metal fans as more self-centered and utilitarian, but in his vision, Death Metal philosophy is just as negative. According to Christenson, fans of metal "tended to demonstrate higher levels of Machiavellianism, implying in Hansen's words, 'a greater likelihood of engaging in social behaviors that most people would judge to be manipulative, cynical, or amoral'" (105). Christenson sees the metal culture as especially cynical and mistrustful. This seems to be the extent of research into the philosophy of metal fans. None of these theories were confirmed by the findings of this study.

Analysis of the metaphysical beliefs of Death Metal fans in this study completely contradicted the original hypothesis that metal fans would tend to look at the universe as a chaotic or hostile place. On the contrary, there could not have been more variation in metaphysical beliefs about the nature of the universe. The survey was designed so that respondents could check all of those metaphysical theories with which they agreed, including mysticism, deism, rationalism or Cartesianism, existentialism, skepticism, and chaos theory.[12] Of those surveyed, 56.7 percent subscribed to a mystical, spiritual view of the universe. This is the sort of metaphysical view that one would expect to prevail among religious devotees, and yet a majority of respondents saw the universe as a place full of miraculous wonder and mystery. A greater percentage reported adhering to this mystical view than to any other metaphysical view. The next most popular choice was the rationalistic, Cartesian, or deistic vision of the universe. 52.2 percent subscribed to this view that envisions the universe as a rationally ordered and comprehensible system, which humans are capable of understanding, manipulating, and controlling. Surprisingly, the view chosen least frequently was the existentialist, skeptic, or chaotic vision of the universe. Only 28.8 percent believed the universe to be incomprehensible or at least not under the control of a rational force, be it man or God. This is a very low percentage. Once again, this evidence supports the idea that metal fans are not as pessimistic or hopeless as they are portrayed to be. Instead, there is strong faith in the rational ordering of the universe. This counters the chaos theme that certain researchers, like Steven Stack, expected to find as dominant in the metal scene. The results also challenge the hypothesis that Death Metal fans would be drawn to music with negative or disturbing images because they themselves are negative or disturbed and view the universe as an unfriendly place. This does not appear to be the case. The metaphysical views expressed by the metal fans in this study seem very healthy, and relatively optimistic, although there was great variation such as one might find in the population at large.[13]

Data about the faith of Death Metal fans revealed similarly vast variation. Few (19.4 percent) expressed strong faith in a higher power or felt that a higher power was actively involved in their lives. Some (22.4 percent) expressed that they had some faith in a higher power but it was very uncertain. Remember, this is to be expected because there is very low involvement in organized religion, and there is also little likelihood that metal heads accept the status quo or traditional, authoritative opinions.

They are outside of traditional belief systems and would therefore feel less certain of their current belief systems. Perhaps this uncertainty is not indicative of a social ailment but of healthy and positive questioning. Many agreed with the statement that there may be a higher power in the lives of others but it plays no part in their own lives. Very few expressed hostility towards any higher power, and yet lyrics of bands such as Deicide are extremely hostile toward God. This shows that metal fans are no more willing to accept the opinions of compatriots and musicians in the scene than of outside authority.

The most prevalent response on faith was rather Deistic, envisioning any higher power as merely an overarching ordering force, not particularly involved in life. About 31.1 percent subscribed to this rationalistic viewpoint. Many checked the response: there may be a god but it is not involved in my life and it really is not necessary. There is no sense of loss, negativity or pessimism at the absence of a spiritual force in life. This is not post-modern or existentialist. It is much more representative of Enlightenment-style atheism or agnosticism, which views lack of God as freeing, not tragic, and as further indicative of man's power to order his own life and universe. This is optimistic, frequently humanistic, and highly rational. Some see the world as chaotic or hostile, but most view it as fundamentally orderly, comprehensible, and ruled by humans.

The original research hypothesis on ethics was disconfirmed. The survey tested respondents using several indicators for each of four primary ethical systems. Respondents were confronted with hypothetical situations and asked to make choices. They were also asked about their perceived method of ethical reasoning and decision-making. The final breakdown of responses for all categories was as follows:

Category[14]	Frequency	Percentage
1. Natural Law/Kantian Ethics	27	41.5
2. Legal or Moral Positivism	4	6.2
3. Cultural Relativism	8	12.3
4. Subjectivism	26	40.0
Total	65	100.0

Metal fans were not highly subjectivist and relativistic in moral reasoning, contrary to the initial hypothesis. Initially, there was no expectation of a major difference between cultural relativism and subjectivism, because they are lumped together in most ethical commentaries, since both reject absolutes and see ethics as something that changes and is not objective. However, analysis of survey results showed a major difference between perception of cultural relativism and subjectivism among metal fans. Cultural relativism places the opinion of the society or culture as the criterion of ethics, whereas subjectivism places the opinion of the individual person as the criterion of ethics. Metal fans overwhelmingly rejected cultural relativism and overwhelming accepted subjectivism. The majority declared that they felt they personally created their own ethical systems, without guidance from absolutes or from society. Similarly, almost no participants displayed positivistic ethical reasoning from either the legal or religious realms. It seems that among metal fans, there is a strong rejection of authoritative prescriptions of right and wrong, whether dictated by religion, law, or custom. Metal heads are very individualistic, value thinking for themselves, and are highly unlikely to simply accept the views of society or culture. This would explain the high levels of subjectivist reasoning and the rejection of cultural relativism and positivism.

One of the most interesting aspects of this ethical examination is the major distinction between professed subjectivist reasoning and projected behavior in different ethical scenarios. In short, the subjectivism of metal fans placed the opinion of the self at the center of the decision-making process, but did not reflect selfish conclusions at all. The course of action which most fans predicted that they would take in different situations was perfectly in line with natural law ethics or even Kantian ethical standards. A number of individuals did openly recognize the existence of moral absolutes, but most of those who did not recognize absolutes and insisted instead on a purely subjectivist standard of ethics nonetheless made the same choices as natural law adherents. There was a strong respect for other persons, if not for law. Nearly every response could be boiled down to the Golden Rule: treat others as you would have them treat you. "My philosophy?" asked Brian Jimenez, "Do unto others..." Killjoy from Necrophagia wrote, "I don't intentionally try to fuck with people and I want the same in return. Treat others as you'd like to be treated." Perhaps legal, cultural, and religious positivism are rejected in favor of a higher ethic discovered by the self. Thinking for oneself and rejecting authoritative dictates and cultural norms does not necessarily mean a negative downturn in ethical behavior. In this case, it seems to have inadvertently produced a return to behavior that is in line with a natural law belief system.

Is there any explanation for these positive results when the only other inquiries performed have drawn such negative conclusions? The primary reason for the disparity in results may lie in the unit of analysis. Others inquiring into the philosophy of Death Metal have looked primarily at lyrics and, if anything beyond that, at the perceived modus operandi for ethical decision-making. This study has attempted to look at decisions themselves in addition to perceptions. We have not looked at lyrics as the unit of analysis for research of ethical decision-making. Is this justified? Are the ethical systems of metal fans tied to the lyrics that they listen to? During the interviews, I asked respondents how they felt about the lyrics, whether these reflected their own philosophies, and how they felt about the perceived Satanism of Death Metal fans. The results led me to believe that it is unfair to look at lyrics as the primary unit of analysis.

I asked respondents, "Do you think the lyrics in most of the music you listen to are reflective of your personal beliefs?" No one responded emphatically "yes," but a few said that some of the lyrics represent their beliefs on certain levels. When I asked which lyrics, they generally pointed out the political ones. No one said that the violent or gory lyrics had any literal relation to their personal beliefs. As Nile's Karl Sanders put it:

> I think the Death Metal lyrics are intended for the Death Metal people who take them, not with a pinch of salt, but in their proper context. When you talk about Satan cutting someone's head off and desecrating their body, I don't see that anyone takes that literally. No one in their right mind takes that literally. When you're writing about serial killers or whatever, it's not supposed to be taken literally. Certainly, no one is glorifying serial killers when they write about Jeffrey Dahmer on their Death Metal album. It's just another horrible brutal tale, much like you would see in any gore flick.

Christenson and Roberts point out that there is a major distinction between music that places lyrics in the foreground, and music that places them in the background as Death Metal does. They admit that fans "ground their music preferences and purchase decisions first and foremost on these auditory elements of style, not on the complexion of the messages or stories converged in the lyrics. Indeed, what most of us probably think of as the story or the 'message' is often — perhaps usually — ignored during music listening" (116). According to Christenson and Roberts, this points out the extreme irony of the political battles against such music. Opponents of metal put the focus on lyrics that are often not even discernable beneath the music. Most interviewees rejected the idea that the lyrics literally reflected their beliefs. The following are some of the responses to the aforementioned question regarding whether lyrics are reflective of personal beliefs:

> Generally, no, it seems that the majority of the lyrics are meant just to shock, and given that they are an acceptable accomplice to the music, this works for most people. Myself, however, I enjoy lyrics which use language itself more creatively and challenge both the lyricist and the reader to take

communication through the lyrics to both an entertaining and possibly artful/enlightening level. That is very difficult to do, and most of the time, the lyrics do not have a place in metal beyond shock value, but there is such a wide variety of topics being covered that it is hard to generalize.—Jason Netherton, Misery Index, Dying Fetus

The music we create comes from the heart and psyche. ... On the outside, we are everyday normal people, but down in the guts of it all, we have an attachment to the gloom and darkness of our songs. We have these inner feelings of death and morbidity. I know, being the lyric writer, that I have always put my feelings onto paper and wrote with all my emotions. Deceased songs never have a happy ending. Every song has a "fork in the road," the final scene of terror and horror. That's how I see it.—King Fowley, Deceased, October 31st, Doomstone

The lyrics for Incantation are my personal beliefs. They are very blasphemous. ... I am not a Satanist, just a blasphemer. ... I cannot live the Christian lies.—Kyle Severn, Incantation, Wolfen Society, Acheron, Funerus

In the broader sense, the anger and pessimism of the lyrics and music do reflect my beliefs and identity to an extent. The recurring themes on gore, Satanism, misogyny, etc. do not always coincide dead-on with my personal beliefs, but regardless, I still find them a significant and intriguing part of Death Metal.—Iris Duran, WSOU

Although I do write in the first person sometimes, I am not necessarily exposing my feelings toward any of it. Sometimes I am. If you peel back the layers, sometimes I am working out my own personal angst.—Karl Sanders, Nile

No, they are more reflective of my personal love for horror and gore. Even the darker and more Satanic based lyrics are only done from a horror angle. I don't believe in God or the Devil.—Killjoy, Necrophagia

No, not at all. We just write about guys who do this stuff. We don't go out and kill people. We're just warning people kind of. Read our lyrics and you'll know what's actually out there. Protect your children. Maybe early on, when we were younger, maybe it was to shock a little bit. [But] we always had that mindset, that we could inform people about this. Kind of like the news.—Nefarious, Macabre

The lyrics are more reality-based than hope-fed like modern music. A lot of lyrics today are for shock and that's the whole purpose. I mean, I am sure there are people that go out and do these things they write about. If you want real horror, read the newspaper. It shows the atrocities on man daily.

That's brutally beyond any fairy tale dungeons and dragons story.—Paul Ryan, Origin

Most definitely not. I am not a violent person and I do not like to see people get hurt.—John Dreisbach, With Immortality

I've never been impressed with the lyrics from many of my favorite bands. This might sound strange, but obviously the main effort to metal music is just that: the music. ... [However] as the lyric writer (and bassist/vocalist) in Angelcorpse, I can state emphatically that all the lyrics and lyrical/ideological concepts are 100 percent who and what I am. (Tracks such as "Sons of Vengeance" or "Consecration" are perfect examples of a statement of rising above, of the survival of the fittest, and of the necessary pride and often solitude that results from such a weltanschauung.)—Pete Helmkamp, Terror Organ, Angelcorpse

Our lyrics are usually negative. We have lyrics that support violence. Just read the lyrics to the song Killing on Adrenaline. Not all of our lyrics are violent. We have topics about subliminal messages in the mass media and corporate America, and we have some gory lyrics as well. Personally, I feel that the music and the sound of the vocals are the most important part of Death Metal. I really don't care what someone is yelling into a mic as long as it sounds good.—John Gallagher, Dying Fetus

There are so many subjects written about in Death Metal, so many beliefs, I can only say I agree with part of them. ... Some bands' lyrical content is for shocking value only, and other bands actually believe what they write about. The music of Death Metal is aggressive, and in a sense, horrifying, so the lyrics are only fitting to be aggressive and horrifying also. ... The lyrics in Death Metal are not reflective of my personal beliefs.—Jeremy Turner, Origin

Death Metal is for the music, not for the lyrics. ... [The lyrics just] cover the aggression that's heard in the music.—Erik Sayenga, Dying Fetus, Witch-Hunt

None whatsoever. Ever hear the expression "I'd kill for a cigarette"? It's just an expression, just a form of release.—Brian Jimenez, Funebrarum

[The band] Death does a fairly good job at expressing ideas similar to my own. While [gore bands like] Cannibal Corpse are amongst my favorite bands, I feel their lyrical content is strictly ornamental and does not necessarily reflect anything I would believe or do. It is also the case that the members of the bands do not believe or would not do any of the things depicted in their songs.—Matthew Medeiros, Eschaton

There does not appear to be a direct relationship between the philosophies of individual listeners and the literal content of the lyrics. Indirectly, there may be a relationship in that the lyrics reject social norms and so do the metal heads themselves, placing the stress instead on individual understanding and discovery. Supported by the pattern of ethical subjectivism among metal fans, gore lyrics might serve as a metaphor for endorsing alternative opinions and lifestyles. If one completely devalues traditional ethical norms, then all kinds of behavior become acceptable — it resembles tearing everything down before coming up with a new belief system. In essence, such extreme lyrics bring one close to an ethical ground zero. They force listeners to rethink the norms that are taken for granted. By taking one ethical extreme to an absurd level, it casts all ethics in a different light. For example, it is possible to challenge people's repulsion with homosexuality by presenting something morally beyond the pale, such as necrophilia. This is like putting one moral extreme up against an immoral extreme, forcing onlookers to reassess their standpoint. The result is an ethical subjectivism. (See Chapter 17, Rebellion and Religion, to learn more about ethical ground zero and the non-literal significance of lyrics.)

Despite the symbolic functions of such lyrics, the gore, the murder, and the anti-religious themes portrayed are not literally related to the metal philosophy at all. This study has found nothing in the personal philosophy of metal heads that reveals a low respect for life or an emphasis on hedonism.

Why then are such gruesome tales the topic of Death Metal lyrics? Brian Jimenez called it the "true alternative," stating that "it's not happy; it's not loving; it's not cheesy, bitchy teen angst. It's a release for its sheer brutality." Matthew Medeiros, who has written such lyrics for his own bands, had more to say on the topic:

> Many people criticize the various metal forms for their violent topics, depressing attitude, antisocial stance, and their overall bitterness toward the masses. But by the very nature of the music itself, it is dictated that these sets of lyrics be of a similar nature. The music is often dark and aggressive and brutal, and the lyrics must follow suit. So while so many people in the metal community are quite well-adjusted and friendly, the lyrical content of their bands will be anything but. Most of the music I listen to has strictly ornamental lyrics.

Killjoy, Karl Sanders, and Jason Netheron had similar comments. According to Killjoy, "When I started writing lyrics there was no one else writing exclusively around horror and gore. ... I just wrote about what I was into and I would say that gore has become the universal concept of

Death Metal and I think it's a perfect concept to go along with hideous music." Sanders concurred, commenting that "the lyrics have to keep up with the music. The music is almost horrifying itself and you can't have lyrics that don't live up to the music in some way. They have to carry some sort of shock value or weight or aggression in and of themselves or it would just be silly." As to the function of such lyrics, Jason Netheron writes that:

> Most likely it is the shock value, which when joined with the extremity of the music itself, compounds the intensity and overwhelming power of the musical style. Death Metal is a form of music that is active, not passive. It actively seeks to engage the listener and demands a response be it good or bad; you cannot just consume Death Metal neutrally. Its very nature is to disturb, and depending on how the listener reacts to such things, they will love it or hate it. Therefore the "function" is to help conjure the imagery that the music has laid the groundwork for, and add to the overall intensity. Lyrics vary in their offensiveness and extremity in many ways across genres and bands, so again it's hard to generalize.

The brutality of the lyrics is thus seen as a response to the extreme nature of the music itself. Yet what is the function of such brutality, such meanness? One is immediately reminded of earlier comments about metal's purity and exclusivity. Says Sanders, "In Death Metal, one of the innate thrills is knowing that you're probably horrifying the normal person in the car next to you or in the next apartment." It is likely that the lyrics serve the role of keeping the metal scene exclusive, and they are only indirectly reflective of a metal philosophy.

Is there a metal philosophy apart from the philosophies of the individual scene members? According to those interviewed, there does not seem to be an official metal philosophy. John Dreisbach wrote, "I don't think there's really a 'philosophy' in the scene. I believe it's more along the lines of people seeking the most intense music out there and fiending for that adrenaline rush that we all love so very much." Said Origin's Jeremy Turner, "There are so many different 'philosophies' in Death Metal; it would be impossible to have just one." Other interviews revealed a similar rejection of the idea that metal involves a particular philosophy. According to Karl Sanders, "So many people have so many different ideas about what metal is, what a metal lifestyle is. ...I think there's a certain rebelliousness and freedom in metal that defies [definition]. I think it would be out of the spirit of metal to clamp a bunch of preconceived ideas on what it ought to be." Nicole Zaretski writes, "I don't think that there is nor can there be a metal philosophy. While there may be musical trends, lyrical similarities, and like-minded people attending shows, it would be unfair to say there is some overhanging philosophy that governs them all. People are all different and will do what they feel, whether metal or not." As Matt Medeiros believes:

> Metal culture is nothing but a smaller sample of regular society. I've encountered the same percentage of pleasant friendly people and mean assholes in the metal scene as I have in any other social situation. Metal is not a controlling factor for personality. There is no overwhelming metal philosophy, although there are some common shared beliefs like "support the underground" or "keep it brutal." We want to perpetuate the culture, but that culture involves people with different philosophies.

There is, however, a common declaration that each person should think for himself or herself, and many interviewees brought this up during the interviews. John Longstreth summarized it well: "One philosophy holds true to all types of metal: individualism." "Don't ever categorize yourself!" exclaimed Brian Jimenez. "I love individualism!" wrote John Dreisbach. "Be yourself," said Jason Netherton. For some musicians, gore lyrics are just an extension of the classic metal philosophy which endorses the determination of one's own life and the refusal to be molded by society into simply accepting what is presented as good or right or correct. As King Fowley put it, the only metal philosophy is to "be yourself — no gods, no masters! Always stay dedicated to yourself. Never follow the leader; strive to be a leader!" This is very Enlightenment-style reasoning. It meshes perfectly with the rationalism expressed in the metaphysical and spiritual views already examined. Thinking for oneself is hardly an easy escape into personal preference. It is, on the contrary, a demanding search for values. Along with subjectivist ethical standards comes a great deal of responsibility — a willingness to own up to one's lifestyle and personal convictions. Often this ties in with an acceptance of responsibility for one's fate. Such emphasis on thinking for oneself prevents a uniform prescription of a metal philosophy. Nonetheless, the philosophies of individual metal heads are united in the stress they place on the role and value of the self in making decisions and finding truth.

14

Behavior

Our glance into the world of Death Metal has revealed much about the sort of people who belong to the Death Metal scene, their basic demographic characteristics, and the nature of their culture. We have achieved insight into the minds and motivations of metal heads through our analysis of their attitudes, philosophies, and ethical systems. In short, we have laid the groundwork for an informed and insightful analysis of actual behavioral norms and tendencies. This section will include faithful reports of behavior in the areas of sexual activity, alcohol use, drug use, suicide, and violent behavior. In many ways, it is the heart of the project because it directly addresses the social illnesses which politicians and popular culture attribute to metal music and its fans.

Christenson and Roberts write that fans of metal show a high instance of "self-reports of specific reckless behaviors, including drunk driving, casual sex, and marijuana and cocaine use" (105). Other statistics are equally disturbing: 96 percent of white students in a school for youth with behavior problems claimed that Heavy Metal was their favorite type of music (Christenson 106). Also, 50 percent more metal fans than pop fans admitted to using illegal drugs (106). Metal fans are also believed to have more casual sex and premarital sex than other groups (107). Christenson and Roberts caution their readers, however, not to assume causality or exaggerate the correlation. Looking at the variety of characteristics associated with a taste for metal might help one to predict that an individual likes metal music; however, the actual patterns in behavior are so low that one absolutely cannot, on the basis that someone is a metal fan, be at all confident in predicting that he or she will be violent, deviant, or depressed (109). For this reason, Christenson reports that "if there is a 'syndrome' at work here, it is a 'troubled youth syndrome,' not a heavy metal syndrome" (108).

The results of the surveys collected in this study did not reinforce or support many of the negative conclusions drawn in previous studies. First, let us look at sexual behavior, keeping in mind that the aforementioned statistics place metal fans in the sexually devious or promiscuous category. In this study, survey respondents were asked whether or not they were sexually active and how many sexual partners they have had in the past year. The range of responses extended from 0 to 7. A full 31.7 percent of those surveyed were not sexually active. Another 53 percent had only one or two sexual partners in the past year; this is not at all indicative of promiscuity. No more than 9.5 percent had three or four sexual partners, and only 4.8 percent had five to seven sexual partners in the past year. The mean number of sexual partners was 1.365, with median 1.000 and mode 0.000. Thus, there are incidences of promiscuity, but they are neither extreme nor prevalent. In general, levels of sexual activity were very low, and so were levels of promiscuity. (These surveys were completely anonymous, so there was little reason to be dishonest about sexual behavior.)

Why then did others who conducted surveys of the metal population find so much more deviance? Perhaps this is related to their research methods. If a researcher were to enter a metal environment and ask fans to fill out surveys about themselves, they might feel like the objects of study for a society that largely rejects them (and which they in turn reject). Metal heads generally wish to keep metal exclusive; they want to scare away the sort of people who they anticipate would want to study their "alien" lifestyles. They might even be tempted to present themselves as more frightening and deviant than is actually the case in order to scare away outsiders. These problems really did not arise in this study because the research assistants have attended shows for years and are an accepted presence among metal heads. In general, they are respected members of the metal scene, able to enlist the friendly and honest aid of fellow Death Metal fans. Metal fans would likely be more cooperative or honest if they felt they were helping out a fellow fan conducting research.

There is reason to believe that the responses regarding behavior that are reflected in this study are more accurate or valid than any results found by outsiders who attempt to enter the scene just to do research. One of the research assistants expressed the same feeling. He stated that he found this research project to be particularly valuable because our access to and familiarity with the scene would enable us to obtain honest answers that no outsider would get. As he said, if a professor approached him at a show proclaiming to study the metal scene and asked him to fill out a survey, he would be strongly tempted to amuse himself by declaring his behavior to be ultra deviant, violent, and all else which he suspected that the outsider already assumed.

Drug and alcohol use among metal fans is typically reported to be high, and these results were neither confirmed nor disconfirmed through this study. Survey participants were asked three separate questions about alcohol use, marijuana use, and use of other illegal drugs. For alcohol use, responses ranged from drinking 0 times per month to drinking 20 times per month. This reveals great variation. The mean number of times which respondents reported drinking each month was 2.415, with median 0.00 and mode 0.00. Those who drank regularly drank about once a week, but almost half did not drink at all. This is certainly not deviant for the age group examined. Rate of marijuana use was slightly more atypical, with 17.5 percent reporting regular use (approximately once per month or more). Illegal drug use showed great variation as well. Respondents were asked how many times per month they used illegal drugs other than marijuana. The responses varied all of the way from 0 to 20 times per month. Of respondents, 92.4 percent did not use any illegal drugs (not including marijuana). The mean was 0.424, the median was 0.000, and the mode was 0.000. Overall, drug and alcohol use were neither low nor high. Drug use was relatively low: only 7.6 percent used drugs. However, those who did use drugs used them fairly often, typically 1–4 times per month. Overall, these rates are slightly higher than average, and may reflect one of the negative sides to the rejection of social norms and dictates. Extreme subjectivist openness to traditionally unaccepted behavior could lead to a willingness to try something dangerous, and in the case of illegal drugs, this can easily become an addiction. It is important to note, however, that drug use is not very high, and that the overwhelming majority of metal fans in this study reported no illegal drug use.

There are other negative behavioral characteristics frequently attributed to Death Metal fans. Several studies have been conducted in order to assess the relationship between Heavy Metal and suicide. In fact, a preference for Heavy Metal music has sometimes been used as an indicator for suicide risk. There is not much basis for this, however. In 1999, Roslyn Heights conducted a study about the relationship between suicide and metal music. Heights emphasizes what she perceives to be the hopelessness presented in metal lyrics. Heights goes on to hypothesize that Heavy Metal fans will be more likely to commit suicide. Her findings did suggest that there is a higher rate of suicide and suicide attempts among Heavy

Metal fans, and that metal fans express less strong reasons for living. At no point, however, does Heights suggest that metal music *causes* suicidal tendencies: "Adolescents with preexisting problems (in this case, personal and family psychopathology) may seek out rock or heavy metal music because the negative themes reflect their own feelings" (Heights 254). There is no way to establish causation, because time order is indistinct, and the correlation does not indicate which is the cause and which is the effect.

Yet, if anything, it seems that metal music is not the cause. According to Heights, the results of her findings "suggest that the source of the problem may lie more in personal and familial characteristics than in any direct effects of the music" (Heights 253). Heights found that fans of metal music tend to come from homes with an exceptional amount of disruption and distant relationships. In fact, her study found that listening to metal music has a *positive* affect on most fans. This has led authors such as Jeffrey Arnett to argue that sometimes negative feelings precede listening to the music; however, the music itself "may serve a positive cathartic function" (Heights 255).

Steven Stack conducted a similar investigation about suicide and Heavy Metal music. He introduced the factor of religiosity to find very telling results. Like Heights, Stack focuses on the lyrics presented in the music. He, however, notes the theme of chaos (388–390). (Perhaps he envisions chaos as a uniting factor of all of the nonsensical gore lyrics.) Stack also emphasizes the fact that metal deals with topics like depression, loneliness and isolation: "an immutable part of the human condition" (388–390). Naturally, such lyrical themes would attract persons with depressive feelings because they provide a means of identification or an indication that one's pain is understood. Stack's analysis of metal lyrics is very insightful, and he even considers those lyrics that comment on the social order. According to Stack, "Metal also deals with *social* chaos and social problems: war, environmental pollution, and political corruption, to name a few. ...The lyrics often capture the psychological essence of the unhappy, lonely individual in modern society" (388–394). Stack believes that such lyrics promote hopelessness. He fails to see the prescriptive nature of a great many lyrics and thinks they may have a negative effect. He admits, however, that a number of metal heads come from disrupted families or lower class neighborhoods, and that "for these teens, metal may have provided a means of catharsis, a means of expressing individual and social chaos" (388–394). Although the suicidal tendencies of metal fans seem higher than those of non-fans, it makes sense to believe that "heavy metal may, nevertheless, save lives through catharsis. Some of the fans interviewed by Weinstein (1991) claimed that the only reason they had not committed suicide was metal" (388–394).

Stack found, however, that suicide acceptability was higher for metal fans than for non-fans, and he wondered at the reasons for this. Stack made a major discovery when he introduced the factor of religiosity into his study. When he controlled for religiosity and church attendance, metal fans showed no greater acceptance of suicide than non-fans. This led him to believe that the relationship between metal music and suicide was indeed spurious, and that the truly influential factor was religiosity. Stack goes on to explain his hypothesis:

> If fans in the metal subculture are less likely to have ties to traditional religion, this may be of key importance, since traditional religion represents, in part, the culture of hope. Religion, for example, may reduce the intensity of all manner of human suffering by promising the reward of a blissful afterlife. The hope for an afterlife and hope for change in adverse current conditions through such means as prayer are thought to reduce suicide risk. To the extent that a group is removed from religion, it would be expected, if all else is equal, to be at higher than average suicide risk. Possibly, a low level of religiosity among fans may result in a spurious association between metal and suicide acceptability. That is, the metal subculture may not be directly related to suicide acceptability. Instead, a low level of religiosity may cause both the attraction to metal and an accepting attitude toward suicide [388–394].

In conclusion, it seems unfair to classify the population of Death Metal fans as more suicide-prone than the average population when key demographic factors are held constant. We can thus conjecture that Death Metal fans are not more self-destructive than the mainstream population. Are they, however, more destructive towards others?

In answering this question, we arrive at the most important topic of this study: violent behavior. The survey results confirmed the research hypothesis that metal fans are not highly violent people. The survey was designed so that respondents were confronted with a number of highly provocative hypothetical situations and asked how they would respond. An impressive 74.2 percent would respond nonviolently when either verbally or physically provoked. The remaining 25.8 percent would respond violently only when physically provoked. None would respond violently when provoked only verbally. This is strongly supportive of the hypothesis that listening to music that portrays violence does not lead to violent behavior.

The majority of respondents were involved in no violent confrontations in the past year, and the vast majority of survey respondents (75.8 percent) were never arrested. Of those who were arrested, all but one person was arrested only once or twice; 97.0 percent were never convicted of a violent crime nor spent any time in prison. Only 3.0 percent were convicted of a violent crime once, and 0.0 percent were convicted of more than one violent crime. These rates are just about on target in terms of national averages. For instance, those convicted of crimes were all male. The national average rate for violent crime conviction is 3.4 percent for males and 0.5 percent for females according to the Department of Justice (www.doj.gov). Therefore, the rates of violent criminal behavior for fans of metal are just about average.

The results of this study are not atypical. No previous studies have ever found solid evidence correlating violent actions with interest in music that has violent themes (*The Nation*, Volume 271, Issue 10, p 3). A recent study reported by *Future Frame News* obtained results similar to those found in this study. The study was conducted by the University of Oldenburg in Germany, and 200 adolescents were surveyed. Their musical preferences were not at all linked to their level of aggression or tendency toward violence. According to *Future Frame News*, although those who listen to aggressive music do not tend to be more violent or aggressive themselves, "in certain situations of anger or sadness, the adolescents show clear distinctions in their choice of music. The higher their tendency to aggressive behavior, the more the youths tend to process their anger with aggressive music. However, there appeared to be no link between musical preferences and personality traits. Thus, listening to aggressive music does not translate to violent tendencies" (Ossietzky www.futureframe.de/news/000714-3.htm). There is no evidence linking violent activity to interest in Death Metal music.

15

Concluding Opinions on Death Metal and Violence

If there is no evidence to link violent behavior to interest in music with violent themes, then why do such stereotypes exist? Why do politicians continue to blame and denounce metal music? Representatives from the Recording Industry Association of America speculate that metal is a very useful scapegoat for politicians who can blame the entertainment industry for violence while ignoring the real correlations between violent behavior and factors like race or poverty (Jones www.wirednews.com/news/print/print/0,1294,19464,00.html). After the infamous *Albuquerque Journal* article already mentioned, metal fans wrote to the editor to defend their beliefs and to criticize the opponents of metal. Metal DJ Reiner Bunning parodies his opponents: "Blame the music! It can't possibly be the lame school system who is telling our kids that they are worthless accidents of life, or the divorced, alcoholic parents, or even the drugs. It's gotta be that darn devil music!" Bunning goes on to defend the music he loves:

> If you have some sense, you already know that musicians can't *possibly* be responsible for the weak constitutions of others. ... I could go on and on about how positive heavy metal is to listen to for many people in many ways, in many countries all over the world. ... As far as violence goes with us metal heads, I will tell you here and now that, unlike rappers and their

fans, we do not carry guns, and the worst it ever gets is a good old-fashioned fistfight, where both parties live and often forgive and forget [www.alibi.com/alibi/2000-05-18/letters.html].

Other metal fans wrote into the *Albuquerque Journal* in defense of metal music and metal fans. Eric Egenes, president of a metal radio station, writes, "I've been a fan of metal for almost 20 years. I've watched horror and gore films. I've been to an endless amount of Death Metal concerts. I've never killed anyone or sacrificed anything. It's entertainment and nothing more." As far as the violence in society goes, Egenes points to the problem of kids raised by the TV and the media instead of by their disinterested parents. Egenes concludes with a comical yet insightful mockery of those who blame metal music for violence in society:

Teenie-bopper music causes brain death. I suggest you also really attack that. It's a major problem in this country: teenage brain death. It's caused by listening to mindless corporate pop like the Backstreet Boys, N'Sync, or Britney Spears. Has any of them put an intelligent thought on disc yet? I think not. Oh yeah, don't forget that Classical music has caused narcolepsy in children for years. Blues causes depression. Jazz causes reefer and heroin usage. Folk music causes people not to bathe properly. Disco causes bad fashion sense, etc., etc. ... And if you don't like it, tough cookies, it's called freedom of speech. Read the Constitution sometime. It's a written document that has caused dissension for many years [www.alibi.com/alibi/2000-05-18/letters.html].

These may not be scholarly words, but they are highly representative of the passionate opinions widespread among Death Metal fans. The interviews conducted during this study yielded similar commentary on the trend of blaming the media for violent behavior. Interviewees sometimes got emotional; it was evident that some felt hurt and disturbed by society's reaction to them. The topic of the Littleton, Colorado, tragedy is always pertinent, and is quite a sore subject. After the horrific school shooting incident and the revelation that the assailants wore black trench coats and listened to industrial music, America turned with glaring eyes toward the teenagers who dressed in black and listened to such types of music. In a local public high school, days after the incident, a few of one researcher's friends were called into the guidance office for questioning. One student, who had worn a black trench coat every day, long before the Littleton incident, was chastised for wearing the coat to school and forbidden from wearing it again. Some metal heads reported that, while walking down the street, people shouted "Trenchcoat Mafia!" at them, associating them with the killers. It is very painful to be an innocent person on the receiving end of such hatred. Matt Medeiros brought up the Colorado incident during his interview:

> After Littleton, the perpetrators committed suicide and thus there was no one to question about their motives, so society looked for scapegoats while the real catalyst of the crime lay within the student body's constant rejection of these individuals based solely on the fact that they were different from them. Had the Trenchcoat Mafia been of a different race than the majority of the white Columbine High School students and they were excluded in the same way, then it would have been an act of racism on the part of the majority. This racist act would've prompted immediate intervention, but because the prejudice was not based on race, religion, or gender, it went by unattended and it has been shown historically that people can only be pushed so far before something violent happens.

As discussed earlier, although there may be some validity to the view that metal is a useful scapegoat for violence, it does not seem fair to say that no politicians are sincere in their crusades against metal. Nonetheless, many of arguments against metal music which congressman and other critics of metal present are very flawed. *New York Times* author Denise Caruso presents a common argument when she says, "Ultra-violent media systematically employ the psychological techniques of desensitization, conditioning, and vicarious learning. ... they teach us to associate violence with pleasure" (www.nytimes.com/library/tech/99/04/biztech/articles/ 26digi.html).

These arguments are flawed, but not entirely invalid. There is the potential for desensitization, but it is not fair to say that violence is really associated with pleasure in Death Metal lyrics.[15] Violence is presented, and while it is often portrayed as "pleasant," it is also presented in its gruesome, horrific reality. One might also argue that desensitization possesses its own value. In a very violent society, it can provide a coping mechanism for the sensitive inhabitants of a violent world. Martha Bayles writes that it "teaches troubled youth that they are not alone, that others feel the same disturbing, sometimes terrifying emotions" (260). In this sense, metal may have a positive value. Tom Werman believes that "heavy metal works by allowing its adherents to vent negative feelings that would otherwise cripple and distort their personalities. In other words, heavy metal can be defended ... as an escape valve, an 'outlet'" (Bayles 260).

Metal fans themselves do not seem to view the music in such a serious light. A number do state that it is a "release," but more think of the music as a "rush," a fun activity. Interviewees were asked how they felt about the current political battles over entertainment forms that are believed to promote violent behavior. The responses were very varied:

> Bullshit!—Adrianne Buchta, WSOU

> Silly! Life is life, people are people. Anything can set anyone off at anytime. [Efforts at censorship are] an excuse to slow down society and the times. It isn't going to work. It only points weaker human beings right [in that negative direction]. People are gonna live as they live.—King Fowley, Deceased, October 31st, Doomstone

> I think the violence in music and films is just a reflection of violence in everyday life.—Kyle Severn, Incantation, Wolfen Society, Acheron, Funerus

> People think Death Metal causes violence. We've had violence even since the beginning of our species, like in 2001: A Space Odyssey when the monkey picks up a bone and realizes he can kill another monkey by smashing him over the head with that bone. Certainly, he didn't get that idea from Death Metal. It's an innate and unchanging part of human nature. People have asked does life reflect art or does art reflect life. Well, art just reflects life. The idea that art is influencing life to any meaningful degree is just silliness.—Karl Sanders, Nile

> Upbringing, social learning, the environment, and a ridiculously complex mixture of other things influence aggression and violent behavior. The argument about 'violent' forms of entertainment promoting violent behavior doesn't seem to do a good job explaining the vast amounts of people who are exposed to it and don't behave violently. The belief that violent forms of entertainment such as Death Metal are responsible for violence is simply a way of scapegoating and avoiding the more complex issues.—Iris Duran, WSOU

> I have no doubt that the music I listen to could be damaging to certain types of people. Those people are not going to listen to metal! Fortunately, I am not one of them. Angry kids need someone to be angry with. They have a lot of confused feelings and not a lot of outlets. The government should not be the one to decide whether or not a person is capable of that. Censorship hinders discourse, and "protection" is the ideal excuse to restrict freedom. Fuck the PMRC! And since the First Amendment hasn't been abolished, I'll say it again: Fuck the fucking PMRC!—Matt Medeiros, Eschaton

> It's good, clean, friendly, violent fun. It doesn't hurt anyone! The efforts of Tipper Gore and the PMRC are fruitless. They're gonna fail because what makes the kids want to buy it? The parental advisory label.—Brian Jimenez, Funebrarum

15. Concluding Opinions on Death Metal and Violence 143

Cannibal Corpse owes a good deal of their prominence to that fact that Bob Dole mentioned them as being reprehensible. Their album (*Vile*) that Dole referred to was the only Death Metal album ever to appear on the Billboard charts. ... This instance clearly demonstrates that moral outrage and censorship only serve to inflame the interest and curiosity of the public at large.—Matthew Harvey, Exhumed

Any person can see the danger of censorship. But ... highly publicized instances of oppression seem to be free advertisement for the albums/mags in question.—Bill Zebub, The Grimoire

I hate censorship in any form; music takes a lot of unnecessary shit. The lawsuits are horrible. If I write about murder and a kid says my lyrics inspired him, I'm gonna get sued, but the same kid can watch it in a movie or read it in a book and that's never brought up. But regardless, for someone to actually mimic those acts then there's something really wrong with that person that goes way beyond any responsibility that any musician should be held liable for. ... There is such a double standard in our society.—Killjoy, Necrophagia

I think that whoever thinks that the movies or music "promote" violent behavior should look into the past and at the people performing the actual violent acts before blaming the entertainment. The whole "see no evil, hear no evil, speak no evil" philosophy is wrong anyway. It is the people performing the actual acts of violence that are to be blamed. It is they who choose to do the acts, not movies or music.—Jeremy Turner, Origin

[Death Metal is] just like a horror movie to me. It's entertainment. It can be funny. I think when you hear this brutal Death Metal, it makes you feel good and more mellow. Some people, it might make them feel violent. For me, Blink 182 [a pop band] is something that would make me want to go kill someone. <laughs> If you like something, it's not going to make you violent. ...I think music has nothing to do with what a kid's gonna do when he grows up. In a way, extreme music, like playing a brutal video game, it's like an outlet. The parents want to blame the music all the time, but [violence] doesn't really have anything to do with that.—Erik Sayenga, Dying Fetus, Witch-Hunt

Some of the lyrics do affect me in different ways. ... It's a positive release of negative energy. Some people don't have that, and they are not around anymore.—Paul Ryan, Origin

[Death Metal] is just like other kinds of music. It might be relaxing to someone and not to someone else. Yeah, there are some sick people. There's nothing you can do about it if you've got a kid who's already sick, manic, bipolar, or whatever.—Seth Newton, Witch-Hunt

144   IV. CONFRONTING THE CONSUMERS OF CARNAGE

> It's all about that adrenaline rush we love to go crazy on. ... Pardon my French on this, but fuck those who oppose metal and think it's our fault for having some kid blow his brains out or slit his wrists! The "outsiders" and the government should keep to themselves if they don't like what we're doing. Like Dying Fetus says ... "You don't know what our shit is all about, so don't even try to figure it out!"— John Dreisbach, With Immortality

> There are people in the metal culture as well as in the mainstream world that are impressionable, weak-minded, and ignorant, and some of these people may go and do various things which are depicted in the bands' lyrics. For example, most of the violent individuals involved in the Norwegian black metal scene, a scene known for its excessive violence, were impressed by the lyrics of Venom, and while the members of Venom themselves didn't do or believe the things they sang about, this particular part of the subculture took it to heart, and violence followed. It is also my belief that the people who committed these acts are the same types of people who will find inspiration for violence in anything from movies to TV to their neighbor's dog!— Matt Medeiros, Eschaton

> There might be a little relationship between interest in Death Metal music and violent behavior. [Violent people] might find more personal meaning in it because they identify with it. I think that the music itself, the medium, is neutral. It's benign. I think it might attract people who engage in violent behavior. They might find it more accessible because they identify with it more. You see all kinds of people at Death Metal shows, all across the spectrum. I think people, first and foremost, are attracted to the music. The lyrics are secondary. They could be singing about almost anything and people could get into it.— Jason Netherton, Misery Index, Dying Fetus

Metal fans clearly believe that their music is blamed unfairly for violence in American society. The American Civil Liberties Union agrees with the concerned metal fans and points out the injustice and danger of censoring music forms like metal and rap. The ACLU believes the attempts at censorship, mandatory labeling, and restricted access to be attempts at the imposition of personal moral standards on an entire nation. According the ACLU, labeling can be quite harmful to the artists whose music is labeled because these albums are often boycotted or receive bad publicity even though there is absolutely no proof that their product is harmful. The standards for labeling and restriction are very vague; they leave too much room for prejudice and injustice. For instance, rap and metal will likely be targeted whether or not their lyrics are offensive, and country or pop music with offensive lyrics is likely to be overlooked as harmless. More fundamentally, censorship and other restrictions directly violate the First

15. Concluding Opinions on Death Metal and Violence

Amendment. They also prevent the free expression or release of passion and the discussion of controversial social issues. According to the American Civil Liberties Union:

> No direct link between anti-social behavior and exposure to the content of any form of artistic expression has ever been scientifically established. Moreover, scapegoating artistic expression as a cause of social ills is simplistic. How can serious social problems like violent crime, racism, or suicide be solved by covering our children's ears? If suppressing creative expression were the way to control anti-social behavior, where would you stop? The source of inspiration most frequently cited by criminals has been the Bible. ... Throughout American history, popular music has mirrored the thoughts and yearnings of young people. ... celebrated change, and challenged the "establishment" [www.aclu.org/library/pbr3.html].

It seems clear that much of the opposition to Death Metal music has been based on uninformed assumptions and hasty conclusions. Not only do crusades against metal music lack any basis in research, they are also largely ineffective in combating those ills that they propound to stamp out. As several of the interviewees pointed out, the disturbed and demented will be disturbed and demented regardless of the entertainment forms with which society provides them. They will seek out what appeals to them, and if it does not exist, they will create it. As for the impressionable youth with whom Congress and most conservative groups seem most concerned, there is no indication that censorship labels and parental advisory stickers turn away anyone other than parents. Those who are likely to rebel and behave anti-socially will be further attracted by such labels.

One could also argue that metal rating labels are more useful than harmful to musicians. In fact, in some cases, such as the one involving Cannibal Corpse and Bob Dole, censorship has an effect opposite to that intended. In general, however, labeling of Death Metal music is not very useful at all, while labeling of other entertainment forms might make more sense. Films are marketed to the public at large, thus the need for a rating system. Death Metal is not. It is extremely unlikely that anyone who did not wish to know about new releases or other occurrences in the Death Metal scene would ever have knowledge of them. Indeed, many fans constantly have to seek out information on even their favorite bands due to the underground nature of the music and the subculture. This negates any need for a rating system since uninterested parties would most likely be completely unaware of a Death Metal album's existence.

Even if metal were harmful to some individuals, which cannot be proven, is it wise to fight against such a force by undermining the First Amendment when there are more effective and more logical means of addressing anti-social material? Ralph Nader made a great deal of sense when he said that the only way to fight the ills permitted by the First Amendment is through the use of the First Amendment. Those who disapprove of metal and its messages should feel completely free to profess the reasons for their disapproval and to produce material that is to their liking. After all, one will never find a metal head petitioning for the illegalization of gospel music.

From this liberal perspective, the point is that all opinions, even very negative and distorted ones, must be permitted to exist and to be professed. This is not out of regard for the perverse and the criminal, but for the good of society itself. Our nation was built on the libertarian philosophy of John Stuart Mill who professes that the negative effects of a repressed society and a restricted media will be far more negative than anything that a given person or group could produce. Truth and rightness are only truly known and understood if their defenders can stand up to false and wrong opinions. Similarly, no truth is complete, and even wrong opinions and negative philosophies might possess some hint of truth that can improve upon existing opinions. The ACLU argues that even songs which seem to sanction vile behavior, such as Ice T's "Cop Killer," may serve an essential function by forcing society to confront its dark and overlooked problems such as racism, violence, and poverty. Real defenders of truth should not fear wrong opinions. Instead these opinions should be analyzed — their positive aspects embraced and their negative aspects dissected and rejected. Simple acceptance of opinions does not yield truth, yet open discourse brings man ever closer to it. Knowledge of truth can only be born of open, progressive dialectic. Such are the opinions of Enlightenment philosopher John Stuart Mill as expressed in his treatise *On Liberty*. Mill warns us that censorship may provide a sort of "pacification" for those who feel secure in the truth and goodness of their own beliefs; however, "the price paid for this sort of intellectual pacification is the sacrifice of the entire moral courage of the human mind. ... The greatest harm done is to those who are not heretics, and whose mental development is cramped, and their reason cowed, by the fear of heresy" (295).

The generalizations made by many Americans and the steps taken by politicians to censor or restrict music are not based on scientific evidence, are not effective, and are not harmless. We have seen how the battle against metal music can be detrimental to society, and its potential to harm the individual should not be overlooked. Ironically, the animosity of mainstream

15. Concluding Opinions on Death Metal and Violence

culture towards fans of metal may increase their alienation and contribute to the perpetuation of negative trends correlated with Death Metal, such as depression or anti-social attitudes. When politicians and society choose to crusade against some "evil," they should take care to recognize that their words, actions, and attitudes are directed towards people and can be hurtful and harmful. Matt Medeiros mourns the effects of the current crusade against Death Metal music:

> Metal culture is not for everyone. It never will be, but people need to acknowledge that people in the metal culture are still people. While some may be monsters, not all are. Media and society have stigmatized a large number of people based on the isolated actions of a very select few, and due to ignorance and disinterest, the majority of American and world culture has done nothing to degrade these barriers, and as time goes on, it becomes harder and harder for people to remain active members of the subculture as a result of society's misunderstanding.

Matthew speaks here of barriers, and these are the most tangible product of efforts geared towards censorship. Senator Byrd complained that "violent" entertainment forms and the media in general were creating "a subculture within a culture, a nation within a nation," yet it seems that it is the rejection and condemnation of such subcultures by mainstream society which has made them largely irreconcilable with the nation at large. If Americans are disturbed by the preoccupation of Death Metal fans with violent themes and dark images, perhaps they should confront them and attempt to understand their source. Perhaps this will prove more rational and more positive than attempts at erecting barriers and destroying something that is both a product of our culture and a functioning, integral part of American society.

Part V

The Mind of the Metal Head and the Heart of the Underground

16

The Subcultural Phenomenon

Our study has provided us with a wealth of information about the demographics, attitudes, philosophies, and behavioral tendencies of Death Metal fans. Much of this data was drawn directly from survey results. The words offered within the interviews provided further insight into the person of the metal fan. We have not yet discerned the personal and psychological factors that help to explain why one chooses to join the Death Metal scene. In this section, we shall attempt to use the information attained thus far, as well as the words spoken in various interviews, to enter the mind of the metal head. Our words will necessarily be brief and vague, for it is dangerous and unjust to draw sweeping generalizations about the psychological makeup of any population. In this section, we are exploring, but not explaining. We shall seek to develop questions and possible hypotheses, but not to draw conclusions. The significance of these cautioning words is perhaps best presented in the interviews themselves, for they reveal a stunning array of answers and varied opinions which betray the inappropriateness of drawing firm generalizations about a group composed of diverse individuals.

For many metal fans, metal is merely one of many forms of entertainment embraced and enjoyed. For such individuals, "metalness" is not an exclusive or defining characteristic of their personalities. Nonetheless, "metalness" is more often than not an integral or essential part of one's social life and activities. The most common reason for becoming a part of the Death Metal scene was cited as entertainment. The interest in the music itself preceded the interest in developing any social life grounded in the scene. Most interviewees claimed to have become fans of metal simply because the music is technically more complex, more unique, and better than popular music. "It is the true alternative," said one fan; "It's just good stuff," reported another. Some interviewees said that the reason they maintain active social lives within the Death Metal scene has to do with the people as well as the music. "The people are very down to earth," said Bill Zebub in description of what he most likes about the metal scene. The interviews yielded a variety of responses about what fans find most attractive about the Death Metal scene. While there is a general consensus that the music itself is the first and most powerful source of interest, metal fans find other reasons for embracing and enjoying the scene. The following were some of the reasons fans gave for their involvement in the Death Metal scene:

- For the experience, for yourself. Also, to support the scene.
- Sheer aggression — [metal] being the heaviest, the most extreme speed with detuned guitars.
- Just the music!
- The incredible power of the music itself.
- It makes me feel happy.
- The music is good, and the guys are hot, especially the Swedish men.
- The metal scene is a recreational place, like a sort of social club, and I can think of no better place for me to go to unwind and have a good time.
- It's great entertainment.
- Musically, it is some of the most diverse, talented, and interesting music out there. ... The variety presented by the various bands in the metal community far surpasses any sort of so-called diversity which is found in any pop culture genre.
- I've been involved in metal for half my life. [There's] no reason to leave it. I have a great time at the shows, enjoy the music, make a lot of friends.
- The factor I like about the Death Metal scene it that it is a very wild group. People are who they are and are not afraid to show it.
- It's aggressive. I enjoy the atmosphere and the experience.
- It's all about that adrenaline rush we love to go crazy on.
- Seeing your influences live and in your face is just such an adrenaline rush! In fact, a lot of the stuff I listen to is better live than on CD.

- I like the intimacy at the shows, where bands actually come into the audience and talk to their fans. There's a sense of camaraderie between the fans and the bands. There's a surprising amount of respect that someone will get just because of the music they write.
- I love how the scene is based on heart, the sheer love for the music is what brings people out to the shows. They want to know everything about the bands.
- The life and the energy in the people, you look around at a show and you see people (for the most part) who know that there is something wrong with the culture we live in, and want to live and breath outside of it as much as possible.
- The two things I like most about the Death Metal scene are its uncompromising style and its refusal to change just to be more marketable. I respect that in the scene and in a way expect those things of myself.
- One of the first things that attracted me towards the scene was the fact that it was like open territory. There were a billion bands each doing their own thing. And whatever it was, you could be judged on your own merit. No one was telling you exactly what you had to listen to. You didn't have to be anybody or anything. I saw it as quite a bit of freedom, freedom of expression, especially in the early days.
- Metal stands in opposition to that plastic and candy-coated world painted by the likes of corporate music companies.
- What I'd say I like most is probably how it takes everybody to make the scene happen. I like seeing everybody walking around with the [metal] shirts on. You know it's kind of hard walking around when you've got gore, blood, and all that shit on your shirt. Also, going to shows, and seeing more and more people come out. It's almost romantic in a way, I think. It takes everybody to make the scene happen.
- People who are heavily into Death Metal tend to make being a Death Metal fan a defining feature of themselves. I think this creates a union between Death Metal fans from all over the world. If you meet Death Metal fans from the U.S., Europe, South America, Asia, or any other part of the world, they are all very similar regarding fashion, interests, and the belief of being in an elite subculture.
- The only society in the scene [is] the fans. We grow stronger as a unit, and it's always been and will be that way.
- There is a unity of metallers. Death Metal is an underground scene, and the underground metallers have to stick together.
- I like the togetherness: bands working together, sharing gear, booking shows for each other. The kinship part is great!
- The whole vibe of knowing you did things on your own is great —

no big wigs, no fucking "head honchos" running it. It is all about getting up and fending for yourself, as it should be!
• A good number of us are pretty complicated people. I would say that this music is very much so a type of catharsis for us personally.
• Death Metal music serves as an emotional release for the striving souls who have found it. It's a place in time and in mind for people with a craving for this lifestyle and genre to truly be themselves.

There is great variety in these responses, but certain trends do emerge. For instance, it seems that the primary reason for interest in metal is the music itself. The other often-cited reasons for attending shows center on "the experience" which provides an adrenaline rush or a release. Metal fans themselves were not specific about the nature or function of this release, except to indicate that it is a relief of tensions and an expression of uninhibited freedom. This seems to mesh well with the theory that metal music and mosh pits provide a form of catharsis.

During the interviews, metal fans were asked not only what attracted them to the Death Metal scene, but also what they liked least about the scene and would like to see changed. While many different answers were given, a prevalent response was aggravation with the occasional bouts of violence at shows. It should be noted that those interviewed seemed to agree that most of the perpetrators of such violence were not "metal people," but outsiders assuming that Death Metal is all about violence and wishing to take part in it. Although this was a common sentiment reflected in the interviews, it seems most appropriate to let the words of those interviewed speak for themselves. The following were some of the responses to a question about the least attractive aspects of the scene:

• Stupid people who get into asinine fights and stupid little girls who get into fights over guys.
• I hate neo–SOD listeners and a lot of the people who drink too much at shows and get into stupid fights.
• The fighting in the crowds.
• Unfortunately, some people can't handle this kind of music and they take it the wrong way. They like to talk shit, and, for some reason, this kid of music makes them some kind of Robert Deniro tough guy. I don't get it.
• I don't like the fighting between the bands. Like, "Oh, we're Black Metal, and Death Metal sucks." Hey, we're all metal. It all came out of like Black Sabbath, Judas Priest, it all came out of that. There's no point in fighting.

16. The Subcultural Phenomenon 155

- People who take elitism to the ultimate extreme ... [and] violence within the scene.
- Egos, rock-star idiots who are nobody thinking they are in KISS.
- Extremist elitist assholes that run around and place rules and boundaries on music, [on] what you can and can't do.
- The thing I don't like about the scene is the elitism or separatist attitude, like everything you do sucks and I am better than you.
- Despite the unity in the Death Metal scene, there is often fierce competition and animosity between rival bands/industry people/etc. It would be nice if more energy could be put into furthering the genre as a whole as opposed to people in the same scene taking stabs at each other.
- There's so many wanna-be's and not enough individuals.
- 100% of the people who follow some sort of ideology supposed to be influenced by metal are the biggest posers of all. That has nothing to do with the music.
- People/bands thinking a certain sound or look is all they need to "fit in." People need to earn their wings and bust balls to better the scene. Respect is much needed. Too many "here today, gone tomorrow" fools.
- As soon as people start trying to limit the underground as to what it ought to be, it starts becoming pretentious and it suffers. Art has to be allowed to breathe. One of the things I didn't like seeing was all these bands trying to be the exact same thing ... I already have Cannibal Corpse and Suffocation records. I like to hear the bands that are doing something a little different, that have something musically to offer, like Cryptopsy and Krisiun.
- There's too many people I find fake, such as singers who cup the mic or drummers who do blast beats that aren't crossed over.
- Lack of talent in musical playing.
- There are too many bands and promoters looking to be greedy and shoot the entire underground in the foot.
- Like anything underground, it becomes infested, corrupted, diluted, downsized, and it can and will become commercially viable. ... Metal in the year 2000 has become a parody of itself.
- The ease with which it [metal] is commercialized, popularized, and bastardized.
- The fruity hairdos! They are beyond gay!

It is evident from these responses that metal fans are capable of being critical of the scene, and that, if those interviewed are at all representative of the greater population of metal fans, there is a strong distaste for violence in the scene and a desire to change that aspect of metal shows. In my own experience of the metal scene, I have witnessed very little of the aforementioned violence; however, the occasional fight does occur, and when it does, the entire atmosphere of the show is ruined. (As previously mentioned, hostility is not the norm, but rather a disruption.) Besides the condemnation of violence, a few of the interviewees provided responses that reveal a conflict between the technical elitism of some scene members (who are often skilled musicians engaged in a continual battle against the reputation of metal as mere noise) and the desire of others to make the scene as united and as large as possible (therefore accepting metal music forms which some musicians find inferior and detrimental to the quality of the scene as a whole). None of those interviewed had a great deal to complain about, but, on the other hand, nearly every interviewee did find at least one thing about the scene which he or she wished to change. As stated, this was most often the violence factor.

The interviews revealed that metal music can be an essential or integral part of life without defining or dominating life to the exclusion of other activities and endeavors. Even in the realm of music, when metal fans were asked what types of music they listened to, most readily offered more than one response, ranging from classical and opera, to new wave and jazz. While some of those interviewed stated that most of their friends were fans of the same music, others replied that this was not at all the case. The Death Metal culture itself may be an exclusive realm, but this does not generally translate into an elitism, exclusivity, or lack of open sociability among individual fans of metal. As the survey results indicated, fans of metal are generally active, functioning members of society who lead daily lives much like those of anyone else. According to one interviewee, "Metal heads are part of regular society. They have jobs or go to school. Life depends on interaction with regular society." Brian Jimenez expressed a similar view: "It's a hobby and a personal choice, not so much of a lifestyle as some make it. Everyone has to categorize groups within society, [but] you're just making your life harder if you're emphasizing disharmony between your lifestyle and society."

This evidence of practical realism should challenge some of the assumptions about metal heads, but should not be taken as a disavowal of the passion that most fans of metal have for their music. First of all, most are not only listeners, but also musicians. Whether or not most have any success in their pursuit of musical prowess, it is difficult to come across a metal fan who has not made some attempt at creating music or starting a band of his or her own. This seems to testify to the importance of metal for the individual fan and to the high degree of involvement found among metal scenesters. Although most metal fans are aware of reality and accepting of their place in the social order, they nonetheless do find a hobby and an identity in the Death Metal culture. Some of the very persons who emphasized the importance of recognizing and accepting the regular social establishment also affirmed the vital significance of metal music within their own lives. As Brian Jimenez always says, "Metal is the beef of my life."

A few interviewees volunteered personal tales of their interest in the Death Metal scene and its personal meaning for them. In hearing their stories, it seems impossible to condemn the Death Metal scene as a negative force in the lives of young people. In many lives, Death Metal has been a saving grace:

> I got into metal for all of the wrong reasons in society's way of looking at things: the craziness, the devil, the drug and alcohol abuse, the violence. But I used it as a way of venting my frustrations. I call it a positive release of negative energy. I had music to create that I truly love. Sure, some of my buddies didn't have that and they killed people or got killed living the wild life. But [the Death Metal scene] kept me out of trouble. I had a goal to make it in this scene.—Paul Ryan, Origin

> November of my freshman year of high school, I went to my first show, Gwar, at Studio One in Newark. Never had I experienced anything like it. A live metal show is unmatched, and Gwar is an exceptional one at that. It was crazy and I loved every minute of it. In metal I had found something that I enjoyed listening to, and people and ideas that I gravitated towards. I was an angry directionless kid with a lot of problems and a lot of questions and no one giving me answers. Dave Mustaine, James Hetfield, and Phil Anselmo [metal musicians] were my surrogate older brothers, who knew how I felt. Just knowing that there were other alienated people out there made me feel better. I might have been weird, but I wasn't the only one.—Matthew Medeiros, Eschaton

> Speaking for myself, Death Metal enabled me to find strength and fulfillment in a preadolescence marred with feelings of sadness and helplessness. Being from a very broken family with neither a mother nor father around, it was extremely difficult coping with issues beyond my control and understanding. Death Metal was like a catharsis, giving me the ability to channel all my rage on life, fate, my parents, etc. In addition to being an outlet for suppressed rage, Death Metal to me was a source of adrenaline for the psyche. It's like your soul feeds off of the energy and intensity of the music, and it becomes transferred into you. I guess for Death Metal fans in general, it is the periphery of music for those searching for extremity. I can safely assume that other fans also can channel rage and aggression through the music. The Death Metal mosh pit is a good example of people feeding off of the energy and intensity of the music. I think for many fans, Death

> Metal has higher value than just being kick-ass music to listen to. Because it is so exceptional and unlike any other existing genre of music, it attracts a unique and elite portion of the general population. I think that the elite few feel empowered to identify with and be able to experience the sonic intensity.—Iris Duran, WSOU

Metal is, after all, not only a form of music, but also a subculture. It serves a role that is grounded in entertainment but ultimately transcends the music itself. Everyone seeks a social life; everyone seeks entertainment. Not everyone, however, becomes a part of a subculture — particularly not one that seems overtly offensive or "brutal." We can thus infer that there is something unique about those individuals who become a part of the Death Metal scene, but one can only hypothesize about the potential psychological elements that draw one to enter a particular subculture. For some it is as simple as rebellion. Comments Nefarious, "I think deep down everyone likes heavy music. They think they're a rebel when they listen to it." For others, the Death Metal scene has a deeply significant role and value as a subculture. Writes Jason Netherton:

> This extreme form of music (as compared to moderate, more commercially acceptable forms of music) reflects my personal belief that extremist innovation is what ultimately forwards history, meaning change comes from the fringes of society. In this case the music and the subculture to which it is connected reflect very much my understanding and view of how truth and alternative viewpoints are given birth. Basically Death Metal's sound and dark worldview is concomitant with my own extremist view of society, and what it will take to change this society for the better.

Clearly, the role and value of Death Metal as a subculture has a strong personalized element for each individual involved. The primary unifying factor discovered among those interviewed (and even those merely encountered at shows) was a sense of individualism. A longing for uniqueness seems to play a role in the choice to dismiss the mainstream in favor of a subculture. At one recent New York City show, a band member spoke of a "sense of otherness" which he had always felt and which drew him to do something different, something "special." Although no one else expressed this sentiment so directly, the very personalities and characters encountered at Death Metal shows, as opposed to the supermarket or the local bar, emanate a spirit of individualism, of uniqueness and freedom.

Adolescents and young adults often attempt to express their individuality by adopting yet another label and joining yet another group, and it seems that the Death Metal scene is in some ways an example of such a group. At the same time, it does permit a far greater degree of individualism and freedom than the typically restrictive and elitist social cliques of adolescent society. By entering the metal scene, one can gain an identity and join a group without sacrificing a great deal of individuality. Moreover, entrance into the Death Metal scene, or any subculture which is not deemed socially acceptable, automatically guarantees that the standards and judgments of the outside world will not come into play. For the socially awkward, for those who are not beautiful, for those who could never succeed at sports, the metal scene provides a community that will not judge based on such factors. Metal is very much about enthusiasm and degree of individual involvement rather than about natural talents or inherent traits. There is no impossible-to-meet criterion of judgment and no mandate that scenesters conform to an ideal mold. By its very nature, metal permits individualism by discouraging judgment and declaring acceptance of the socially unacceptable.[16] Metal may thus be a haven for the unique.

The rejection of social standards may have some negative as well as positive effects. More than a mainstream social group, the metal scene could perhaps be attractive to the anti-social or to the disturbed. This may explain the correlations found in some studies between a preference for metal music and negative attitudes or antisocial behavior. However, as this study clearly demonstrates, it is in no way rational to assume that a given metal fan is disturbed or antisocial, because the vast majority of fans do not fit this description at all.

Martha Bayles does not recognize that metal music can appeal to persons who are not "troubled." Nonetheless, she does provide a vision of one role which metal music plays to assuage the pain of difficult times in life. Bayles writes that "heavy metal is therapeutic because it functions as the modern equivalent of a puberty rite. It's 'a vital and reliable rite of passage,' writes Mikal Gilmore of Rolling Stone. It's 'a community ritual,' writes Pareles, that teaches troubled youth that they are not alone, that others feel the same disturbing, sometimes terrifying emotions" (260). Bayles envisions Heavy Metal as a sign of a troubled spirit and a disturbed soul, but perhaps she is missing the fact that every adolescent, every human being, experiences times of trying emotions and distressing feelings. Every teenager seeks out a rite of passage. Metal music is not just therapy for the "disturbed" but can be therapy for anyone who does not live in a crystal palace or a snow globe. Life is difficult — particularly for adolescents who do not look like Britney Spears and Justin Timberlake and have no desire to wear Tommy Hilfiger or Calvin Klein clothes to impress others. When the rite of passage in modern society is so centered on materialistic and superficial attributes, it seems a sign of integrity to seek a viable rite of passage elsewhere.

Christenson and Roberts write that "heavy metal is central to the alienated and disaffected youth who seek it out. It provides a crucial source of personal identification and group solidarity, and articulates as no other set of cultural texts can their opposition to the cultural mainstream and their quest for alternative modes of self and peer acceptance" (110). It seems that there is certainly some truth to this statement, yet one might add that youth need not be especially "alienated and disaffected" to long for an expression of individualism and freedom that surpasses the mundane and conformist reality of mainstream culture. In other words, metal may be crucial to teens with severe social problems, but it is just as attractive to and crucial to any youth who feel unfulfilled and repressed by critical and typically superficial social norms.

Authors like Bayles, Christenson, and Roberts have pointed out some of the functions of the metal subculture, but they step too far when they use these potential functions to make generalizations about the members of the metal scene. There is something in the search for or identification with a subculture that can be examined as a phenomenon in itself, rather than a sign of disaffection and dementia. Dick Hebdige looks at the complex phenomena of subcultures themselves. He does not attempt to pigeonhole and classify what he has observed. Instead, he is open to discoveries that seem rational, profound, and compatible with the results of this study. Hebdige writes:

> The "subcultural response" is neither simply affirmation nor refusal, neither "commercial exploitation" nor a "genuine revolt." It is neither simply resistance against some external order nor straightforward conformity with the parent culture. It is both a declaration of independence, of otherness, or alien intent, a refusal of anonymity, of subordinate status. It is an insubordination. And at the same time it is also a confirmation of the fact of that powerlessness, a celebration of impotence. Subcultures are both a play for attention and a refusal, once attention is granted, to be read according to the book [35].

Hebdige neither idealizes nor condemns the phenomenon of the subculture. His explanation of the "subcultural response" hints at the natural and often healthy motives for rejecting the mainstream. Consistent with the findings of this study, Hebdige's words seem to confirm the role of firm individualism, of "otherness," in the choice to embrace a subculture such as the Death Metal scene.

There is something extraordinarily valuable in this phenomenon. And to those who find in the Death Metal community an identity that meshes camaraderie with individuality, it is essential. The mold of the mainstream ideal is not all-inclusive, and some individuals must duck out to maintain their integrity and perhaps their sanity. These individuals are not "sucked into" subcultures; they are naturally drawn to them, and they in turn mold and define them. Writes Pete Helmkamp, "For those of us who listen to metal, it is because it has become (or *is*) a necessary element of our existence. It predicates our being. Whether it is because we took the music and filled a certain niche in our psyches or because the music allowed us the release that we so desired, it matters not. What matters is that it simply is." The Death Metal subculture is not a group or an organization that recruits members; it is the spontaneous response of those youth who demand such a phenomenon for the fulfillment of their natures and the preservation of their individuality. The Death Metal scene was not "created;" it arose and continues to develop and evolve as a progressive and perpetual response of its members, who do not conform to it but allow it to conform to them. A subculture is a natural phenomenon, not the invention of some perverse rabble-rouser. Its spontaneous rather than artificial nature testifies to its significance and its necessity.

Author David Walley recognizes the natural essence of the subcultural phenomenon and criticizes those who attack and condemn it. Subcultures are a naturally occurring and recurring phenomenon, common throughout the ages and ultimately necessary. David Walley compares metal heads to the greasers and hoods of the 1950s. He believes that they fit the same psychological and sociological profile (175). According to Walley, "Each generation salvages what artifacts remain from the last, then adds its own little twist" (175). Walley's view is unique in that he visualizes the subcultural phenomenon as a positive or at least healthy response of certain youth to the larger social order. Jason Netherton views the Death Metal scene in this light:

> In metal, people don't like the mainstream culture, and they just opt out. [What motivates this depends on] each person's understanding, their own perception. They know something's wrong. They don't feel comfortable in their given setting in life. They see how mainstream culture works, and they don't want to go along with it, so they opt out. People opt out into different subcultures, whether it's punk, or gothic, or Death Metal. ... [Unfortunately they rarely] connect their discontent to the greater discontent of others, the greater society. The Death Metal scene is a scene in itself, rather than a scene for itself. It is a class in itself. Death Metal people know they opt out, they know they don't want to deal with mainstream culture, and at the same time, they just sort of become a scene. But it's not a scene conscious of why it's a scene. It's not a scene with a direct purpose. It's a scene that came about as a result of the conditions that led to [the "opt-out"].

A few other scholars recognize that such cultures and communities would not have developed if they did not serve some function for their constituents. Author Betty Houchin Winfield presents the view that one cannot really judge music aesthetically because it is about culture and taste, which are unique to certain groups and persons. Others will not understand the music of a given culture and are therefore not justified in dismissing its artistic value (10). For Winfield, powerful evidence of the importance of music like Death Metal is found in the complete and utter failure of attempts at censorship in the United States, such as Tipper Gore's PMRC (11–12).

Winfield is optimistic about the fate of subcultures because she believes them to be necessary, unavoidable, and largely indestructible in the sense that, if one cultural response is suppressed, another will naturally arise through the voice of those who by nature require it. Yet in the absence of the constitutional guarantees of free speech, this response may be suppressed with dire consequences. It seems ridiculous to think that in the United States, the bastion of the free world, the First Amendment could be in any danger. However, we are reminded not to take such freedoms for granted in light of the unanimous passage of the Brownback Amendment and the current consensus of opposing political factions as to the evil of Death Metal music and other violent entertainment forms. Congressmen and conservative groups believe that in advocating restrictions and censorship, they are saving society and discouraging violence by hampering the production of music with violent themes. However, there is no evidence of a correlation between violent behavior and an interest in such music, nor is there any evidence that fans of Death Metal music hold particularly negative or destructive attitudes. There seems to be a great deal more evidence, found in the words and the persons of those who actually embrace the subculture, that it serves a positive and cathartic function for them. Death Metal music defines a community and represents the response of a unique and individualistic minority to a mainstream society that is itself superficial and unfulfilling. To stifle and ban such a response, to tear away someone's culture and identity, is no small matter. The consequences of such an action will likely be far more destructive and hurtful than the effects of even the most vile art forms.

But metal is "ugly and useless!" exclaims Martha Bayles. She is evidently as removed from the culture as its political opponents, for she is unable to recognize its positive function and is drawn to lament its negativity and perversity: "Heavy metal offers ritual death, but at the end of the ordeal, there is no rebirth" (261). Fans would argue that Bayles is mistaken — indeed, that they are reborn at every show.

17

Rebellion and Religion

At the heart of any political and social controversy surrounding Death Metal music, one can only find the disturbing and disgusting lyrics that the genre has latched onto with ferocious pride and defiance. The lyrics spoken of here are those with gore-based, pornographic, or anti-religious themes. While lyrics with a socio-political message about environmentalism, drug use, etc. might also be disturbing to some, they do not warrant the same thoroughgoing analysis as the former. Instead, lyrics with social or political themes present their messages literally; their reform-oriented agendas are both more overt and more easily digested by the respectable masses. On the other hand, there is mystery and fear surrounding the tendency to bash religion or to horrify with revolting images. The motivations for producing such material are unclear, and the allure for listeners is even more unclear. For this reason, two chapters of this book will be devoted to exploring anti-religious and gory/pornographic lyrics, respectively. Each chapter will examine the motivations of musicians in creating these lyrics and of listeners in consuming them. This chapter will look at anti-religious lyrics because they are slightly more literal and thus more easily analyzed than horror/gore/porn. Anti-religious lyrics are a staple of the Death Metal genre, and even bands that embrace other themes often allow the Satanic or otherwise anti-religious sentiment to invade their lyrical compositions.

Sometimes, sacrilegious lyrics are attractive merely for aesthetic appeal. Often, the elaborate gothic paintings and images utilized by bands discussing or bashing religion are quite beautiful. The same paintings one might find on the ceiling of the Sistine Chapel could work their way onto the cover of an anti-religious Death Metal album. The use of archetypal images of angels and demons, and the relation of tales about hellfire, punishment, and divine or demonic retribution is fascinating on a number of levels. Any archetypal stories appeal to the universal human consciousness, as Jung might say. Such sacrilegious art and tales hold the same allure as much pro-religious material: they explore in a creative manner extremes of good and evil, purity and sin.

Any discussion of religion invites the supernatural into the equation. Listeners are lured into a fantasy world, which is appealing simply by virtue of its fantastic nature. It is an escape from the mundane, a vacation from reality. Whether or not listeners agree with the anti-religious themes being discussed or sympathize with angel-raping demons is not necessarily significant to the mere allure of fantasy for fantasy's sake. But why choose dark, sacrilegious themes just to attain entry into the fantastic realm? Ironically, one might suggest that perhaps this is a more accepted or reputable form of fantasy. Dragons and unicorns are quite evidently fictitious; not so with heaven and hell. While children can ponder the existence of fairies and trolls, adults cannot. They can, however, indulge in fantasies about angels and demons without the stigma attached. It is immature or perhaps insane to be seriously enthralled by the fantastic, unless the fantastic is a brand of supernatural which contemporary adult society has stamped with approval. Religion is precisely this brand of the supernatural. For this reason, it is possible to make the case that Death Metal fans enjoy lyrics with sacrilegious themes and archetypal religious images because they provide an ostensibly "adult" trip into the realm of fantasy.

This theory is supported by the fact that dominant religious and anti-religious images are not the only ones utilized by Death Metal artists. Other forms of the occult are used frequently as well, but all of them bear some connection to a modern or ancient religious rite, which makes the fantasy adult and not childlike. The band Nile, for instance, has explored ancient Egyptian religion and myths. Morbid Angel has also centered many of its lyrics and album concepts around strange occult religious images and themes. In general, the fantastic itself holds a great allure for Death Metal audiences as for most other people. Religion provides merely one means of indulging in fantasy without departing from the acceptable adult psyche. It might be "cool" for a teenager to know the rites of an ancient vampiric cult or other bizarre religious sect, but it is could never be "cool" to know too much about Leprechauns or Santa Claus. The religious foundation lends credibility or at least acceptability to the fantasy: it is dark, it is sedate, it is mature. Therefore, it is a particularly attractive fantasy.

17. Rebellion and Religion

There are certainly possibilities that listeners feel deeper, more direct forms of identification with anti-religious lyrics. The lyrics of bands such as Deicide and Immolation often present extremely angry accusations against religious persons and against God himself. The highly emotional, non-intellectual nature of such lyrics suggests that they are a mere angry lashing-out, a product of feelings of betrayal or abandonment at the hands of religion and God. Often, religious persons are accused of hypocrisy and derided for their tendency to be judgmental. The angry backlash found in Death Metal lyrics may be a consequence of negative personal experiences that Death Metal musicians and fans have had with the religious. A few negative personal experiences can easily slip into bias and outright prejudice when one's social climate seems to validate feelings of outrage against a particular group. This bias, like all bias, is, of course, fundamentally irrational. It is a gut-level expression of discontent and anger lashed out upon those imagined to be a source of that discontent.

In this context, it is not a large leap to equate the religious with the bourgeoisie and the heathen with the proletariat. To lash out against persons of the dominant religious persuasion is not far from lashing out at the class system itself. This is supported by the fact that the trait of the religious attacked most frequently within the context of Death Metal lyrics is their feigned superiority, be it moral, material, or otherwise. Religion and class are strongly tied together. Therefore, anger at the high society itself can be translated into anger at a religion embraced by that society — a religion which sanctifies the existent order and excludes the dirty, the imperfect, the uncouth, the lower classes. Into the latter categories fall a vast number of Death Metal fans.

This analysis makes sense on a macro-level, but there is also something more personal than social which causes anger against religious persons, religious norms, even God himself. This involves feelings of rejection. There is great pain in rejection by one's peers, rejection by adults, rejection by the clergy who are supposed to embrace "all of God's children." When life itself is extremely painful and one feels particularly abandoned by the entire existent order, the consequence is tremendous anger that demands an outlet. That anger is naturally directed toward those who do the rejecting and towards those who make false promises of happiness or security. Religion, to many youths, seems the origin of these false promises, and religious folk form the army that spreads lies.

The ultimate betrayal, of course, is that at the hands of God. Where is God in the life of the rejected, alienated teenager? The popular, content children with decent families and pleasant lives are God's children; the angry young boy in dire financial straits, unable to get a date to the prom, is *not* a child of God. God's children, on the contrary, are the source of his pain. For him, God does not exist at all; God is a lie. Or worse yet, God rewards *his* children and ignores the pain and suffering of others. God himself becomes odious, a father who has abandoned his neediest sons. The anti-religious and anti-God lyrics produced by some Death Metal bands reflect a deep anger rooted in personal feelings of betrayal and rejection.

Sometimes, the messages of such bands are more than mere rants. There is a possibility that some aim to do more than merely blow off steam or express their own philosophies. Such bands are not merely ranters; they are advocates. Their message is that old value systems should be destroyed. (This is perhaps analogous to: "The system which makes me suffer should be overthrown.") The frightening thing about this message is not its tendency to merely question values, but to suggest an actual replacement or substitute value system. What is to replace dominant, bourgeois, Christian values?

The substitute ethical system most frequently proffered by Death Metal bands is Satanism. This is basically a not-so-creative inversion of traditional Christian ethics, where evil becomes good, sin is virtuous, and selfishness replaces altruism. It is particularly attractive because it attempts to reintegrate man's animalistic tendencies into his lifestyle. (Unfortunately, his humanity might be sacrificed in the process.) Satanism allows the "beast" in man to come to the forefront, and this is appealing for several reasons. First of all, it appeals to that which is repressed (and is actually a very safe outlet for it). Secondly, "there is a kind of defiant pleasure in regression, in wallowing in dirt as a way of rejecting social constraints" (Paul 314). Satanism might seem very frightening and threatening to critics of Death Metal, and it might be indeed, if it were adopted as a serious philosophy. It, however, is not. The research undertaken for this study suggests that even those who profess to adopt a Satanic ethical system do not behave accordingly. If Satanic theory is pervading the ranks of Death Metal fans, it seems that it has had little or no impact on behavioral norms. (As mentioned earlier, the ethical systems actually practiced by most Death Metal fans are Kantian or quasi–Christian.)

Sometimes, bands that advocate the destruction of existing value systems suggest that ethics be replaced with a void. Because of the somewhat laughable nature of professed Satanism, the advocacy of this nihilistic substitution should perhaps be viewed as more threatening. While a denial of Christianity is not necessarily a denial of humanity, pure nihilism is precisely this. The elimination of all religion is a much more serious transgression than the attempted replacement of one religious system with a reactionary substitute (*a la* Satanism). "Religion [in general] assures us of the elevation of the spirit over the flesh" and gives humanity some sort of dignity (Paul 292). Religion ensures that there is an ethical foundation for humanity: even in the midst of extreme subjectivism, there are some fundamental rights and wrongs.

Nihilism challenges human dignity, challenges the existence of right-and-wrong itself. This philosophy does not belong exclusively to Death Metal. In fact, even Death Metal lyrics that are strongly suggestive of nihilism do not overtly own the title. Instead, nihilism has subversively pervaded the Death Metal genre as it has many aspects of contemporary Western culture—from horror and science fiction films to scientific dissertations on Darwinian theory. Nihilism is a morbid shadow that hangs over contemporary philosophy and society. To present nihilistic imagery and suggest nihilistic themes in Death Metal music is not so much a departure from mainstream society as an exploration of an underlying part of it—a part that seems to grow as the years progress.

In light of this fact, one can see the appeal of nihilistic sacrilegious lyrics. They offer some semblance of identification for listeners, who feel the terror of nihilism on the heels of Western culture and are tempted to explore this forbidden yet inevitable philosophy. The world, for many Death Metal listeners, and many adolescents in general, seems wholly barren of spirituality. This is a devastatingly frightening fact, and is thus addressed in art and music. In Death Metal, the void of spirituality is sometimes mourned, but it is more often celebrated. If nihilism is an inescapable fact, then how should it be confronted? The answer, according to many Death Metal musicians, is that nihilism should be embraced, confronted, examined, and thus tamed. Sometimes, it is rationalized, welcomed, even worshipped—an ironic attempt to make sense out of an utter lack of sense, to build a system out of the void. The defensive nature of this reaction is evident.

More often, however, nihilism is made into a light and laughing matter. Nihilism is not so scary if it can be sung about in the context of zombies and demons, if fans can flock to it and laugh about it. Speaking of horror movies that adopt similar tactics in confronting nihilism, Freeland wrote: "Evil is taken seriously ... only in the sense that it is combined with powers that enable us to laugh at it and deny it" (271). In the following chapter's discussion of "self-defense" through horror, the idea of taming the terrifying by making a joke of it will be further explored.

Often, however, sacrilegious lyrics are not highly nihilistic. In their listeners, they spur neither Satanism nor nihilism as a substitute for ethical systems. On the contrary, for most Death Metal fans, attacking religion is simply another means of flouting a tradition, of embracing a taboo to the shock and horror of many conservative adults. Sometimes, taboos are violated simply because it is fun to shock one's parents and others. Other times, taboos are violated with more progressive intentions and results.

First, the glory of violating tradition for its own sake should be explored. It is a known yet perhaps inexplicable fact that "there is some sense in which we enjoy having our values attacked" (Paul 263). The violation is both thrilling and shocking for the gut-level reaction that it produces in the listener himself and in those who are horrified that he would choose such fare. Sometimes, it is simply entertaining to shock and annoy other people, particularly people with whom one does not identify (for instance, parents) and wishes to contend (such as authority figures). There is a thrill in watching their reaction that adds substantially to the personal thrill obtained from the mere observation of a taboo being shattered. Freeland has suggested that in horror, "we encounter a kind of amoral sublime, an enjoyment of cosmic combined forces of creation and destruction" and perhaps the same applies to the challenge of traditional religious values poised by many Death Metal musicians (271).

Of course, a challenge to values is not always poised merely to achieve a cheap thrill. On a deeper level, such challenges to tradition promote questioning and reassessment of personal and cultural values. At this time, the concept of ethical ground zero must be introduced. Ethical ground zero is both an end point and a starting point for ethics. A person is said to achieve ethical ground zero if he disowns all culturally-imposed values in favor of a purer ethical system discovered by himself. The idea of ethical ground zero implies that the individual should be the source of his own value system, that only he can discern true right from wrong, and cultural norms and values actually cloud the path to virtue. One must reject all that he was taught in his childhood before building his own ethical system, for simply following traditional ethical norms is not "true virtue." Although only a mythical concept popularized by Cartesian individualism, the allure of achieving ethical ground zero is strong in highly individualistic cultures such as that of the contemporary United States. Here, the endorsement of a return to ethical ground zero is extremely common in the population at large, certainly not just among Death Metal fans. American culture ironically teaches its children to reject cultural values in order to "find themselves" or discover truth on their own. Of course, the values that they ultimate do own are heavily influenced by culture (as are all values), but proponents of ethical ground zero retain the notion that they have discovered true objective right and wrong on their own by destroying all existing ethical foundations and subsequently rebuilding their own. Although no one actually achieves this impossible task, there is certainly some value in attempting to achieve it. It is only by challenging cultural norms that individuals and cultures continue the search for noble ethics and progress towards more just and good ethical norms.

It is in the devastating of traditional values preceding return to ethical ground zero that Death Metal lyrics enter the picture. Anti-religious lyrics, like gore lyrics and horror movies, can help to "reduce life and its values to a nearly absolute minimum" (Dillard 27). In the wake of this destruction, there is an implied need for reconstruction, an assessing and refiguring of ethics on hopefully more just and more noble terms. Challenging traditional ethical norms through sacrilegious lyrics and other taboo topics encourages the same exploration and redefinition. (This may be even more poignantly expressed in the taboos violated with gore and porn lyrics. Together with anti-religious lyrics, they do help man move toward ethical ground zero.)

Throughout this brief chapter, a number of possible values and attractions of sacrilegious Death Metal lyrics have been explored. There is little existing literature on the matter, and there are surely many additional possible values and attractions that have yet to be pondered. Even in light of the few theories explored here, it is evident that there are a wide array of potential motivations for listening to and composing anti-religious lyrics. These include but are not limited to: aesthetic appeal, fantastic allure, venting of anger, expression of personal philosophy, confrontation of nihilism, attempts to shock, and progressive challenges to imperfect ethical norms. The diversity of these theories should make it clear that any wide generalization about the meaning and effects of anti-religious Death Metal lyrics should be made only very cautiously, if at all. One should even hesitate before labeling such lyrics as either destructive or constructive. If, because of their essentially ambiguous nature, they cannot be understood, then they clearly should not be condemned.

18

Horror, Gore, Porn, and the American Mind

Themes of violence, horror, death, and destruction are not unique to Death Metal, but pervade many forms of entertainment. An obvious parallel can be drawn between Death Metal and video games or horror films. Widely popular video games contain at least as much graphic horror and violence as the standard Death Metal fare. Steven King constantly tops the best-seller list, and people who buy his books are not characterized as "violent." It is perfectly acceptable for anyone to see movies like *Scream*, *Hannibal*, *Seven*, *The Bone Collector*, and any number of other successful Hollywood blockbusters that deal with serial killers, violence, murder, and other horrific topics. Violence, gore, and horror have an appeal that extends beyond this particular style of music.

Although music is not the only source for this kind of entertainment, politicians and others tend to react more strongly against the violence expressed in music than in other media. Matthew Harvey has suggested that people perceive music as a more honest representation of the people creating and patronizing the art form. Lyrics are often assumed to be a literal relation of the artists' thoughts or feelings. Ironically, pop songs are often written by someone else, although the feelings expressed in such lyrics have been felt by most people. The same certainly cannot be said about many Death Metal lyrics, and thus censors may be more likely to target them. Moreover, music is one of the major factors around which young people base their identities, making Death Metal — with its images of murder and rape — particularly threatening. The failure of censors to distinguish between artistic expression and literal expression of a belief system is at the root of their fear of Death Metal.

The fact remains that Death Metal music is far from unique in its tendency to use horrific, gory, disturbing, and even pornographic images. Forms of entertainment that utilize these same sorts of images are often mainstream and acceptable. The closest parallel is that between Death Metal and horror movies. Rather than comparing Death Metal to pop, it would be far fairer to place it in the vein of the horror movie, which speaks to people in a figurative rather than a literal fashion, and which explores the repressed and the forbidden.

For this reason, it is useful to examine psychological and sociological theories on the allure of horror films in researching the appeal of Death Metal lyrics. Although there are no official sources on the topic of Death Metal lyrics, countless studies have been performed on horror movies and horror movie audiences. Thus, in this chapter, the relationship between horror movies and the gory/pornographic lyrics of Death Metal music will be explored. The parallels as well as the differences between the genres will be discussed. Are they truly related in terms of themes, styles, etc.? Why are horror movies considered more acceptable than Death Metal music? Most importantly, what makes horror attractive? What is the appeal and the function of gore and pornographic images?

Before this analysis is launched, a closer look at the similarities and differences between horror movies and Death Metal lyrics is necessary. Horror films and Death Metal share similar audiences, themes, images, and techniques. For both art forms, audiences are primarily young males (Clover 5–7). Both genres play on elemental fears, emphasize sex, and focus on misunderstood or alienated characters (Iaccino 22–23, 27; Dickstein 70). In the following lists of horror film prototypes by reputed critics of the genre, notice the common elements in theme between the most popular horror movies and Death Metal lyrics. Reputed feminist critic Robin Wood provides this list of prevalent themes: The Monster as human psychotic or schizophrenic; the revenge of nature; Satanism, diabolic possession, the Antichrist; The Terrible Child; and Cannibalism (Wood 1984, 181). James Iaccino notes three horror prototypes: Slasher, Zombie, Possessed Child (32–34). Finally, Morris Dickstein lists the following "elemental fears" addressed through horror films: "fear of the dark, fear of being alone, fear of enclosure, fear of the supernatural, fear of human blood, fear of corpses and cemeteries, the unquiet spirits of the dead, and so on" (70). Each of these lists could easily describe Death Metal lyrics as well.

In both Death Metal and modern horror movies, there is generally no closure (Paul 417). Horror expert William Paul has noted that horror actually resists closure in order to preserve a disquieting ambivalence (419). Similar techniques are used in Death Metal. In both genres, going over-the-top with disgusting images is considered positive or at least a way to attract fans; grossness of the human body is itself a strong selling point (Paul 382). Author R. H. W. Dillard has stated that it is the "unrestrained ... avalanche of atrocities" which makes a horror movie "good" (17). The same applies to lyrics in Death Metal.

In horror movies since the 1970s, as in Death Metal, the victims and perpetrators are regular human beings rather than fantasy monsters (Paul 262–263). Cynthia A. Freeland and Vera Dika have contended that horror movie audiences identify with the victim whereas Death Metal audiences are invited to identify with the perpetrator (Dika 88, Freeland 271). This, however, is not really the case. Horror movie analyst William Paul notes that, in the films, there is a "mobilization of conflicting antipathies set up in the audience, one that is conventionally felt against the monster, but also ... one that is unconventionally felt against a victim who has otherwise engaged sympathies" (265). It is as plausible to say that audiences identify with both the victim and the perpetrator as to say they identify with only one or neither.

Most horror films are as pornographic as most Death Metal lyrics. Explicitness belongs to all forms of media nowadays, and is only increasing (Kendrick 253). As early as the 1950s, horror was labeled the "new pornography" (Kendrick 241). Since then, it has grown increasingly "exploitative" and "sex-obsessed," and has recently been described as a "hardcore pornography of violence made possible by the virtual elimination of censorship" (Derry 165; Dickstein 66). The "continuously whirring phallic chainsaw" is a staple of both genres (Wood 1984, 189). There are vast parallels in the way that sex and sexuality are presented in horror films and Death Metal. Horror films like *Halloween* frequently feature the displacement of sexuality into aggression (Dickstein 66). As Robin Wood has noted, "The release of sexuality in the horror film is always presented as perverted, monstrous, and excessive. ... Sexuality is totally perverted from its functions, into sadism, violence, cannibalism" (Wood 1984, 189). Sexually disturbed characters are common, and victims are frequently killed immediately before or after engaging in illicit sexual behavior (Clover 28, 33).

In the wake of these many similarities between Death Metal and horror movies, there are also several differences. First, the images conjured up in Death Metal songs are sometimes more graphic. Is this a sign of greater extremity and sicker audiences? It is very doubtful. One must keep in mind that Death Metal relies on the ear, while horror movies have the privilege of appealing to both the eyes and the ears. The bi-sensual strategy clearly affords its exploiters the privilege of shocking and disturbing more easily than the uni-sensual approach. A case for the idea that Death Metal has to be particularly brutal due to its solely auditory nature could be made by looking at the extra grotesque imagery of silent films in the early twentieth century (Iaccino 19). The absence of either the visual or the aural element seems to entail that the other be much more abrasive to deliver the same effect. More importantly, one must remember that horror movies are limited in their degree of explicitness by what technology allows them to portray on film. Before special effects were well developed, films had to be significantly less explicit because it was simply not possible to make a realistic image of, for example, a person's head exploding. Death Metal, due to its exclusively auditory nature, is not limited by the same technical constraints. In Death Metal music, one can sing about disgusting scenes that cannot technically be portrayed on film. These factors account for the extra gruesome nature of Death Metal.

Although both genres rely upon "an attraction in revulsion," audiences of horror films are far less likely to acknowledge that it is the revolting which attracts them (Paul 312). It has been said that horror films and comedies (in which attraction is overt) both appeal to "poles of disgust," and "if disgust inevitably involves an ambivalence, a simultaneous attraction and repulsion, then the comedies play to the positive pole of disgust, the horror films to the negative" (Paul 292). But what happens when the positive and the negative poles are united, as they are in Death Metal? What happens when gore is overtly acknowledged as pleasant to look at and even *comedic*? This is totally unacceptable — the ultimate taboo — and Death Metal audiences openly ascribe to it. Death Metal fans admit to and celebrate the attraction in revulsion, while the typical fan of a mainstream horror movie does not. Even pleasure in the sado-masochistic elements of Death Metal is overt and celebrated. In the genre of the horror film, the response of the audience is ostensibly terror; in Death Metal, it is gratification. Do both audiences really feel pleasure in watching horror, yet only Death Metal fans admit to it? This is a huge value breech, a major anti-social act. Why do Death Metal fans take this stance?

To answer this question, it is important to refer back to the previous chapter's analysis of value of taboo-breaking. People, particularly youth, enjoy shattering taboos, and their efforts to do so can actually have progressive implications after old value systems are destroyed and new ones must be created. Also, it does seem that there is more outright honesty among audience members who openly admit to their gratification at seeing a limb chopped off. Gore itself must be appealing to the general audience. Why else would the most graphic films attain the largest audiences? Perhaps Death Metal fans' overt admission of pleasure in repulsion is simply an honest version of what the typical American covertly admits by paying to see the most explicit films.

Having reviewed the similarities and differences between horror films and Death Metal music, it is now possible to launch an analysis of what makes horror in either genre so appealing. Many horror film critics have noted that there is a purely aesthetic appeal to horror films, and the same can be said of Death Metal (Freeland 243). As Gregory A. Waller notes, in horror films (as well as Death Metal) explicit violence is "undertaken with an air of 'top that!' ingenuity and lovingly explicit detail" (5). Cynthia A. Freeland suggests that the aesthetic appeal of horror is twofold, and both of the elements she notes could also be applied to some Death Metal music: "First, despite what might seem a mere vulgar emotional kick, the graphic spectacles contribute to the plot and to the cognitive-emotional content of horror film. And second, for the real genre (or subgenre) fans, the pleasures of graphic visual [or auditory] spectacle are associated with delight in a certain sort of cinematic [or lyrical/musical] creativity" (256). Clearly, fans of Death Metal and horror films may have an aesthetic appreciation for the graphic horror depicted in either genre.

Aside from aesthetic appeal, there is another element to the allure of horror that is not nearly so respectable. Many theorists have mentioned the "scopophilic drive as a major source of cinema pleasure — the viewer [acts] as voyeur" (Giles 41). What is scopophilia? The horror film *Peeping Tom* defined it as the "morbid urge to gaze" upon the shocking and disgusting (Clover 169–172). In some ways, fear/shock/disgust is a pleasurable thrill. Several theories exist as to why this is so.

Some theorists have suggested that thrilling images of gore, sex, and terror produce some sort of sensory excitement. Their allure may even have its root in human biology and the production of adrenaline with the experience of a thrill. And what is the source of this thrill? "We remain effortlessly balanced between belief in fiction and detachment from it. When a head explodes, however, or an arm gets yanked off, our detachment shrinks to zero" (Kendrick 250). Therein lies the thrill. According to Morris Dickstein, "Fear and desire are our most primitive impulses, both ridiculously easy to arouse" (68). Dickstein speaks of "elemental fears" piqued by the films—feelings that subside quickly after the experience is over. This creates the drive to experience the thrill again; it becomes a "repetitive compulsion" (70–71).

Perhaps the most basic and insightful theory suggests that watching horrific scenes is a form of play, and that play is pleasurable in itself. William Paul has developed this theory extensively in his book *Laughing Screaming*. For Paul, experiencing "gross-out" is a form of indulgence, and indulgence is simply fun (421). Paul asks why we need to explain the pleasure of screaming any more than the pleasure of laughing. Both, in his opinion, are self-explanatory "ends in themselves" (270). Paul later notes that "intensity of, and absorption in, play finds no explanation in biological analysis. Yet in this intensity, this absorption, this power of maddening, lies the very essence, the primordial quality of play. ... This last-named element, the *fun* of playing, resists all analysis, all logical interpretation" (270). Maybe being shocked is just fun.

Exploring the nature of the horrific shock lends more insight into its potential allure. Horror entails the glorification of the physical in "brutal simplicity" (Clover 116). Like pornography, horror is centered on the body and flesh of man. Man is often shown, not as a dignified human being, but as a beast or a chunk of meat. His humanity is rejected; he is "without dignity; ugly; unworthy" (Paul 294). The return to man's bestial nature is enticing because it appeals to the repressed. In the previous chapter's discussion of Satanism, the enticing nature of the bestial was explored. Disgusting body-based horror—involving vomit, excrement, etc.—refers back to a more primitive time "when bodily wastes ... were not seen as objects of embarrassment and shame" (Clover 13). The rejection of reason in favor of grossness evokes a "repelled fascination" because it allows this forbidden journey into the repressed realms of the beast. According to Paul, "there is a kind of defiant pleasure in regression, in wallowing in dirt as a way of rejecting social constraints. We take fierce pride in our body's ability to produce disgusting emissions, finding pleasure in them precisely because they are disgusting" (314). Death Metal lyrics, like horror films, permit a vacation into man's repressed bestial nature.

There is also a sense in which the glorification of the physical, the presentation of man as flesh and bones, may promote greater vitality. In late medieval Europe, after the plague, images of death pervaded art in an effort to "remind [man] of life's brevity" (Kendrick 260). Exposure to death could translate into awareness of life. In horror, man is made to feel his physicality and mortality (Waller 6). Celebration of the physical—alive and dead—may produce greater vitality in its audience. Paul has stated that a "surge of vitality" can accompany "the sudden onset of any strong feeling" (422). When life is boring, vitality slips away; when boredom is ameliorated with thrills, man is reinvigorated (Dickstein 77–78). Thus, Death Metal lyrics may ironically produce greater vitality in listeners.

Many theorists have suggested that film audiences are attracted to movies because they feel a sense of identification with the characters and situations presented. In Death Metal and horror films, audiences may identify with characters' anger, aggression, evil, even nihilism and hopelessness. This is not necessarily negative, as long as fans recognize the figurative nature of the relationship between their sentiments and the characters' behavior. (Clearly, because horror films and Death Metal lyrics have prompted no surge of mass-murders, fans do understand this.) Paul has compared horror films to mirrors which reflect the fears, desires, and sentiments of audiences in exaggerated proportions, allowing audiences to feel understood, even normal, when compared to the over-the-top characters in movies or Death Metal songs (313). Horror film director John Carpenter admitted that horror films are popular because they "toy with the rage and anger we have within us" (Dillard 67). Horror films and Death Metal songs evoke disgust but also often give their audiences the twisted psychological perspective of the perpetrator, making them feel some sort of sympathy for or identification with him (Iaccino 20).

Most often, the identification between the audience and the film or Death Metal song is an identification with underlying sentiments rather than specific characters. Nihilism and hopelessness pervade horror films and Death Metal lyrics. According to Dillard, life is shown as "ugly and cheap ... when someone dies, his value dies with him" (26–27). The bad is presented "with great force, but what good we reach in the end is small and frail indeed" (Dillard 28). Many modern horror films share a common and disturbing conclusion that emphasizes the futility of man's attempts to escape annihilation (Wood 1984, 187). Robin Wood recognizes the nihilism in horror that contemporary audiences identify with:

> As a "collective nightmare" [horror] brings to focus a spirit of negativity, an undifferentiated lust for destruction, that seems to lie not far below the surface of the modern collective consciousness. ... What the horror film has come to signify [is] the sense of a civilization condemning itself, through its popular culture, to ultimate disintegration, and ambivalently (with the simultaneous horror/wish fulfillment of nightmare) celebrating the fact [Wood 1984, 191].

Although Wood's comments undoubtedly place horror in a negative light, there is a sense in which they also reveal a redeeming quality within the genre. If nihilism does indeed pervade the "collective consciousness" as Wood has suggested, then it is probably not a negative thing to explore it, or even to be comforted by the fact that others feel the same sense of fear and hopelessness that each of us feels at times. Identification with the nihilistic metaphysics of horror, or even the anger and aggression of characters in horror films and Death Metal songs, can be comforting and cathartic rather than incendiary.

How does this catharsis work? The audience experiences the pain and terror of evil and chaos along with the characters in the play/film/song/etc., and as the horror unfolds and reaches its resolution, the original feelings of fear/evil/chaos/etc. are released; the audience is psychologically purged and freed from the terror. Classical tragedies employed this Aristotelian notion of catharsis. Friedrich Nietzsche offers a spin on it. Nietzsche "considered the plots of tragedies 'optimistic' because they testified to the basic human resilience even in the face of an acknowledgement of evil and destruction. ... The Dionysian art shows a primal unity of good with evil, of pain and contradiction" (Freeland 269). This formula of catharsis can certainly be applied to horror movies. According to Barbara Creed, "purification of the abject through a 'descent into the foundations of the symbolic construct'" is the "central project of horror" (14). This theory might be applied to some Death Metal songs as well. Both genres certainly hold the potential for cathartic effects. As Charles Derry has stated, "Horror can be revealed not as reactionary, but as a release of social tensions, perhaps even a necessary first step toward a more liberated society with more responsive social and familial structures" (165).

Many analysts have argued that horror is simply a framing and examination of the nature of evil in all its forms. This examination may be launched because of curiosity and scopophilia, or it may be a somewhat progressive or intellectual exploration. Defending the idea that we examine evil to sate our scopophilic drives, Freeland believes that horror is appealing because villains and monsters provide the audience with various manifestation of evil that confuse and entertain (276). She also points out, however, that horror movies "stimulate more complex emotional and intellectual responses. They provide visions of a world where action may or may not have meaning, where a monster may or may not be sympathetic, where evil people may or may not win out in the end" (273–4). Other theorists also find something rather intellectual in the drive to examine evil. According to Waller, "Taken as a whole, the entire [horror] genre is an unsystematic, unresolved exploration of violence in virtually all its forms and guises" (7).

In the previous chapter, the taboo-breaking tendency of anti-religious lyrics was explored. In this chapter, the same taboo-breaking tendency of horror movies and Death Metal lyrics will be addressed. Horror movies represent an attack on cultural norms and values as do lyrics featuring porn and gore. In horror, "we encounter a kind of amoral sublime, an enjoyment of cosmic combined forces of creation and destruction" (Freeland 271). Religion, sex, and violence are combined simply because it is thrilling to witness the destruction of all the taboos (Derry 168, Paul 305). In addition to witnessing vile and forbidden acts, audiences are invited to identify with both the killer and the killed, the villain and the victim (Creed 12). The violence in horror transcends the physical to attack the psychological; "the grossness, then, explicitly relates to some taboo, and the pleasure in horror that these events occasion derives from a desire to see the taboo broken at the same time that we feel the horror of that violation" (Paul 262). Therein lies the thrill of seeing reason ditched in favor of bodily wastes (Creed 13).

Because the modern horror film or Death Metal song "reduces life and its values to a nearly absolute minimum," it is particularly effective in helping man move toward ethical ground zero (Dillard 27). Horror in all its forms may also help people to explore confused or broken value systems. It challenges dominant ideologies, undermines traditional values, and makes a mockery of law and government (Polan 210; Dillard 28). Gregory A. Waller has found in post-1970 horror a "thoroughgoing critique of American institutions and values" including families, couples, individual heroes, government bodies, etc. (4). According to Waller, horror movies have provided a stage for the American "debate over the status of the independent woman in a society dominated by men" (5). In fact, they force their audiences to question the very nature of good and evil, positive and negative, monstrous and human (Paul 375).

This may be valuable in the assimilation of old and new values and the progression of ethics (Dika 98–99). Values must be knocked down or at least challenged before new and better systems can be developed. In this sense, horror—whether it takes the form of films or lyrics—plays an important role in society. Waller succinctly explains this view:

> Horror defines and redefines, clarifies and obscures the relationship between the human and the monstrous, the normal and the aberrant, the sane and the mad, the natural and the supernatural, the conscious and the unconscious, the daydream and the nightmare, the civilized and the primitive—slippery categories and tenuous oppositions indeed, but the very oppositions and categories that are so essential to our sense of life [12].

Feminist critics such as Robin Wood and Vivian Sobchack have suggested that occasionally horror poses an attack on patriarchal bourgeois capitalism because it endorses such a disruption of the system (Wood 1984, 192; Sobchack 178–179).

In general, feminist critics have a lot to say about horror movies, and most of it is very negative. It is not a stretch to assume they would react similarly to Death Metal lyrics. Robin Wood and Carol J. Clover see horror films as ideologically representative portraits of collective dreams or nightmares that make manifest the repressed (Clover 11, 20; Wood 174; Derry 163). Often, feminists find in horror movies a reaffirmation of patriarchal values (Fischer 66). Slasher films and many Death Metal songs feature relentless exploitation of females. Clover equates them with pornography and suggests that they are a direct, brutal representation of cultural attitudes about sex (22). Wood finds horror themes "depressingly reactionary," and Clover notes that victims (even when male) are always feminized, and villains (even when female) are always made masculine (Wood 1987, 82; Clover 12–13). Indeed, many horror films and Death Metal lyrics actually reinforce traditional sexual mores and values (Fischer 77). Patriarchal ideals are reasserted when, for instance, a woman is viciously raped and murdered because she is perceived as a "whore" or an unfaithful "slut." Such images are not uncommon in either horror movies or Death Metal lyrics.

Many critics have found in horror movies the expression of repressed desires for sex and violence: "These films represent not only a rebellious rejection of adult values, but also a titillating glimpse into the forbidden contents of the id, especially the sexual and violent impulses that so dominate the contemporary genre" (Derry 163). Horror movies and Death Metal lyrics readily provide the means to live vicariously through violent and sexually brutal characters. Horror is mixed with porn to make women absolute victims as well as mere objects of men's sexual fantasies (Fischer 64–65). Some have argued that this is dangerous, but it seems wiser to argue that experiencing such things vicariously is far preferable to experiencing them actually. If innate desires for violence and sex must be expressed, it is far better for society that they be expressed only in art such as songs and movies (Wood 1984, 177).

Many critics have suggested that horror helps audiences to process repressed fears. Among these are deep-rooted, subconscious fears of sex and women. Horror in general tends to display a general fear of or disgust with sex and sexuality. As previously mentioned, victims are often killed before or after sex; they are punished for their sexuality (Paul 324). "Sexual arousal is in itself never seen as something positive. It only has the power to punish" (Paul 306). In many films and songs, sexuality is perverted and gender identity is in question (309). The characters in horror films are unable to process their sexual desires properly; the chainsaw is their phallus and the victim is their partner (Freeland 251). According to Clover, "the reason she must be killed, rather than fucked, is that slasher killers are by generic definition sexually inadequate — men who kill precisely because they *cannot* fuck" (Clover 186).

This brings us to a central theory of many horror analysts: gory pornographic material that is highly exploitative of women is a reaction to extremely strong fears of the female. In horror, "women are punished for being women" (Wood 1987, 80). Female sexuality is portrayed as the paramount source of filth and evil; her sexual drives and desires are literally monstrous (Clover 47). As Paul has stated, "The girl's sexual organs are themselves an object of terror because they explicitly suggest a wound. Sexuality is it itself a kind of punishment" (306). Male fears of castration create a loathing of the "castrated" female. Even babies and small children are frightening because they come from the female body (Paul 281). (Note Polanski's *Rosemary's Baby* or Cannibal Corpse's "Butchered at Birth.")

This terrible fear of castration and of women is thought to entice men into objectifying women as an attempt to bring the fear under control. In porn and in horror, the presence of the penis and the void of vagina are exploited and celebrated because the female's "lack affirms the male's potency" (Giles 47). Once objectified — a mere image suited to his fancy — the woman is not so threatening to the man (Giles 46). Castration fears are only stamped out with a reassertion of male dominance through the slaughter of the woman. Male fears and inadequacy are thus at the root of the drive to kill women (Fischer 70; Dika 97).

Some critics have developed these ideas into a complex theory of male sado-masochism. This theory, presented by Clover in her book *Men, Women, and Chainsaws*, suggests that horror films allow young males to work out their fears as well as their heterosexual and homosexual desires. Young males enjoy the perspective of both male and female, perpetrator and victim, rapist and raped (Clover 48–49). For instance, when a woman is raped by a man in a movie that builds the male audience's sympathy for and identification with the female character, the act is really one of homosexual sex. In slasher movies, which commonly feature the survival of only one emasculated female protagonist, the "Final Girl" is a "homoerotic stand-in" (Clover 52). Despite their sado-masochism instead of mere sadism, such films are ultimately anti-feminist. All of the feminine girls are killed off, and the girl who survives does so because she is masculine (think *Halloween*). The killer is ultimately victimized because of what is feminine in him. The message remains that the female should be destroyed and the male should be the powerful destroyer (Clover 50).

This look at slasher films is especially pertinent because of the close parallels in theme and images between slasher films and Death Metal lyrics. If Clover's theory is accurate, it suggests that such forms of entertainment are alluring because they provide a safe, vicarious release for repressed sexual desires (which is probably not something negative, as mentioned earlier). Of course, Clover herself recognizes that several questions are unanswered by her theory. For instance, males are not the only ones present at horror movies, nor are they the only consumers of Death Metal. What about female fans? Dennis Giles has suggested that maybe both males and female viewers are bisexual when watching fetishistic horror (46). Another question that one is tempted to poise is why must audiences identify with *any* character? Does it not seem more likely that the gore and the violated taboos are themselves a sufficient thrill and release? These questions remained unanswered. Nonetheless, Clover's theory is a fascinating look at one potential allure of horror.

Perhaps theories rooted more in the tangible than the repressed possess greater power to explain the appeal of horror and gore. Horror movies and Death Metal lyrics may be reactions to more conscious fears, to social phenomena, and to the socio-political atmosphere. There are various physical and metaphysical threats which confront human beings on a daily basis or which linger in the atmosphere of everyday life. William Paul wonders whether increasing medical technologies and new concepts of the human body have evoked fears and questions that are addressed through horror. In modern horror, the body itself became much more gross after medical technology allowed for increasingly evasive procedures, blurring the boundaries between inside and outside, self and other (Paul 381, 385–387). Horror certainly reacts to new and disturbing realities: "New perceptions of ourselves gained from interfering with reproductive anatomy, invasive medical procedures, and the drug culture overdetermine an annihilation of boundaries, erasing distinctions by which we have defined our individual bodies in the past" (Paul 387). Such threats require a response and an examination; horror provides this in the form of torn-open bodies. According to Freeland, "Horror films have appeal because they continue a lengthy tradition of making art, addressing human fears and limitations, forcing confrontations with monsters who overturn the natural order — of life and death, natural/supernatural, or human/non-human. They depict vivid threats to our values and concepts, our very bodily and mental integrity" (273). Apparently, they also help man to understand and cope with those threats.

Threats to humanity abound in the field of epistemology as well. Paul believes that horror responds to scientific challenges to dualism, resulting in a psychosomatic fascination within the horror genre. This seems very plausible. Recent theories in philosophy of mind have grown increasingly materialistic: the mind is just an extension of the body; man is but a physical entity, and a very fragile and destructible one at that. Gore is a clear reaction to this presumed and threatening reality. Paul believes that grossness in horror comes as a result of the blurred boundaries between the psyche (mind) and the soma (body). This also translates into confusion between the subjective and the objective (Paul 400). Such modern ideas poise tremendous threats to the very notion of human dignity, never mind human ethics and values. Perhaps Paul expressed the threat best in *Laughing Screaming*: "If an organ that defines an aspect of our individuality could be transplanted, it became inescapable that we must be made up of interchangeable parts. ...Cut us open and we all look like the meat counter in a supermarket. ...We are all just slabs of meat" (386). This terror is confronted full-force by gore bands and their disgusting Death Metal lyrics.

Many horror film analysts believe that entertainment forms like horror movies and Death Metal lyrics display the tensions and dysfunctions just beneath the surface in American families (Derry 168). Robin Wood thinks that violent entertainment might be "a reflection of America's increased dissatisfaction with its traditional sexual roles and the nuclear family" (Derry 165). Vivian Sobchack has found in horror interesting themes of patriarchal failure, self-hatred, and rage: "Apocalyptic destruction and villains themselves seem generated by familial incoherence and paternal weakness" (Sobchack 183). The family structure is no longer there to serve as protector, and even the villains seem "oppressed and vulnerable" (Sobchack 183). This is often true of the "villains" in Death Metal lyrics as well. Horror provides one means to deal with the "literal sickness at the core of both the family and society" (Paul 260–1).

Beyond the basic family structure, modern life provides many greater socio-political threats that are addressed through horror. According to Derry, "The hallmark of the contemporary horror film" is the "exploitation of everyday anxiety, in all its guises" (172). Often in horror, it is not only the individual body that is out of control, but also the body-politic or society at large. Vigilante justice, for instance, is common in Death Metal songs, and murder is met with no judicial consequence. A zombie movie like *Dawn of the Dead*, for example, "aims to induce a feeling of hysteria in the viewer, to create the sensation that we, effectively deprived of our ability to understand exactly what is taking place in all this chaos, are also without governance" (Paul 395). Paul explains that gross-out horror was most popular during periods of radical change or inversion in American society. For instance, gore became huge after the Watergate affair because the President's crime signified a defilement of something respected: "high became low" (Paul 420). Paul goes on to theorize that gore thrived in the 1980s because there was a significant backlash against the liberalism of the 1960s (420). There are different types of horror to respond to nearly all social shocks, including economic difficulties. Horror always responds to the major issues of its time. Modern horror, for example, has come to emphasize the terror of real life over the fear of death, especially in times of race riots, assassinations, and other major social turmoil (Derry 164). Many analysts have even theorized that the rampant exploitation of women in horror since the 1970s is a reaction to the feminist movement (Wood 1987, 81; Derry 165). Derry has suggested that perhaps horror that shows sexuality as something terrifying and deserving of punishment is a reflection of the liberal sexual revolution and its aftermath of widespread venereal disease (Derry 165). Apocalyptic stories and images — extremely common in Death Metal — are said to be "inspired by atomic bomb anxieties. ... The world is destroyed by proliferating, nonindividualized, nonhuman creatures" in many films and lyrics (Derry 171). Gregory A. Waller believes that horror confronts all of the major cultural fears and issues of its time on the moral, social, and political level (12). Waller writes:

> The horror film has engaged in a sort of extended dramatization of and response to the major public events and newsworthy topics in American history since 1968: fluctuations in "key economic indicators" and attempts to redirect domestic and foreign policy; Watergate and the slow withdrawal from Vietnam; oil shortages and the Iranian hostage crisis; the rise of the New Right and the Moral Majority; and the continuing debate over abortion, military spending, and women's rights. Further, contemporary horror can and has been interpreted as an index to and commentary on what have often been identified as the more general cultural conditions of our age: its "crisis of bourgeois patriarchy," to borrow Sobchack's phrase; its narcissism, postmodernism, and sense of the apocalyptic; and its attitude toward technology, death, and childhood.

Clearly, horror throughout the ages has responded to socio-political conditions and temporal concerns. However, the greatest concern tackled by horror, and most specifically by Death Metal lyrics, is a universal concern that knows neither temporal nor spatial boundaries: the fear of death. The notion that death is the end is a legacy of contemporary science and philosophy. Death is biologized or factualized and simultaneously ignored by modern American culture. As Walter Kendrick has pointed out,

Western culture began a slow turn away from the fact of being dead that has continued for three hundred years. The reality of corpses, their sight and especially their smell, came to seem disgusting, obscene, dangerous to health. The spectacle of rot—for centuries a familiar spectacle—was moved from the centers of cities to their peripheries. ...Today, at least in Europe and North America, no one ever sees or smells a rotted corpse except by lamentable accident; even morticians and gravediggers evade the experience, thanks to the chemicals that are routinely pumped into the dead [260–1].

The most elemental fear of man, the deepest universal concern, lies almost entirely unaddressed in contemporary reality, leaving art to take up the burden as it has so many times in the past. (In Europe, for instance, after a "long recoil from deadness, images of rot rose up in art" and became quite popular [261].) Kendrick has recognized that horror, more than anything else, has helped man in his Heideggerian endeavor to confront his own being as being-towards-death.

Whether this is always a genuine confrontation is questionable. Could it be that horror movies and gore lyrics present death as ridiculous and even funny so that man can "face it" and simultaneously run from its reality? In fact, horror films and Death Metal lyrics are often quite comedic. The more extreme and far-fetched the gore, the faker and funnier it is. Ironically, the more perverse, excessive, and bizarre the graphic presentation, the more "cartoon-like" and evidently fictitious it becomes (Freeland 269–271). Many Death Metal artists openly admit to the outlandishness and humor in their most disgusting lyrics. Comedy is also deliberately worked into horror films by many directors (Paul 312). The most serious topics that horror addresses may indeed be presented as jokes. According to Freeland, graphic horror is less skilled at truly confronting fears and evil than at "poking fun at it, denying its power and permanence" (271).

Perhaps horror does help man to face his fears but simultaneously makes them digestible. Horror films confront terrifying real issues in a fantastic realm because these issues are too difficult to confront on a conscious level (Derry 162). Horror could be a form of self-defense which enables man to attack real, justified fears in a safe and even light environment. According to Giles, "At the same time that it threatens to transgress prohibitions, the industry promises a vision which the viewer knows will be psychologically and ideologically *safe*. By the terms of the viewing contract, desire will be engaged then domesticated by the textual strategies; fear will be aroused, then controlled" (39). Perhaps images of death provide a defense against real-life violence. Dickstein has likened watching horror movies to placing an "aesthetic bracket" around the things that most terrify man (69). Other critics suggest that horror could teach lessons about difficult situations that men fear in everyday life: "The horror film functions in a decidedly instructive fashion, much like a morality play, teaching us to accept 'the natural order of things ... and to cope with and even prevail over the evil in life" (Telotte 115). Sometimes, all horror teaches is that it is possible to live and laugh even in a world where chaos seems to reign and violence is a threatening reality. Horror might "desensitize" its audience to some of the terrors of life, but this could actually be a self-defensive, beneficial desensitization. According to J. P. Telotte, "The terrors confronting us in these films are neither gratuitous nor designed merely to effect a catharsis; they also drive home lessons regarding our resolution of those personal and cultural problems that we are often reluctant to face outside the theater" (115).

To understand the multi-leveled self-defensive value of horror, perhaps one should assume the proverbial shoes of the typical Death Metal fan. A high-school boy, not very popular, probably suffering from acne, is likely to feel that his life is quite out of his control. He may have difficultly handling his relationship with his parents, and his social life is yet another battlefront. He may feel devastated when he cannot get a date to the prom, when he is rejected from the basketball team, or when he seems to be good at nothing in school. Compared to the prom king, the football hero, the pre-med student, he looks and feels weak. Death Metal music contains images of chaos and destruction that are far more terrible than anything he or any of his peers must face. Anyone who can watch a vicious murder and still maintain a straight face — or better yet, a smile — is tough. Anyone who wears black T-shirts featuring splattered guts is not to be messed with or laughed at. The attire, the music, the gore itself provide a protective barrier, while at the same time allowing their host to laugh in the face of his own greatest fears.

Ask any young Death Metal fan what the ultimate compliment is, and the response will probably be "brutal." The more insecure the boy, the more he wants to be brutal ... and *nothing* is more brutal than Death Metal. Horror provides the perfect vehicle for the young angry teen to work out his fears and still uphold his image of toughness, masculinity, invincibility. Dickstein has mentioned that it is common for children to make games centered around the very things that terrify them, and horror entertainment is a "safe, routinized way of playing with death, like going on the roller coaster or parachute jump at an amusement park ... but this death trip is essentially vicarious" (69). For Tellote, horror entertainment is a reaffirmation for its fans that they can deal with life's "traumatic encounters," that they are indeed brutal. Cynthia Freeland recognized that in most horror, "evil is taken seriously ... only in the sense that it is combined with powers that enable us to laugh at it and deny it" (271). For many Death Metal fans, the horror lifestyle is, above all, about reaffirming one's brutality, one's capacity to face and even mock terrors that others shrink from.

Although it is impossible to draw any bold generalizations about all horror fans, it is evident that they need not be perverse or disturbed to enjoy a good dose of porn-gore. The potential functions and allures of horror are countless and varied. Nearly any human can find in the genre some element that appeals to his desires, his curiosity, his intellect, and — above all — his fears. Perhaps it is senseless to label Death Metal lyrics (and horror in general) either reactionary or progressive, gratuitous or intelligent, desensitizing or cathartic. Horror's potential effects are as numerous and diverse as its fans. For every negative criticism brought against horror, for every denial of its value, one can argue that it is most obviously a key element in American culture. Horror cannot be stifled because it will rise again. Whether its themes are glorified or condemned, it undeniably lies very close to the surface of what Wood called the "collective consciousness" in contemporary America. Horror, disgusting and terrifying as it may be, is an unassailable part of the American mind.

Epilogue: Personal Reflections on Death Metal

One of the standards of social science research states that researchers ought not become emotionally involved in the topic of their studies. I can emphatically state that I failed miserably in adhering to this simple rule. In fact, it is only fair to divulge that I was personally interested in the Death Metal scene long before this study was launched. It was through this project, however, that I truly delved into the underground and explored the culture that had intrigued me as an outsider. In my explorations, I soon found myself enveloped by the atmosphere, by the camaraderie, by the sheer exhilaration of a true underground movement. Following bands on tour, listening to the breathtakingly powerful music in crowed halls night after night, wearing skimpy clothes to get backstage and on tour buses, and even occasionally growing enamored of dashing musicians, I lived the Death Metal life as deeply as any fan. As the months progressed, I had made significant emotional investments, found friendships and conflicts, allies and enemies, cooperation and antagonism, nobility and sexism, joy and pain in the Death Metal community. At the launch of the project, I had no idea what I was in for.

The thing that first drew me to "metal heads" was their complete lack of concern for what anyone thought of them — an escape from the teenage world of appearance emphasis and social hierarchy. Most people see this as a defiance of authority, but I tend to believe that the primary authority combated by the metal scene is that of the homecoming kings and queens, the cliques, and the rules of behavior that emphasize appearance over action. In the words of King Fowley of the band Deceased, "Metal ain't meant to be pretty." Metal is real.

And yet at the same time, through its lyrical content, Death Metal is inextricably tied to illusion. There is a surreal emphasis on rape, on murder, on war, on destruction. Cannibal Corpse and Macabre do not sing about the deaths that occur everyday on street corners. Instead, they choose the most horrific subject matter, emphasizing serial killers, pedophiles, necrophiliacs—in general the most demented persons and actions of all. How can this be the emphasis of a scene that supposedly combats the falsity and phoniness of society? Is it not even more misrepresentative of the world than Britney Spears' sugar-coated pop? If taken literally, yes. However, a slightly deeper analysis may hint at something very truly human in these twisted words, sounds, and images—a search for answers.

Serial killers may not be an integral part of the social order, but they are an integral part of reality. They evoke morbid curiosity and force the world to wonder *why*. What in the human soul could provoke such sickness? If one listens to the lyrics of a Death Metal band, he or she will find a description of the acts of these people, but this is seldom unaccompanied by some psychological analysis, some attempt at comprehending the incomprehensible. Metal heads are not just gore fiends, although they do want to face the gore *and* to understand it. Often, this means making a joke out of it. However, most of the time, horror is graphically presented and analyzed. Cannibal Corpse—perhaps the only thing Congress' Democrats and Republicans unite in despising—provokes questions with perverse lyrics and provides some hypothetical answers. Death Metal lyrics rarely display any literary value or showcase poetic talent, but they very vividly present a portrait of something most people would rather not think about, yet cannot help but ponder if seriously seeking answers about humanity. Who and what is a serial killer? However one chooses to respond to the question, it undoubtedly exists. Most people run from it. Metal heads seem to obsess over it. Where the more healthy response lies is anyone's guess.

Metal is a philosophical response, whether conscious or subconscious, to terrifying questions about nebulous human nature. In this way, the fantasy of the metal realm is a response to reality. However, there are more concrete ways in which the most fantastic lyrics can be explained in terms of the psychological reality of listeners. Those bands that do not sing about murders and perverse human beings usually sing about a hostile and evil world. Bands like Deicide, Morbid Angel, and Mortician present a sort of dark metaphysics. Sometimes shadowy scenes of horror and destruction are attributed to real-life events like war and pollution. Other lyrics seem to discard reality entirely ... but do they? When listening to Deicide's surreal album "Legion," one is transported to some dark and frightening realm of "caco-demons" and Satanists. It is a lonely, hostile, and terrifying world. In fact, it might be even worse than the hallways of Anytown High, but the metal head, who feels lost and frightened while sitting alone in the cafeteria, can face the world of Deicide without flinching an eye. In this sense, the words are never without some true-life basis. Even the most far-fetched and fantastic content of a Death Metal album has some foundation in reality, be it physical or psychological. Metal heads can sing about the bizarre and the otherworldly while very firmly embracing, expressing, and examining their own reality.

I would not claim that most metal heads are consciously seeking to come to grips with reality by listening to these lyrics. In fact, more often than not, lyrical content is not at all important to listeners. In light of this, however, two points must be made. Firstly, the music itself is meant to be expressive of the same dark metaphysics and longing epistemology that is expressed in the lyrics. Secondly, the authors and composers of this music are undoubtedly conscious of their own creations, and they are likely drawing their inspiration from experience and reality. It is difficult to deny that metal is the product of inspiration and is the true expression of the artist. This can be affirmed with more certainty when speaking of metal than when speaking of any popular music. Metal is not highly marketable. It is not made merely to lure an audience. The lyrics are thus derived from something more pure than marketability. It is my belief that they are drawn from real questions, real experiences. One does not sing about serial killers and demons to reel in a large fan following. One sings about serial killers because serial killers are on the mind. One sings about demons because they somehow reflect his life experiences. Thus, despite the seemingly escapist and fantastic nature of metal music, its source is perhaps grounded in actual reality. It is certainly more real than the proms and pageants of high school. Even Death Metal with its bizarre and surreal images is a means to stay true.

In a final word on the terrifying lyrics of Death Metal, I would like to challenge the assertions of Tipper Gore, Orrin Hatch, Joseph Lieberman, and probably a hundred other authorities who have declared emphatically that Death Metal lyrics glorify violence. They undoubtedly present it and they sometimes tell the stories from the point of view of individuals who derive pleasure from the pain that they inflict. However, these individuals are not glorified at all. They are not presented as heroes, but as demented freaks of human nature, to be pondered and examined. There exists in metal lyrics a preoccupation with violence, but not a glorification of it. These horrors are presented as horrors.

I remember that when I first became interested in Death Metal music, I was quite disturbed by the lyrics. Other than the few metal friends I had at the time, I wondered what sorts of people were attracted to this music. I thought perhaps the ethically upright and relatively well-adjusted Death Metal fans with whom I was associated were the exception rather than the rule in the scene. I was very apprehensive when, as a young teenager, I decided to attend my first metal show. I will never forget that night although I never actually got into the 18+ show. I learned a great deal about the metal scene in those few hours of waiting outside with other disappointed teens too young to enter the building. I had traveled two hours to get to a hole-in-the-wall club, The Saint, in the rundown ghetto of Asbury Park, only to find out that minors were not allowed to see Cannibal Corpse that night. My older friend got into the club, but I sat down on the filthy sidewalk, prepared to wait outside for the next few hours. It was not long before I began conversing with the other kids outside. I found them very friendly and nice people, even in the midst of their great disappointment. (After all, some had traveled over three hours just to see this band and had already purchased tickets to the show.) Like me, they were probably stuck waiting for others who had managed to get in. They were relatively optimistic despite the night's letdown, and were ready to strike up friendships with one another. We chatted about music and a few other things. It was a genuinely pleasant experience. When the first band came on, we tried to peer through the tiny windows high on the wall, and boosted one another up to catch a glance at the show inside. We finally gave up in that endeavor and simply sat, backs against the outside wall of the club, listening to the muffled sounds that reached our ears.

That was when a well-known figure emerged from the bus parked near the sidewalk. It was a member of Cannibal Corpse! Starstruck, none of us approached him. But we did not need to — tall, lean guitarist Pat O'Brian caught sight of us and walked over to greet us! "Why are you guys out here?" he asked, brushing his long black hair out of his eyes. We explained that they would not let us in. He told us he would see what he could do. The impressive figure dressed in black from head to toe went into the club and came back out a few minutes later saying that there was no way that the club owners would let us in. Pat apologized and expressed his sympathies before returning to the bus. A few minutes later, a diminutive man with long, blonde hair wearing ripped jeans emerged from the bus. It was Alex Webster, the bassist and the author of most of the band's lyrics. One boy approached him, telling him how much Cannibal Corpse's music meant him. Alex Webster smiled a boyish grin and reached out to shake his hand saying, "*That* really means a lot to me." His blue eyes shone with gentle sincerity as he thanked us for coming and said he was very sorry that we could not enter the club to see them play. Yet somehow I think most of us were plenty satisfied with the experience we had out on the sidewalk.

"Wow!" exclaimed one fan, "He's exactly the kind of guy you want to bring home to your family for Thanksgiving dinner!" Everyone was reveling in the kindness and humility of these band members, who have repeatedly invoked the wrath of politicians and other social leaders by simply producing their music. I could not help but remember a study I had read, where psychologists lamented that most metal heads were so enthralled with their favorite music that they named metal musicians as their role models. Is that really so terrible?

Remember that most youth do not have role models. In fact, I recall searching for one as a kid and feeling very let down. In an age of divorce, broken families, and day-care, most children are not presented with heroes in the family. As a generation left home alone and raised by the TV, many are incapable of seeing the economically successful as their heroes because they witness the vacuous and alienating consequences of that economic success. If they look outside the home and family, who are they to admire? George W. Bush? Bill Gates? My point is made. Yet kids need role models, and they *will* find them. Where do most kids find heroes to worship? Television. The child who grows up with Britney Spears or Justin Timberlake as his or her hero will inevitably be disappointed. Statistically speaking, it is nearly impossible to emulate the success of these stars, and it is often unhealthy to try. Britney and Justin are on MTV because they are very attractive and, in the opinion of some, their voices are pleasant to listen to. The average kid cannot, no matter how hard he or she tries, ever become a Britney Spears or a Justin Timberlake. Secondly, Britney and Justin are not going to return the gratitude and love with which their fans deluge them. These stars will not step off stage and have a conversation with a fan. They will not establish communication or join the unit that they have created. Their fans are essentially leaderless.

These are typical role models, and yet psychologists and politicians are concerned that metal heads look to metal musicians as role models? Contrast a musician like Alex Webster with a typical pop star. First of all, a fan can attempt to follow in the footsteps of Alex Webster, hoping to attain moderate success through personally fulfilling work. Alex Webster is not on stage because he is extraordinarily good-looking or because he was born with an incredible talent. He is on stage because he worked very hard to become the accomplished musician that he is. His success is a measure of how much time he put into his work and how much devotion he has to the music. Alex Webster and other metal musicians present realistic models for fans to aspire to. Just about anyone who works hard enough in the metal scene could find himself or herself on stage. In metal, success is a function of effort, not beauty or luck. More importantly, heroes like Alex Webster are real. They are not unattainable, media-produced images of perfection. They are a part of the scene that they have created. They actually care about their fans. They want to converse with them, to learn from them, to be among them. The appreciation and the adoration are reciprocal. This seems a much healthier sort of hero.

In my experience, the members of Cannibal Corpse are not atypical. In fact, I have met a friendly "star" at almost every show I have attended since that first one years ago. The producers of this "filth," as Senator Hatch likes to call it, are generally really nice guys. I saw Origin three times one summer, and at the last show, one of the band members went of his way to thank me for coming to support them so many times. I have had similar experiences with all the musicians I interviewed and with Sean from Impaled, George from Skinless, Karen from Crisis, Ross from Immolation, Chris from Internal Bleeding, April from Dark Supremacy, Josh from Cephalic Carnage, and many, many others. The American Death Metal scene is not a place of vicious hostility; it is a place of brotherhood, camaraderie, and fun, tempered by the darkness that forms the backdrop of the metal reality.

The shows themselves are ground-zero of the metal scene. You could own every metal album on the planet, and still not be truly metal if you have not attended a show. Metal shows are a place to lose yourself in the crowd and in the darkness, to become a part of something exhilarating and communal. No one cares what you look like, because it is probably too dark to tell anyway. There is no pressure to come up with the right words during an awkward conversation, because the boisterous music itself provides the conversation. There is complete freedom to *be* yourself and to *lose* yourself at the same time. Dress, dance, and sing as you wish. No one will judge you the way you are constantly judged in outside world.

Are metal shows violent? Usually. Of course, that depends on your definition of violence. Metal shows are very physical, and the dancing looks like fighting. However, there is no hostility involved. If someone falls to the ground, anyone standing nearby immediately helps to lift him or her back up. Does anyone hurt another person intentionally? With very few exceptions, absolutely not. Even in the course of the rough-housing, people are only very rarely injured, and I have never witnessed a severe injury at a Death Metal show (one that would cause someone to get out of the pit). At a metal show, no one enters the infamous mosh pit unless he or she chooses to. Bystanders are not drawn in unwillingly. As previously mentioned, if violence is defined as physicality, then shows are violent. However, if violence is defined as the hostile attempt to injure another person, then Death Metal shows are overwhelmingly nonviolent. I feel safer standing on the outskirts of a typical mosh pit than standing outside on a typical street corner.

Mosh pits are crucial to metal. Their physical, perhaps furious, nature is an unsurpassed agent of aggression-release and expression. They are emblems of freedom and passion. If you want to know what it is to be alive, step into a mosh pit. Mosh pits are about human contact and animalistic release. In the pit, touch is electric, and bodies are no longer restraints. Slayer's advice to "step outside yourself and let your mind go" is taken. What could better express the paradox of simultaneously being supremely alive and yet separated from the self as a part of something shared? These experiences are essentially united. A true pit is pure exhilaration.

Lest my words sound entirely too optimistic, I must temper them with a call to reality. My boundless praise of the Death Metal scene should not obscure imperfections and problems in the scene. I've certainly experienced them, first-hand on several occasions. I started my research of Death Metal as a naïve college student who had spent far more hours with her head in the books than her feet on the ground. Many of my innocent, rose-tinted notions of the world and its people were shattered during the time I spent in the Death Metal scene. At times, I learned far more than I cared to. Placing trust in the wrong persons and taking risks based on idealistic assumptions about other human beings landed me in more trouble than I care to discuss. The Death Metal scene is by no means a scene devoid of self-seeking and cruel individuals. It has its fair portion of untrustworthy villains like every other group, scene, or culture.

Yet the villainy of a few cannot suppress the goodness of the masses in the Death Metal scene. In fact, the togetherness of a tight subculture serves as an antidote to a "real world" where self-interest outweighs camaraderie. Granted, part of this impression is illusive, for the scene is host to many less than decent people. Nonetheless, as a whole, the scene represents an attempt on the part of the vast majority to reject the selfish, negative elements of contemporary western society. Having endured deception and hurt in the course of my involvement in the Death Metal scene, I, as much as anyone else, would be predisposed to emphasize its negative elements. Nevertheless, I confidently and sincerely proclaim that the Death Metal scene, in itself, is a positive force in contemporary society.

In short, Death Metal is a group or a scene much like any other group or scene. It has its negative elements and certainly possesses quite a few of those individuals who lead Senators McCain and Byrd to proclaim that a cultural crisis is on our hands. However, there are probably quite a few such individuals in the '*NSYNC* fan club. Metal heads on the whole have not acted to warrant the hatred that they receive. Yes, our culture is frightening, but that keeps it safe from infiltration and dilution. Yes, our culture emphasizes violence, but that is a reflection of social reality. Most fundamentally, our culture provides us with an identity and helps us to feel joined in a brotherhood where we are neither judged nor held to social standards. It is a powerful means of expression. Americans are very worried about what Death Metal will do to American culture. I am very worried about what its absence could do to the thousands of youths who find identity and expression in its harsh chords.

The Death Metal scene does not harm American culture or values. It does not lure youth into a life of debauchery and hopelessness, or present tempting images like most popular entertainment forms. No one becomes a fan unless he or she feels naturally drawn to it. If these inherent tendencies are stifled, what will become of the youth who feel outcast and alone? Does it make sense to destroy a viable form of expression in hopes that expressions of actual violence will decrease?

I feel confident in my defense of the Death Metal scene because I have been personally transformed by my experience of the scene. I have encountered its best and worst elements. I spent a few of my formative years in the midst of the bustling underground and learned valuable lessons about myself and about other human beings. In many ways, I began this project as a child and finished it as an adult. I am pleased with the role that Death Metal has played in what I have learned and in who I have become.

Appendix A: Project Goals, Implications, and Methodology

This study examined characteristics, orientations, and actions. The characteristics investigated were at the demographic, economic, political, and social levels. With respect to orientations, a number of political, ethical, and philosophical traits were examined, including apathy, sociability, relativism, subjectivism, rationalism, existentialism, and optimism-pessimism. The analysis includes a look at perceived chances of success in the contemporary American system. The behavioral aspect of the research focused on social interactions and violent tendencies. The primary unit of analysis was the individual fan of Death Metal. Further analysis was undertaken with social artifacts that are pertinent to the scene, such as metal music CDs, lyrics, and magazines. At the Death Metal shows themselves, informal group interactions were observed and analyzed. Some aggregate data was utilized in the overall comparison of the American Death Metal population with the normal American population of non-fans.

This was to be a cross-sectional study of the current Death Metal scene. Most of the data collection itself took place during a period of approximately three months. Although the theoretical population consists of all fans of Death Metal in America, it was impossible to draw a truly random and representative sample of this population, because there are no records of the identities of members or even the number of members. Convenience sampling thus had to replace random sampling. It was not possible, due to restraints of time and finance, to attend Death Metal shows throughout the United States. Fortunately, interviews with band members have consistently revealed a consensus that New York City possesses one of the most thriving and largest scenes, and the vast majority of data collected at shows was collected in or near New York City. Some data was gathered from other areas throughout the United States in order to make the sample more representative. Participants who were not from the New York area were found with the assistance of the editor/publisher of a prominent Death Metal magazine, the Grimoire, through Death Metal "chat rooms" on the Internet, and through member profile searches on America Online.[17]

The basic means of data collection involved surveys of demographics, philosophy, and behavior. The surveys consisted of sixty-four items and were ten pages in length. They were both anonymous and confidential. Most were distributed to persons met at shows, to be completed at their convenience and returned to myself or one of the research assistants who helped with the survey distribution. Others were sent out to Death Metal chat room participants and AOL users who described themselves as fans of Death Metal in their member profiles. These surveys were filled out and returned by e-mail at the participant's convenience. The total number of surveys collected was sixty-seven.

The second means of data collection involved intensive interviews with dozens of Death Metal fans, band members, and icons of the scene. The interviews were only somewhat directed by my questions, and remained quite open in order to keep the data unbiased and to gain as much insight as possible. The prepared portion of the interview involved questions about: Death Metal music itself, reactions to lyrics, experience of shows, impressions of the people in the Death Metal scene, reasons for joining the scene, positive and negative impressions, insight into the "metal philosophy," view of metal's supposed relationship to violence, and a description of the influence and personal meaning of Death Metal in the interviewee's life. The intensive interviews were not restricted to a given time frame, but lasted as long as the interviewee desired to continue the discussion. I also engaged in informal field research by attending shows and making note of behavior, interactions, and any other noticeable aspects of the underground metal scene. Some analysis of secondary data took place in the comparison of the aggregate data collected in this research of the Death Metal community with aggregate crime/violence statistics. The research methods employed within this study were therefore numerous.

Due to the small sample size for surveys, interviews, and field research, the methods utilized in this study are even less generalizable than they would be in better circumstances, and they therefore cannot be used to draw conclusions about the population at large. An accurate and reliable description of the population of Death Metal fans will not be obtained from this study, although some insights into the makeup of the population can be inferred as long as a high degree of variation is expected and a low confidence interval is accepted. The results of this study may be employed to cast doubt on claims that interest in violent entertainment forms is related to actual violent behavior. The modest scope of this study cannot aim to disprove these hypotheses, but can perhaps call them into question and encourage further study on the matter. This research is not sophisticated enough to establish or deny causality, because there are no means to identify and eliminate interfering variables, nor are there any grounds to generalize the conclusions found through this research.

Appendix B: Topics of Focus and Research Hypotheses

This section contains a lengthy overview of those major hypotheses which were addressed in this study, with an explanation of the techniques and indicators utilized to measure the presence or absence of given traits and variables.[18] While glancing over this chapter, it is crucial to keep in mind that it lists merely the hypotheses tested, not the results found. Some of the hypotheses listed here were confirmed, and others were disconfirmed by the research. The actual results of the research were presented in previous chapters, not this one.

1. *There is a relationship between interest in Death Metal and age, gender, and race.* Past research has suggested that the overwhelming majority of Death Metal fans are young, white males (Christenson 103). I expected my research to support this hypothesis for the most part. However, my attendance at shows during the past few years suggested that the label of "overwhelming majority" might not be appropriate, because there are a number of females and minorities in attendance at Death Metal shows. The Death Metal scene is not exclusive, and females and minorities are not rejected. This hypothesis was tested by determining raw percentages for the attributes of each demographic variable addressed in the survey: gender (male or female), race (white, black, Hispanic, or other), and age (within the range of 10–40).

2. *There is a negative relationship between interest in Death Metal and education level/GPA.* Christenson cites statistics which suggest that metal-

heads do worse in school and drop out earlier than other persons (103). To test this hypothesis, statistics were drawn from survey responses to questions about the highest level of education completed or in progress and average GPA while in school (or, if still in school, current GPA). These were compared with U.S. Census data taken from the general population in 1998 to measure education level (www.census.gov/hhes).

3. *Fans of metal are more likely to be from urban areas than from rural areas.* This hypothesis was tested based on a single survey question asking respondents to classify the area where they were from as urban, suburban, or rural.

4. *Fans of Death Metal tend to consider their relationships with family members as "not close" rather than "close."* The survey employed several questions regarding familial closeness. (See survey questions 9a, 9b, 10, 11, 12, 13.) For those who have siblings, the surveys tested for sense of closeness to siblings while growing up (indicated by perceived presence of closeness ["yes"] or absence of closeness ["no"]). Survey respondents were asked to classify their *parents'* relationship as "stable but happy", "stable but unhappy", "unstable", or "divorced." They also answered whether or not they felt close to their parents while growing up ("yes" or "no"). Respondents reported whether they saw their family members often (operationalized as more than once per month) while growing up ("yes" or "no"). Finally, survey participants were asked to classify their relationship with their parents as *predominantly* "loving", "appreciative", "indifferent", or "angry/bitter."

5. *Fans of Death Metal tend to be non-religious rather than religious.* The dimensions of this variable include attitude toward religion in general, personal identification with religion, and degree of participation in religious activities. Responses to two survey questions were used as indicators of religious attitudes among Death Metal fans. In question 15, fans were asked to choose the statement that best describes their attitude toward organized religion among the following choices: "Religion is a good institution; I am religious" (positive and involved), "Religion is a good institution, but I am not religious" (positive but not involved), "I feel indifferently toward religion" (indifferent), "I do not feel that religion is right for me, and I would never become religious" (negative but non-hostile), and "Religion is stupid; no one should be religious" (negative and hostile). Results were reported as the percentage of respondents choosing each of the aforementioned options. Question 32 asked for an open response to the question of whether respondents attend mass or church-related activities, and the answers were coded as "never," "sometimes," or "always." An index measuring degree of religious participation was devel-

oped based on this question. The index is on a scale of one to three, where one is least participation and three is most participation. An answer of "never" was assigned a value of one; "sometimes" was assigned a value of two; and "often" was assigned a value of three.

6. *Attitude of Death Metal fans toward big business and the economically successful tends to be negative rather than positive.* Two questions in the survey address this variable, and responses were coded and transformed into an index of attitude toward the economically successful on a scale of one to five, where one is the most positive and five is the most negative. For each question, respondents checked all answers with which they agreed. Each answer was assigned a positivity-negativity point value on the scale of one to five. The average value of all the responses was taken as the index of attitude toward the economically successful. Question 16 had respondents decide which statements apply to successful businessmen: "worked hard and advanced to successful positions through their efforts" (1), "got their positions because they were born privileged (3), "rose to power or success by exploiting others" (4), or "are the reason that I am not successful" (5). Question 17 asked respondents to check which statements they agreed with regarding Bill Gates: "shows how anyone in America can be a success if he/she works hard enough" (1), "is a genius in technology and business" (1), "has made great contributions to society" (1), "is enviable" (2), "has done a great deal of harm to society" (5), or "is a symbol of what is wrong with the economic system today" (5). Every highly positive response was assigned a value of one, moderate responses were ranked between two and three (depending on the degree of optimism that the respondent implied), and the most negative responses were assigned a value of 5.

7. *Attitude of Death Metal fans toward marriage tends to be negative rather than positive.* Attitude toward marriage must be divided into the dimensions of attitude toward marriage in general (positive, negative, or hostile), or attitude toward one's own marriage or potential for marriage (optimistic or pessimistic). Survey respondents classified their attitude toward marriage by choosing one of the following statements: "Marriage is a good institution; I am married or hope to be married someday" (positive, optimistic); "I would like to get married, but I doubt that I will" (positive, pessimistic); "I feel indifferently toward marriage" (indifferent); "I do not feel that marriage is right for me, and I do not wish to marry" (negative); "Marriage is a bad idea, and no one should get married" (hostile). The percentage of participants choosing each option was recorded.

8. *Most Death Metal fans will be ideologically more liberal than conservative with regard to current social issues.* Five survey questions about

opinions on current issues were used to develop an index of liberalism with a range of one to three, where one is the most liberal and three is the most conservative. Questions 18 through 22 addressed the topics of: homosexual rights, abortion rights, welfare, taxes, and prayer in schools. For each question, three possible options were available to respondents, one expressing a liberal opinion having a value of one, one expressing a moderate opinion having a value of two, and one expressing a conservative opinion having a value of three. The respondent was asked to choose one of the three options. The average value of responses for each survey was calculated and entered as the index of liberalism. Question 25 asked respondents about their political orientation (Democrat, Republican, or Other), and it was expected that, in light of a liberal ideology, more respondents would be Democrats than Republicans.

9. *Most Death Metal fans consider violence to be entertaining in fiction (but not in reality) or consider violence to be a poor solution to problems.* This hypothesis focuses on a single dimension of violence, and that is personal perception of violence as a solution to problems or a form of entertainment. In question 23 of the survey, respondents were asked to check all of the statements about violence with which they agreed. In recording the results, the possible answers were divided into three main categories of violence perception. Category 1 consisted of individuals who believe violence can be entertaining when fictional, but is bad in reality. Category 2 consisted of those who believe violence is entertaining in both fiction and reality. Finally, Category 3 consisted of those who believe that violence is never the solution to any problems or should only be used as a last resort. A participant was considered to belong to a particular category of violence perception if he or she checked *any* of the responses in the given category. (See survey question 23). For each perception of violence, percentages of its adherents were calculated.

10. *Fans of Death Metal will tend to be low in political knowledge, politically apathetic, and low in nationalism.* Questions 24–30 and 34–40 of the survey addressed political apathy, awareness, and pride. These questions attempted to target a number of indicators, such as tendency to vote or identify with a political party, willingness to work on a political campaign or a protest, and self-proclaimed sense of pride in American citizenship. Sense of pride was assessed through responses to the questions "Do you feel proud to be an American?" (yes or no) and "If you could live in any country on earth which would it be?" (America or not America). The nationalism score was on a scale of one to two, where one is most nationalistic and two is least nationalistic. Answers "yes" and "America" each have a value of one. Answers "no" and "not America" have a value of two.

The average of the answers to the two questions was calculated to find the nationalism index score. A political knowledge quotient, on a scale of one to eight, gave participants one point (or two in the case of question 40) for every correct answer given to questions about contemporary political groups and figures which would be considered common knowledge for an educated, adult citizen. For instance, participants were asked to identify the candidates for the Presidency in the year 2000, the legislative body of the United States, the number of justices on the Supreme Court, the organization represented by the letters WTO, the organization represented by the letters IMF, and 4 or 5 powerful nations. The sum of the points accrued by each respondent was used as the index of his or her political knowledge.

11. *Fans of Death Metal will tend to have low, rather than high, perceived chances of achieving success in society.* There is a nearly infinite number of dimensions for the variable of perceived chances of achieving success. Those which were tested in this study are based on the following indicators: projected image of financial situation in the future, projected image of familial/social interaction in the future, and projected enjoyment of future career. Each dimension was tested with a single question, and the possible responses to each question were given a value on scale of one to four, where one denotes extreme pessimism and four denotes extreme optimism. (See survey questions 41, 45, and 46). For each participant, the average value of the responses to each of the three questions was calculated and recorded as the index of perceived chances of success (range: 1–4). A perceived *low* chance of success was considered an average value of two or below, while a perceived *high* chance of success was considered an average value of three or above.

12. *Fans of Death Metal will tend to have a negative, rather than a positive, view of life.* Like perceived chances of achieving success, life view has a variety of dimensions. Those which were tested in this study are based on the following indicators: reported enjoyment of school or work situation, view of death at a young age, and overall classification of life as joyful, painful, or something in between. Each of these dimensions was tested with a single question, and the possible responses to each question were given a value on a scale of one to five, where one denotes extreme pessimism and five denotes extreme optimism. (See survey questions 42, 43, and 44). For each participant, the average value of the responses to each of the three question was calculated and recorded as the index of life view (range: 1–5).

13. *Fans of Death Metal will tend to be more self-centered than altruistic.* Altruism was operationalized as a score from one to four (where one

is least altruistic and four is most altruistic) based on a single question with four possible answers, each given a different altruistic value between one and four. (See survey question 47). A score of one was recorded as self-centered, two or three as neither altruistic nor self-centered, and four as altruistic.

14. *Fans of Death Metal tend to feel depressed sometimes or often rather than rarely or never.* Question 48 directly questioned participants about how often they feel depressed, and each participant chose from the options often, sometimes, rarely, or never.

15. *Fans of Death Metal are low in faith and relativistic or subjective in moral reasoning.* In question 49, respondents were asked to check those responses which best reflected their personal faith (or lack thereof) in a higher power, and, for coding purposes, the responses were grouped into categories of strong spirituality, some spirituality, rationalism/deism, and existentialism/fatalism. (Strong spirituality was denoted by a check next to the option: "*Faith is very important to me....*" Some spirituality was denoted by a check next to the option: "*I have some faith....*" Rationalism/deism was denoted by a check next to the option "*I believe in a higher power, but....*" or "*I have no faith in a higher power....*" Finally, existentialism/fatalism was denoted by a check next to the option "*If there were a higher power, life....*" or "*If there is a higher power, it....*" or "*I have nothing but anger toward....*") In question 50, respondents were asked to check those responses which best reflected their metaphysical vision of the universe, and, for coding purposes, the responses were grouped into categories of mysticism, rationalism/deism, or existentialism/nihilism. (Mysticism was denoted by a check next to the option "*The universe is full of wonder and....*" Rationalism/Deism was denoted by a check next to the response "*The universe operates in an orderly fashion....*" or "*In the world and the universe, what you see is what you get....*" or "*The world is like man's playground....*" Existentialism/nihilism was denoted by a check next to the option "*The universe is pretty bleak. It has no guiding force and neither do humans*" or "*Who can know anything about the operation of the universe....*" or "*The universe is totally chaotic*" or "*The universe is a hostile place.*") In questions 51 A-E and 52, respondents were asked to choose those responses which best reflected what they thought they would do in a particular ethical dilemma and why they would do this. For coding purposes, the responses were grouped into categories of natural law ethics, legal/religious positivism, relativism, and subjectivism. The respondent was recorded as adhering to that ethical theory which he or she chose most often.

16. *Fans of Death Metal will tend not to initiate violent confrontations, and to respond violently only when physically attacked.* Survey questions

53–56 were intended to measure perceived tendency toward violence by asking participants to check the response that best reflects how they would react in a number of different provocative situations. Their answers were coded, where one was nonviolent, two was violent only when physically provoked, and three was violent when physically or verbally provoked. (If answers to questions conflicted for a given respondent, then an average score was assigned.)

17. *Fans of Death Metal do not tend to be more violent than non-fans.* Survey questions 57–60 asked for numerical information on number of arrests, violent crime convictions, prison sentences, and recent (during the past year) violent confrontations. Other survey questions, such as the many sections of question 23, were intended to assess attitudes about and tendencies toward violence. This information was tallied into percentages which can be compared with crime rates for the general population. This hypothesis was of utmost importance due to its social significance, so the instrument employed in this study included a number of questions to measure the different facets of violence. (See Appendix C, the Coded Survey, for more detail.)

18. *Fans of Death Metal do not tend to be more deviant that non-fans in terms of alcohol and drug use and sexual activity.* Questions 61–64 asked for numerical information on the number of times per month that alcohol and different drugs were used, and the number of sexual partners had in the past year. This information was tallied into ratio statistics or percentages that could then be compared with rates for the general population.

Appendix C: Coded Survey

Please answer all of the following questions to the best of your ability:

1. Age_____
   (Variable 1: Question 1. Range: Open)

2. Gender: _____ Male _____ Female
   (Variable 2: Question 2. 1=male, 2=female)

3. Race: _____ Black _____ White _____ Hispanic _____ Other
   (Variable 3: Question 3. 2=black, 1=white, 3=Hispanic, 4=other)

4. Are you employed? _____ Yes _____ No
   (Variable 4: Question 4a. 1=yes, 2=no)

   If yes, please write in your average annual income: _____
   (Variable 5: Question 4b. 1=<15000, 2=15000–40000, 3= 40000+, 4= N/A)

5. Are you in school? _____ Yes _____ No
   (Variable 6: Question 5a. 1=yes, 2=no)

   If yes, please write in the average annual income of your family: _____
   (Variable 7: Question 5b. 1=<15000, 2=15000–40000, 3= 40000+, 4= N/A)

6. You would characterize the place where you live as:
   _____ Urban _____ Suburban _____ Rural
   (Variable 8: Question 6. 1=urban, 2=suburban, 3=rural)

7. Check the one which applies to your current or highest level of education:
   _____ completed grammar school   _____ still in high-school
   _____ completed high-school   _____ completed technical school
   _____ still in college   _____ completed community college
   _____ completed 4-yr college   _____ still in graduate school
   _____ completed graduate school

(Variable 9: Question 7. 1=completed grammar school, 2=still in high school, 2=completed high school, 3=completed technical school, 4= completed community college, 4=completed 4-yr college, 5=still in grad school, 5=completed grad school)

8. What was your average high-school GPA, or, if you went to college, your average college GPA? _____
(Variable 10: Question 8. Range: Open)

9. Do you have any siblings? _____ Yes _____ No
If yes, did you feel close to your siblings when you were growing up? _____
(Variable 11: Question 9b. 1=yes, 2=no, 3=N/A)

10. Please choose the statement that best describes your parents' relationship when you were growing up:
_____ Stable & happy
_____ Stable but unhappy
_____ Unstable
_____ Divorced
(Variable 12: Question 10. 1=stable & happy, 2=stable but unhappy, 3=unstable, 4=divorced)

11. Did you feel close to your parents when you were growing up? _____
(Variable 13: Question 11. 1=yes, 2=no)

12. Did you see your extended family members frequently (more than once per month) when you were growing up? _____
(Variable 14: Question 12. 1=yes, 2=no)

13. Please choose the statement which best describes your current attitude toward your parents:
_____ Loving
_____ Appreciative
_____ Indifferent
_____ Angry or bitter
(Variable 15: Question 13. 1=loving, 2=appreciative, 3=indifferent, 4=angry or bitter)

14. Please read the following statements, and choose the statement that *best* describes your attitude toward marriage:
_____ Marriage is a good institution; I am married or hope to be married someday.
_____ I would like to get married, but I doubt that I will.
_____ I feel indifferently toward marriage.
_____ I do not feel that marriage is right for me, and I do not wish to marry.
_____ Marriage is a bad idea, and no one should get married.
(Variable 16: Question 14. 1=Marriage is a good institution; I am married or hope to be married someday, 2=I would like to get married, but I doubt that I will, 3=I feel indifferently toward marriage, 4=I do not feel that marriage is right for me, and I do not wish to marry. 5=Marriage is a bad idea, and no one should get married.)

15. Please read the following statements, and choose the statement that *best* describes your attitude toward organized religion:
_____ Religion is a good institution; I am religious.
_____ Religion is a good institution, but I am not religious.
_____ I feel indifferently toward religion.

Coded Survey

_____ I do not feel that religion is right for me, and I would never become religious.
_____ Religion is stupid, and no one should be religious.

(Variable 17: Question 15. 1=Relig is good/I am religious, 2=relig is good/I am not religious, 3=Indifferent, 4=never become religious, 5=hostile toward religion)

16. Check all that apply: In my opinion, successful businessmen...
_____ worked hard and advanced to successful positions through their efforts.
_____ got their positions because they were born privileged.
_____ rose to power or success by exploiting others.
_____ are the reason that I am not successful.

(Variable 18: Question 16. 1=worked hard..., 2=got their positions..., 3=rose to power..., 4=are the reason...)

17. Check all that apply: Bill Gates...
_____ shows how anyone in America can be a success if he/she works hard enough.
_____ is a genius in technology and business.
_____ has made great contributions to society.
_____ is enviable.
_____ has done a great deal of harm to society.
_____ is a symbol of what is wrong with the economic system today.

(Variable 18: Question 17. 1=shows how anyone..., 1=is a genius..., 1=has made great..., 2=is enviable, 5=has done a great deal of harm..., 5=is a symbol)

18. Homosexuals...
_____ should have all the rights of marriage, adoption, etc., that heterosexuals have.
_____ should not be persecuted, but should not be given full rights of marriage.
_____ should have no rights.

(Variable 19: Question 18. 1=should have all rights..., 2=should not be persecuted..., 3=should have no rights...)

19. Abortion...
_____ is a woman's right to choose.
_____ is only acceptable in certain situations.
_____ is never acceptable.

(Variable 19. Question 19. 1=is a woman's right..., 2=is only acceptable..., 3=is never...)

20. Welfare...
_____ is an important program, because it is the government's responsibility to provide for the poorest people in our nation who cannot find work.
_____ is a good idea, but it is often misused and exploited or taken for a handout.
_____ is a bad idea, because everyone should be able to find a job and no one has a right to depend on the government.

(Variable 19: Question 20. 1=is an important..., 2=is a good idea..., 3=is a bad idea...)

21. Taxes ...
_____ should be lowered for businesses, so that the profits will trickle down.
_____ should be lowered for all people, even at the expense of public services.

APPENDIX C

_____ should be lowered for the poor, and increased for big business and the rich.
(Variable 19: Question 21. 3=for business, 2=for all people, 1=for the poor)

22. Prayer in schools ...
_____ should be encouraged for those who wish to pray.
_____ should be permitted, but only as a moment of silence.
_____ should not be allowed, because there must be separation of church and state.
(Variable 19: 3=encouraged, 2=permitted, 1=not allowed)

23. Check all that apply: Violence among people ...
_____ can be entertaining when fictional, but is bad in reality.
_____ is entertaining in fiction and in reality.
_____ is a good and efficient way to solve problems between individuals.
_____ should only be used by individuals as a last resort.
_____ is never the solution to any problems.
(Variable 20: Question 23a. 1=checked, 2=not checked; Variable 21: Question 23b, c. 1=either checked, 2=neither; Variable 22: Question 23d,e. 1=either checked, 2=neither.)

Please answer the following to your best ability, and leave blank those answers which you do not know:

24. Are you a registered voter? _____.
    If so, do you vote regularly? _____.
    (Variable 23: Question 24. 1=vote regularly, 2=do not vote regularly, 3=not registered)

25. Do you identify with a political party? _____.
    If so, which one? _____.
    (Variable 24: Question 25. 1=Democrat, 2=Republican, 3=Other, 4=N/A)

26. Do you feel proud to be an American? _____.
    (Variable 25: Question 26. 1=yes, 2=no)

27. If you could live in any country on earth, which would it be? _____.
    (Variable 25: Question 27. 1=America, 2=not America)

28. Would you ever attend a political rally or work for a candidate's campaign? _____.
    (Variable 26: Question 28. 1=no, 2=maybe, 3=yes)

29. If you had the financial means, would you ever invest money in the stock market? _____.
    (Variable 30: Question 29. Ultimately eliminated from study due to low completion rate.)

30. Would you ever attend a protest or work on a petition? _____.
    (Variable 26: Question 30. 1=no, 2=maybe, 3=yes)

31. Do you ever attend social events such as parades or festivals? _____.
    (Variable 27: Question 31. 1=no, 2=maybe, 3=yes)

32. Do you ever attend mass or church-related activities? _____.
    (Variable 28: Question 32. 1=never, 2=sometimes, 3=often)

33. Would you ever belong to any youth groups or clubs? _____.
    (Variable 27: Question 32. 1=no, 2=maybe, 3=yes)

34. The Democratic candidate for the presidency is _____.
    (Variable 29: Questions 34, 35, 36, 37, 38, 39, 40. For 34–39, one point for each correct answer. For question 40, two points for 4–5 powerful nations, one point for 2–3, no points for 0–1.)

35. The Republican candidate for the presidency is _____.

36. The legislative body of the United States is called _____.

37. How many justices are on the Supreme Court? _____.

38. IMF stands for _____.
    Do you support the IMF? _____.
    (Variable 30: Question 38b. Ultimately eliminated from study due to low completion rate.)

39. WTO stands for _____.
    Do you support the WTO? _____.
    (Variable 30: Question 39b. Ultimately eliminated from study due to low completion rate.)

40. Please write the names of 4 or 5 of the nations that you think are the most powerful: _____.

*For each question, please read all of the choices, and choose the **best** answer:*

41. In the future, I expect to be:
    _____ in a very successful financial situation.
    _____ in a decent, middle-class financial situation.
    _____ in a stable, but not very successful financial situation.
    _____ in an unstable financial situation.
    _____ poor.
    (Variable 31: Questions 41, 45, & 46. 4.0=in a very successful…, 3.5=in a decent…, 3.0=in a stable…, 2.0=in an unstable…, 1.0=poor. 4.0=to have a life full of…. 3.0=to value the rare…, 2.0=to keep pretty much…, 1.0=what future? 4.0=challenging, but…, 2.5=fairly dull, but not…, 2.5=above all, a…, 1.5=very unpleasant. 1.0=what career?)

42. My school or work situation is:
    _____ stimulating and enjoyable.
    _____ fairly decent.
    _____ not stimulating in itself, but just a means to do something better in the future.
    _____ not stimulating in itself, but then again, what is?
    _____ where I'll be stuck forever.
    (Variable 32: Questions 42, 43, & 44. 5.0=stimulating…, 4.0=fairly…, 3.0=not stimulating, but…, 2.0=not stimulating…, 1.0=where I'll be…, 1.0=probably a welcome…, 3.0=usually good…, 4.0=sometimes good…, 2.0=no big deal, 5.0=a tragedy, 5.0=full of joy, 4.0=whatever you…, 3.0=good for lucky…, 2.0=a struggle…, 1.0=inevitably painful.)

43. In my view, death at a young age is …
    _____ probably a welcome release.

_____ usually good, sometimes bad.
_____ sometimes good, usually bad.
_____ no big deal.
_____ a tragedy.

44. In my view, life is ...
    _____ full of joy.
    _____ whatever you make of it.
    _____ good for lucky people, and bad for unlucky people.
    _____ a struggle.
    _____ inevitably painful.

45. In my own future, I expect ...
    _____ to have a life full of contact with family and friends.
    _____ to value the rare time I will spend with family and friends.
    _____ to keep pretty much to myself.
    _____ *what future?*

46. I believe my future career will be ...
    _____ challenging but enjoyable.
    _____ fairly dull, but not too bad.
    _____ above all, a big challenge.
    _____ very unpleasant.
    _____ *what career?*

47. In the future, I plan ...
    _____ to get involved in my community.
    _____ to help out when I can, but I doubt I'll have much time.
    _____ to look out for my own interests first.
    _____ to avoid social interaction as much as possible.
    (Variable 33: Question 47. 4.0=to get involved..., 3.0=to help out..., 2.0=to look out..., 1.0=to avoid...)

48. Have you ever felt depressed?
    _____ Often, and I have been treated for depression.
    _____ Often, but I have never been treated for depression.
    _____ Sometimes
    _____ Rarely
    _____ Never
    (Variable 34: Question 48. 1.0=often, and..., 2.0=often, but..., 3.0=sometimes, 4.0=rarely, 5.0=never)

Please read all of the following questions and statements carefully. Many of them require reflection on your part. Take your time in choosing the best answers.

49. Please choose the statement that best describes your personal beliefs:
    _____ Faith is very important. I believe in a higher power that influences my life.
    _____ I believe in a higher power, but it doesn't really affect my daily life.
    _____ I have some faith, but it is very uncertain.
    _____ I have no faith in a higher power, and I certainly don't need one in my life.

_____ If there were a higher power, life would be meaningful, but there is not one.
_____ If there is a higher power, it may help others but it plays no role in my life.
_____ I have nothing but anger towards any power that created this universe.
(Variable 35: Question 49a. 1=checked, 2=unchecked. Variable 36: Question 49c: 1=checked, 2=unchecked. Variable 37: Question 49b, d. 1=either checked, 2=neither. Variable 38: Question 49e, f, g. 1=any checked, 2=none)

50. **How do you think the universe works?** Please read through all of the following, and check *any* of those statements that you feel you can truly identify with. You will probably check more than one, but you may check only one or none at all. Take your time.
_____ The universe is full of wonder and mystery. It operates by rules that are beyond human comprehension, yet man is one integral part of the greater whole.
_____ The universe operates in an orderly fashion. Although humans cannot control it, they can learn about it through reason and experience, and come to live in harmony with it.
_____ In the world and the universe, what you see is what you get. Physical science has explained almost everything, and what it hasn't explained, it probably will in the future. There are no ordering forces or mystical higher powers, but it really doesn't matter because we know enough to operate and survive without them.
_____ The universe is pretty bleak. It has no guiding force and neither do humans. We are on our own, and that is very difficult in a world where we are always grappling for some transcendent meaning that does not really exist. Humans keep expecting to be able to define good and bad or find a purpose in life, but because there is no higher power, there really is no purpose.
_____ The world is like man's playground. It is up to humans to arrange and manipulate it, and to make it into a suitable environment for themselves. This world operates logically because humans have studied it through science and have developed an organized way of understanding it.
_____ Who can know anything about the operation of the universe or the world? It is futile to try. We might as well just give up before we even begin to search for answers to major metaphysical questions, because there are none anyway.
_____ The universe is totally chaotic. Any men who believe that they control or understand it are fools. We do not control the universe, and we cannot even understand it. We are just part of a universal struggle for survival.
_____ The universe is a hostile place. If there are any natural forces, they operate against humans. There's no meaning to life, and survival is a struggle.
(Variable 40: Question 50a. 1=checked, 2=unchecked. Variable 41: Question 50b, c, e. 1=any checked, 2=none. Variable 42: Question 50c, e, f, g. 1=any checked, 2=none.)

51. Many of the decisions that people make on a daily basis have to do with values. They call upon individuals to distinguish right from wrong in order to determine how they *ought* to act in a given situation. Please consider the fol-

lowing situations. Try to decide what you *should* do, and, more importantly, why you *should* do it. Circle the number of the best answer.

A. You are walking down a city street with some loose bills and change in your pockets. You notice a pathetically thin man in tattered clothing reaching up toward you. He is begging for money. What do you do?

   1. Give him money. It's just the right thing to do. He's a human being.
   2. Give him some change. The Bible says you should give to the poor.
   3. Walk by. There's no law that says you have to give him money.
   4. Walk by. Your own wants and needs come first.

B. You are driving late at night in a secluded area, and there are no other cars in sight. You come to a red light. What do you do?

   1. Go through the light. You won't get caught, so who cares?
   2. Go through the light. You know there's no other cars, so you're not endangering anyone.
   3. Stop. It's the law.
   4. Stop. If nobody paid attention to traffic signals when they judged them unimportant, then where would be today?

C. Your country has entered a war against a state that you have never even heard of, aside from the recent talk about the negative effects that the state's trading policies have had on your country. The war escalates and you will be drafted. What do you do?

   1. Find a bogus excuse to get yourself out of military service.
   2. Join protests against the war, and leave the country once you're drafted.
   3. Go to war. It's your duty to your country as a lifelong citizen.
   4. Go to war. It's the law, and if you fail to obey, you will pay for your crime.

D. Your country has entered a war against a state which you know is carrying out a holocaust-style policy of genocide against minorities. The human rights violations are incomprehensible. You are drafted. What do you do?

   1. Find a bogus excuse to get yourself out of military service.
   2. Leave the country.
   3. Go to war. You are willing to risk your life for this cause.
   4. Go to war. It's your duty and it's the law.

E. You go to the store and purchase several bags of groceries, and you must make a few trips back and forth to your car. A security guard is supposed to be watching so that your car and groceries will be safe during your walks from your shopping cart to your car. He has the authority to arrest anyone caught stealing. While the guard's attention is diverted, you notice a woman and child stealing the groceries from your car. You could call to the guard and have them arrested or you could let them run off with your groceries. What do you do?

   1. Let them run off without saying a word. After all, it is groceries that they are stealing, so they must be very needy, hungry people.

2. Run over and confront them yourself. Make them give back the groceries that you bought with your own hard-earned money, but do not alert the security guard.
3. Shout to the guard! Those are your groceries. You paid for them, and they have no right to them. Let that women get a job and pay for her own groceries!
4. Call the guard to have the woman arrested. Stealing is illegal and it's just wrong.

(Variable 42: Questions 51A, B, C, D, E; 52a, b, c, d, e, f. 1=Naturalism: 51A: 1, 51B: 4, 51C: 3, 51D: 3, 51E: 1, 52 a or e: checked, 2=Positivism: 51A: 2 or 3, 51B: 3; 51C: 4; 51D: 4; 51E: 4; 52 b or c: checked; 3=Relativism: 51B: 2, 51C: 2, 51D: 2, 51E: 4, 52 f: checked, 4=Subjectivism, 51A: 4, 51B: 1, 51C: 1, 51D: 1, 51E: 3, 52 d: checked)

52. After considering all of the previous situations, you may have some questions about the validity of moral statements. From where do you derive your values, and why are they valid? What makes you use the word "should"?

    _____ Some things are just right and other things are just wrong. That's the way the world works, always and everywhere. Morality is objective.
    _____ I know what is right and what is wrong because my religion tells me.
    _____ The government decides what's right and what's wrong. I know what I *should* do when I know the laws.
    _____ I create my own value system. There really are no objective standards of "good" and "evil." When I use the word "should," I am basing it totally on my own perceptions and convictions. It's my opinion and my right to decide. No one can judge the true nature of "right" and "wrong" because these are just human creations. My definition of values is as good as anyone else's.
    _____ We can tell what's right and what's wrong just by knowing what it means to be human. Good actions are in accord with our human nature, and bad actions go against our human nature. Everyone has some natural idea of what is right and what is wrong. You can call it a conscience.
    _____ Society decides what's right and what's wrong, and values are different for different cultures. Something is considered morally good if the people of a society have agreed that it is morally good. There are no objective standards, and no one culture has better moral values than any other.

Consider these scenarios:

53. You and 3 friends are sitting at a picnic table in a public park minding your own business when suddenly you get hit in the head with a frisbee. It really hurt. You turn around to discover who did it, and you see someone about your age and size laughing hysterically, along with 3 friends. This is evidently the person who threw the frisbee, and it apparently was not an accident. What do you do?

    _____ Ignore it. Your head will be fine in a minute, and it's not worth it to get into a confrontation.
    _____ Shout at them and call the person who threw it a nasty name, but don't get up from where you're sitting.

_____ Jump up and start a confrontation. After all, you've got 3 friends who have your back, and you're pretty confident that you could take on this crew.
_____ Go report it to the security guard on the other side of the park.
(Variable 43: Questions 53, 54, 55, 56. 1.0=Nonviolent: 53a, 53d, 54a, 55c, 56a, 56b; 1.5=Nonviolent but hostile: 53b, 54b, 55b, 56c; 2.0=Violent when physically provoked: 53c, 55a; 3.0=Violent when verbally provoked: 54c, 56d)

54. You are walking your younger sister to school when some man whistles and shouts a vulgar comment at her. Later on that night, you and a group of your friends come upon the same man. He is quite alone, and there is no one watching. What do you do?

_____ Ignore him. Pretend you don't recognize him.
_____ Shout an obscenity at him from across the street.
_____ See to it that he pays *physically* for his comment earlier.

55. You're in a club when a fight starts up. Within seconds, it seems like more than a dozen people are involved, and someone accidentally gets thrown into you. What do you do?

_____ Join the fight.
_____ Take a few steps back and enjoy the show!
_____ Leave the club rather than deal with these people.

56. You and a friend have been out walking all day, and you're thirsty. You enter a restaurant to buy something to drink. As soon as the owner gets a look at the two of you, she asks you to leave and declares that your business is not needed at her restaurant. What do you do?

_____ Walk out angry, recognizing that there's really nothing you can do. This is a privately owned place, and the owner can legally kick out whomever she chooses.
_____ Walk out after voicing your anger at the owner's action, then do everything in your power to spread the word about the injustice that took place, so that the business will be affected.
_____ Refuse to leave, even though you know it means you'll end up getting arrested.
_____ Come back much later that night and throw a bottle through the window. You know you can get away with it.

57. Have you ever been arrested? _____Yes _____No
   If yes, how many times? _____
   (Variable 44: Questions 57 & 59. 0=no arrests, no prison; 1=1 or 2 arrests, no prison; 2=Arrested multiple times, but not imprisoned; 3=Imprisoned)

58. Have you ever been convicted of a violent crime? _____Yes _____No
   If yes, how many times? _____
   (Variable 45: Question 58. 0=no, 1=yes)

59. Have you ever spent time in prison? _____Yes _____No
   If yes, how long total? _____

60. Have you been involved in a violent confrontation in the past year? _____Yes _____No

Coded Survey 215

   If yes, how many times? _____
   (Variable 46: Question 60. Range: Open)

61. Do you use alcohol regularly? _____Yes _____No
    If yes, about how many times per month do you drink? _____
    (Variable 47: Question 61. Range: Open)

62. Have you ever used marijuana? _____Yes_____No
    If yes, do you do so on a regular basis? _____
    (Variable 48: Question 62. 0=no/not regularly, 1=regularly)

63. Have you ever used illegal drugs other than marijuana? _____Yes_____No
    If yes, do you do so on a regular basis? _____Yes_____No
    If yes, how many times per month do you use such drugs? _____
    (Variable 49: Question 63. 0=no/not regularly, 1=regularly)

64. Are you currently sexually active? _____Yes_____No
    If yes, how many sexual partners have you had in the past year? _____
    (Variable 50: Question 64. Range: Open)

Thank you so much for your participation!

Appendix D: Sample Interview Questions

General Interview Questions

1. What kinds of music do you listen to?
2. Why do you listen to these types of music? What do they mean to you?
3. Do you think that the music expresses your personal beliefs and identity? If so, how?
4. Do you think that the lyrics in most of the music that you listen to are reflective of your personal beliefs?
5. What are the factors that attract you most to the metal scene?
6. What are the factors that you dislike most or would like to see changed?
7. What do you perceive to be the difference between the metal that you listen to and the metal that is played on MTV?
8. Do you dress and act the same when you are at shows as when you are not at shows?
9. Are most of your friends fans of the same music?
10. Why do you go to shows instead of just listening to music at home?
11. What do you think of the "Satanism" that is often attributed to the metal scene?
12. What sorts of personalities do you encounter most at shows? What are the positive trends and the negative trends that you have noticed?
13. Is there a "metal philosophy"? If you think so, how would you describe it?
14. Do you have a personal philosophy? How would you describe it?
15. Is there a relationship between the metal scene and society as a whole? How would you describe that relationship?

16. American Death Metal is often distinguished from foreign and particularly Northern European Death Metal. What do you think makes American Death Metal something uniquely American? What classifies the scene as American?
17. What is your perception of the current political battles over "violent" entertainment forms or films, music, etc. which are believed to promote violent behavior?
18. Would you want metal to go mainstream so it would be more prevalent and easier to access? Why or why not?

Generic Musician Interview

1. How would you characterize the type of music that you create? Has your style changed or evolved over time?
2. Do you think that the style of Death Metal music in general has changed or evolved over time? How so?
3. Do you think that the sound and style of the music you perform express your personal beliefs and identity? If so, how?
4. Do you think that the lyrics in this music are reflective of your personal beliefs? Why or why not?
5. Do believe that the lyrics in Death Metal music serve a particular function? Is there a particular reason why they are horrifying?
6. Many people find Death Metal music offensive or at least shocking. Do you believe the music is intended to shock or offend? What is the purpose of shocking people? Why be offensive?
7. What first attracted you to Death Metal music? What captured and held your interest?
8. Because the type of music you perform is quite underground, it is difficult to market it and for a band to become widely known and respected. What was it like to establish a name for yourselves? What sort of efforts did it entail? What setbacks did you suffer, and what obstacles have you overcome through the years?
9. Please describe your experience of the Death Metal scene. What has it been like to perform, both when you first began and at present? How has the scene changed? Are the fans different? Are the shows different? Is the music different?
10. What are the factors that you like most about the Death Metal scene?
11. What are the factors that you dislike most or would like to see changed?
12. What do you think of the "Satanism" that is often attributed to the metal scene?
13. What sorts of personalities do you encounter most at shows? What are the positive trends and the negative trends that you have noticed?

14. Is there a "metal philosophy"? If you think so, how would you describe it?
15. Do you have a personal philosophy? How would you describe it?
16. Is there a relationship between the Death Metal scene and society as a whole? How would you describe that relationship? Hostile? Friendly? Indifferent?
17. What do you think makes American Death Metal something uniquely American? What classifies the scene as American?
18. What is your perception of the current political battles over "violent" entertainment forms or films, music, etc. which are believed to promote violent behavior?
19. Would you want metal to go mainstream so it would be more prevalent and easier to access? Why or why not?
20. Thank you so much for participating in this interview. Please add any additional comments, reflections, or impressions that you might have.

Appendix E: Criticism of Methods and Suggestions for Future Research

As emphasized throughout this work, it was impossible during the course of the research to obtain a large enough or representative enough sample of Death Metal fans. As a result, the findings are not highly reliable or generalizable. However, as a result of the extensive interviews conducted and of my comprehensive experience of the Death Metal scene, I do believe firmly in the validity of those theories and insights that have been expressed here. The purpose of this study was not to draw definitive conclusions about fans of Death Metal, nor to establish an explanation for violence in society or violence in entertainment. Instead, I hoped only to provide an open window into the scene, which as small as it might be, permits outsiders to glance in and to question the assumptions and prejudices which they may already hold. It is my hope that someone more capable than myself will gain a new perspective in peeking through this window, and will undertake more extensive and scientific research that will ultimately defend the metal community and perhaps help to justify the existence of Death Metal to some of its most powerful opponents.

As mentioned earlier, much of the data in this study was collected via lengthy surveys. Although these surveys were pre-tested, certain potentially problematic aspects of the survey instrument itself were discovered later in the course of the research. For instance, questions 11 and 13 ask about one's relationship with his or her parents. These questions are inherently double-barreled because in both instances, the survey asks about "parents" without differentiating between mothers and fathers. This is particularly significant in a population where rates of divorce are perceived to be high, and the difference between feeling close to one parent and feeling close to both parents should have been noted. Because it was not, the responses to question 13 were not exhaustive and the accuracy of responses to this question suffers as a result. Question 11, which asks for an open response to the question "Did you feel close to your parents when you were growing up?" enabled respondents to differentiate between mothers and fathers. Unfortunately, my established coding process did not allow for this differentiation because I classified each response as either "close" or "not close" to both parents. For those respondents who reported closeness to only one parent, I alternated between "close" and "not close" responses in entering the data codes for analysis. In future studies, greater accuracy and validity can be obtained through the differentiation of relationships with fathers and with mothers.

Question number 21 was particularly problematic because it lacked the quality of exhaustiveness. In reviewing question 21, one may notice immediately that the option of keeping taxes precisely as they are is not mentioned. This oversight should be avoided in future studies. Luckily, it would not significantly affect the results because it is only one of many questions used to formulate an ideological score for respondents, and the score can still be calculated with ease even when question 21 is left blank.

The other major problem with the survey instrument lay in the questions that presented scenarios and possible reactions in order to measure respondents' tendencies toward violent behavior. Responses were coded only as: nonviolent; violent only when physically provoked; or violent when physically or verbally provoked. In some situations, respondents reported nonviolent reactions to physical provocation and violent reactions to verbal provocation. This was unexpected and proved a barrier to the coding process. I dealt with the problem by assigning numerical values to the different responses on an interval scale, where 1 was nonviolent, 1.5 was nonviolent yet hostile, 2 was violent when physically provoked, and 3 was violent when verbally provoked. For each question, I recorded the respondent's answer as one of these numbers. I then found the mean of the numbers recorded for each respondent. Although this may have provided a reasonable portrait of the violent tendencies of given persons, the measurements were highly imprecise and too arbitrary. An accurate and meaningful average value cannot be calculated using such rough interval measures. However, I felt constrained to deal with the data as if it were ratio data in order to develop a recordable and measurable statistic. Such a procedure is improper, and in future studies, a more accurate and more measurable means of quantifying violent tendencies should be developed and utilized.

In a general criticism of the survey instrument employed in this study, I affirm that the length of the survey is certainly its most undesirable factor. Actual rate of response and completion rate could not be calculated because of the snowballing methods which took place beyond the researcher's eyes, and because with surveys sent out via e-mail it is impossible to tell how many persons actually saw the survey and how many began but did not complete it. It is likely, however, given the length of the survey, that response and completion rates were low. Because of the quantity and variety of information that I wished to obtain for this analysis, I felt as though I could not sacrifice any data to make the survey shorter and more manageable. On the other hand, had the survey been shorter, it is likely that more persons would have completed it, and that a larger and more representative sample would have been obtained. I thus had to mediate between the goals of in-depth analysis and generalizability, and depth of analysis took priority in this particular study partly because generalizability was simply not a realistic goal to begin with. The limited resources and time for the research process precluded it from becoming more generalizable and representative. However, for the exploratory purposes of this study, a deeper look into the characteristics of a smaller number of individuals seemed most desirable.

Other than these factors, I can think of no more specific criticisms of my methodology and data collection that could benefit researchers conducting studies in this area. In general, the weaknesses of this project are grounded in the inordinately small sample size and my inability to obtain a reliably representative sample. Future researchers are encouraged to find means of data collection that are less likely to have a class bias than the e-mail methods utilized in this study. In the best of worlds, all data would be obtained from a sample of Death Metal shows across the nation. Although this sample could never be truly random, it would be more representative and more generalizable than any findings of this study.

In conclusion, I would like to point out that it is not as difficult to obtain a large and representative sample of Death Metal fans as it may initially appear. Had I not been bound by financial and temporal constrictions, I would have attempted to do so, and I hope that future researchers will. The amount of cooperation and the great assistance that I received from so many metal fans indicates that an in-depth, more scientific study of the Death Metal scene is a realistic possibility and a worthy endeavor.

Notes

*A great deal of the factual data in this section are drawn from the unpublished writings of Matthew Harvey, with his consent.

1. Before delving into this discussion, it is important to note that although these sub-genres are often titled after different geographic areas, they actually represent different styles of music. The fact that a band is labeled "New York style," for instance, does not mean its members are from New York. For instance, the members of New York style band Dying Fetus come from Maryland. The band still falls under the category of New York Death Metal because its music form is typified by the style that originated in and still hails predominantly from New York. Similarly, the bands listed as "Florida style" are not all from Florida. The members of Florida-style Cannibal Corpse, for example, are originally from New York state.

2. This set of lyrical labels is adopted, with permission, from the set of (unpublished) categorizations developed by Matthew Harvey.

3. The following is just a general classification of the types of lyrics found in Death Metal music, not indicative of their relevance to fans or to society. More will be said about the possible significance of these lyrics only after the population of fans is described.

4. The lyricist who penned the controversial word has maintained in several interviews since that the word was never intended as a reference to African Americans in particular, but to ignorant persons of any and all races.

5. For insight into the intelligent and serious political commentary of the Death Metal world, see the website of Jason Netherton at www.demockery.org. The site is a voice for political, social, and economic theories associated with the lyrics of *Dying Fetus* (when Jason Netherton was a part of the band) and Netherton's current project *Misery Index*.

6. A New Orleans band with the same name (Incubus) also released Thrash/Death Metal albums in 1988 and 1990 respectively.

7. While in California, Death members became acquainted with the members

of Sadus (a Californian Thrash/Death Metal band), and bassist Steve DiGiorgio of Sadus would play with Schuldiner on later Death albums.

8. A note from one researcher: "Once I accidentally dropped a new CD in a particularly crowded and active mosh pit at a Dying Fetus show. I was sure it was done for, but as soon as the moshers noticed the broken CD case and the CD itself on the floor, they moved aside. People picked up the pieces and handed them to me. (Incidentally, the case was broken, but the CD itself worked fine!) These persons interrupted their dancing and went out of their way to help me."

9. Peter Helmkamp (formerly of Angelcorpse and currently of Terror Organ) disagrees entirely. Helmkamp believes that the exclusivity of the scene is proactive, not reactive. That is, true metal fans are the elite and their superiority over and distaste for others is at the heart of their rejection of mainstream culture. Helmkamp writes:

> The entire premise of extreme metal music ... is that of aggression and, as the name implies, extremism. By this token, I feel that it is safe to say that the majority of bands/musicians that hail and have hailed to this banner are mere shadows of who and what they claim to be — posers, as the common phrase so eloquently puts it. Being neither extreme in belief, action, or creativity, they are simply the followers of yet another genre. Thus, it can be stated that within even this fringe element of society, and of musical trends, there is really only a small core of truly extreme metal musicians and fans. This should not come as any real surprise: as in all walks of life, the masses are the cattle that the herdsmen lead to slaughter.

10. Once again, Pete Helmkamp disagrees entirely. For him, elitism is central to the maintenance of a strong and vital scene. He writes:

> The myth of the underground has been one of the main reasons why the scene itself has become so glutted: everyone supports everyone else and there is no natural selection or survival of the fittest. I believe in purity. If a band is crap, they should be told, they should be ignored, they should allowed to wither and die. Unfortunately now they get an album released by some startup chump that is operating a label out of his bedroom, and needs titles to flesh out his catalog. ... I believe that most metal bands are absolute garbage, and I don't hesitate to state that emphatically (often naming names) in interviews and in conversation.

11. On the other side of the political spectrum, Pete Helmkamp has published works explaining his highly conservative ideology. His published works include *The Conqueror Manifesto* and *Controlled Burn*. Helmkamp's views are representative of a small minority in the scene.

12. For those unfamiliar with these terms, rough definitions follow:

Mysticism: The universe is a place of wonder and mystery. It is ordered by some greater natural force or power. This view is generally positive or optimistic, and does not rule out the existence of the supernatural or of a god-like force.

Cartesianism: The universe is a rationally ordered, sensible entity. Everything operates according to scientific laws or rules that are understandable to man. Man is able to manipulate and control his environment, for he is the master of the universe. Generally, this view is optimistic, but rejects any concepts of the supernatural or God.

Existentialism: This is the view that, in Sartre's famous terms, "existence preceded essence." Man is thrown into a physical universe devoid of any meaning. There is no overarching concept of nature or humanity to which he should conform, nor are there any pre-existent concepts of right and wrong. Man, as the only creature for whom existence precedes essence, must define his own essence or nature via his own choices and actions. He creates right and wrong and participates in the collective historical defining of humanity. This view can be pessimistic or optimistic, depending on whether the adherent is willing to accept the responsibility of creating meaning or instead mourns the absence of any objective meaning to life.

Skepticism: Nothing is certain. Neither the physical nor the supernatural can be taken for granted or understood by man. Man probably does not control the universe, but there is no reason to affirm that a God controls the universe either. This view is often pessimistic.

Chaos theory: The universe does not operate in a rational manner, nor does it conform to the plans of some greater being. The only meaning or direction in existence is the inevitable drive toward nonexistence or entropy. The universe can be neither controlled nor understood. Man occupies no special place in the universe, and his life bears no special significance or dignity. This view is often pessimistic.

13. Helmkamp believes that extreme metal is defined by a philosophy of "controlled chaos, animalistic fury, and a Nietzschean worldview." Although his philosophical view is undoubtedly hyper-rationalistic and Cartesian, Helmkamp's worldview is anything but moderate. In summary of his philosophy, Helmkamp writes:

> I speak of a Conqueror that resides within each one of us, and of how to bring forth this being to fully reap the rewards that life has to offer. A philosophy based on the development and exercising of both strength and wisdom in conjunction. A harsh yet natural worldview: no mercy for the weak, no hope—only Will! No 'wait and see', only push forward on one's own accord. Make the world as you would want it. Accept no other's definition of the world as your own. Either rule or be ruled by someone else. My philosophies are based on natural laws, and are as much archetypal ideals as they are realities, but they are attainable and achievable. Man as Conqueror, as Predator—woe to the vanquished!

14. Rough definitions of these categories follow:
Natural Law/Kantian Ethics: Some things are just right and other things are just wrong. That is the way the world works, always and everywhere. Morality is objective. Man can tell what is right and what is wrong just by knowing what it means to be human. Good actions are in accord with our human nature, and bad actions go against human nature. Every one has some natural idea of what is right and what is wrong; one can call it a conscience. The major moral precepts are: (1) Treat every person as an end in himself, never merely as a means. (2) An action

is right if one would be comfortable living in a world where everyone in the same circumstances made the same decision.

Legal or Moral Positivism: A moral positivist would say: I know what is right and what is wrong because my religion tells me. A legal positivist would say: The government decides what is right and what is wrong; I know what I *should* do when I know the laws.

Cultural Relativism: Society decides what is right and what is wrong, and values are different for different cultures. Something is considered morally good if the people of a society have agreed that it is morally good. There are no objective standards, and no one culture has better moral values than any other.

Subjectivism: Each person creates his own value system. There really are no objective standards of "good" and "evil." When one uses the word "should," he is basing it totally on his own perceptions and convictions. It is his opinion and his right to decide. No one can judge the true nature of "right" and "wrong" because these are just human creations. One person's definition of values is as good as anyone else's.

15. Alternatives to this hypothesis abound, and are explored in *Horror, Gore, Porn, and the American Mind*. It is, for instance, possible to challenge the desensitization hypothesis by arguing that even the most vile Death Metal lyrics promote sensitization and awareness rather than lack thereof. Says Matthew Harvey:

> They serve to shock people out of their everyday numbness and apathy. Consider the fact that most people going through life with no ambition, direction, will, drive seem 'dead' already. Perhaps Death Metal lyrics serve to shock these people into reacting to something. People are so desensitized, commercialized, and tranquilized by mass media, mindless jobs, bills, etc. that very little really affects them or ever makes them look outside of their own bubble or within themselves to really think about what it is that they are doing with their lives. Shock treatment is as good as anything.

16. Pete Helmkamp disagrees entirely. See his *Conqueror Manifesto* and *Controlled Burn* for a very different perspective.

17. None of these methods of sampling is as representative as actual attendance and recruitment from nationwide Death Metal shows. For instance, it may cost money to be an Internet user, and thus a sample drawn from Internet chat rooms may taint the socioeconomic data for the population. However, because Internet access is currently very widespread, and because shows themselves cost a considerable amount of money (usually a $10 admission fee), drawing a sample from an Internet population should not have thrown off the results to a very significant degree. The convenience sampling process used to collect data was not truly random, but it is fairly representative.

18 This chapter may therefore only be of interest to those who wish to analyze the technical methodology of this study or to conduct a similar study themselves. For the general reader, a more concise and less technical idea of the hypotheses examined and the indicators employed may be obtained from an overview of the actual survey used in this study, found in Appendix C.

Bibliography

Books and Academic Essays

Arnett, Jeffrey Jensen. *Metalheads: Heavy Metal Music and Adolescent Alienation.* New York: Westview Press, 1996.

Bayles, Martha. *Hole in Our Sole: The Loss of Beauty and Meaning in American Popular Music.* New York: The Free Press, 1994.

Cantor, Joanne, Kristen Harrison, and Marina Kremar. "Ratings and Advisories: Implications of the New Ratings System for Television." *Television Violence and Public Policy.* Ed. James T. Hamilton. Ann Arbor: University of Michigan Press, 2001.

Christenson, Peter G., and Donald F. Roberts. *It's Not Only Rock & Roll.* Creskill, NJ: Hampton Press, 1998.

Clover, Carol J. *Men, Women, and Chainsaws: Gender in the Modern Horror Film.* Princeton: Princeton University Press, 1992.

Cooper, Cynthia A. *Violence on Television: Congressional Inquiry, Public Criticism and Industry Response.* New York: University Press of America, 1996.

Creed, Barbara. *The Monstrous-Feminine: Film, Feminism, Psychoanalysis.* New York: Routledge, 1993.

Derry, Charles. "More Dark Dreams: Some Notes on the Recent Horror Film." In *American Horrors: Essays on the Modern American Horror Film,* ed. Gregory A. Waller. Urbana: University of Illinois Press, 1987.

Dickstein, Morris. "The Aesthetics of Fright." In *Planks of Reason: Essays on the Horror Film,* ed. Barry Keith Grant. Metuchen, NJ: The Scarecrow Press, 1984.

Dika, Vera. "The Stalker Film, 1978–81." In *American Horrors: Essays on the Modern*

American Horror Film. Ed. Gregory A. Waller. Urbana: University of Illinois Press, 1987.

Dillard, R.H.W. "*Night of the Living Dead*: It's Not Like Just a Wind That's Passing Through." In *American Horrors: Essays on the Modern American Horror Film*, ed. Gregory A. Waller. Urbana: University of Illinois Press, 1987.

Dolbeare, Kenneth M., and Murray J. Edelman. *American Politics: Policies, Power, and Change*. Lexington, MA: D.C. Heath, 1971.

Edelman, Murray. *Constructing the Political Spectacle*. Chicago: University of Chicago Press, 1988.

_____. *Political Action: Words that Succeed and Policies that Fail*. New York: Academic, 1977.

_____. *Politics as Symbolic Action: Mass Arousal and Quiescence*. Chicago: Markham, 1971.

_____. *The Symbolic Uses of Politics*. Chicago: University of Illinois Press, 1985.

Fischer, Lucy, and Marcia Landy. "*Eyes of Laura Mars*: A Binocular Critique." In *American Horrors: Essays on the Modern American Horror Film*, ed. Gregory A. Waller. Urbana: University of Illinois Press, 1987.

Freeland, Cynthia A. *The Naked and the Undead: Evil and the Appeal of Horror*. Boulder, CO: Westview Press, 2000.

Giles, Dennis. "Conditions of Pleasure in Horror Cinema." In *Planks of Reason: Essays on the Horror Film*, ed. Barry Keith Grant. Metuchen, N.J.: Scarecrow Press, 1984.

Hebdige, Dick. *Subculture: The Meaning of Style*. London, UK: Methuen & Co., Ltd., 1989.

Iaccino, James F. *Psychological Reflections on Cinematic Terror: Jungian Archetypes in Horror Films*. Westport, CT: Praeger, 1994.

Kendrick, Walter. *The Thrill of Fear: 250 Years of Scary Entertainment*. New York: Grove Weidenfeld, 1991.

Krasnow, Erwin G., and Lawrence D. Longley. *The Politics of Broadcast Regulation*. New York: St. Martin's, 1973.

Krattenmaker, Thomas G., and Lucas A. Powe, Jr. *Regulating Broadcast Programming*. Cambridge, MA: MIT Press, 1994.

Kunkel, Dale, Barbara J. Wilson, James Potter, Daniel Linz, Edward Donnerstein, Stacy L. Smith, and Eva Blumenthal. "Content Analysis of Entertainment Television: Implications for Public Policy." In *Television Violence and Public Policy*, ed. James T. Hamilton. Ann Arbor: University of Michigan Press, 2001.

Mill, John Stuart. *On Liberty*. In *Introduction to Political Thinkers*, William Ebenstein and Alan O. Ebenstein, eds. New York: Harcourt Brace Jovanovich College Publishers, 1992.

Paul, William. *Laughing Screaming: Modern Hollywood Horror and Comedy*. New York: Columbia University Press, 1994.

Polan, Dana. "Eros and Syphilization: The Contemporary Horror Film." In *Planks of Reason: Essays on the Horror Film*, ed. Barry Keith Grant. Metuchen, N.J.: Scarecrow Press, 1984.

Rowland, Willard D. *The Politics of TV Violence: Policy Uses of Communication Research*. Beverly Hills, CA: Sage, 1983.

Sobchack, Vivian. "Bringing It All Back Home: Family Economy and Generic Exchange." In *American Horrors: Essays on the Modern American Horror Film*, ed. Gregory A. Waller. Urbana: University of Illinois Press, 1987.

Telotte, J.P. "Through a Pumpkin's Eye: The Reflexive Nature of Horror." In *American Horrors: Essays on the Modern American Horror Film*, ed. Gregory A. Waller. Urbana: University of Illinois Press, 1987.

Waller, Gregory A. "Introduction." In *American Horrors: Essays on the Modern American Horror Film*, ed. Gregory A. Waller. Urbana: University of Illinois Press, 1987.

Walley, David. *Teenage Nervous Breakdown: Music and Politics in the Post Elvis Age*. New York: Insight Books, 1998.

Winfield, Betty Houchin. "Because of the Children: Decades of Attempted Controls of Rap and Rock Music." In *Bleep! Censoring Rap and Rock Music*, Betty Houchin Winfield and Sandra Davidson, eds. Westport, CT: Greenwood Press, 1999.

Wood, Robin. "Returning the Look: *Eyes of a Stranger*." In *American Horrors: Essays on the Modern American Horror Film*, ed. Gregory A. Waller. Urbana: University of Illinois Press, 1987.

_____. "An Introduction to the American Horror Film." In *Planks of Reason: Essays on the Horror Film*, ed. Barry Keith Grant. Metuchen, NJ: Scarecrow Press, 1984.

Articles

Albiniak, Paige. "Washington Demands Answers." *Broadcasting & Cable*. 17 May 1999.

_____, and Bill McConnell. "FCC Looks for Strategic Guidance." *Broadcasting & Cable*. 17 May 1999.

American Academy of Pediatrics. "Joint Statement on the Impact of Entertainment Violence on Children." Washington DC: 26 July 2000. www.aap.org/advocacy/releases/jstmtevc.htm, 2 Oct 2000.

American Civil Liberties Union. "Popular Music Under Siege." Arts Censorship Project. New York, NY: 1996. www.aclu.org/library/pbr3.html, 2 October 2000.

Blumner, Robyn. "Freedom's Fair-Weather Friends." *Wall Street Journal*. 31 Mar 2000.

Bunning, Reiner. "Heavy Metal Summons the Beast." *Albuquerque Journal*. Albuquerque, NM: 18 May 2000. www.alibi.com/alibi/2000-05-18/letters.html, 2 Oct 2000.

Cockburn, Alexander. "The Gores' Cultural Wars." *The Nation* (New York): 2 Oct 2000.

Cole, Thomas J. "Savage Sound." *The Albuquerque Journal*. Albuquerque, NM: Apr–May, 2000. www.abqjournal.com/news/death/default.htm, 2 Oct 2000.

Colford, Steven W. "Foes of TV Violence Persist." *Advertising Age* 65. 7 February 1994.

"Congress Seeks Media Limits in Wake of Violence." *News Media and the Law*. Summer, 1999.

Congressional Quarterly staff writers. "Congress, FCC Consider Newspaper Control of Local TV." In *Issues in Broadcasting: Radio, Television, and Cable*, Ted C. Smythe and George A. Mastroianna, eds. Palo Alto, CA: Mayfield, 1975.

Egenes, Eric. "Vomit Radio Defends Death Metal." *Albuquerque Journal*. 18 May 1999. www.alibi.com/alibi/2000-05-18/letters.html, 2 Oct 2000

Flick, Larry. "It's Back Big-Time: Metal Returns for a Match with the Mainstream." *Billboard* (New York): 5 June 1999.

Hoerrner, Keisha L. "The Forgotten Battles: Congressional Hearings on Television Violence in the 1950s." *WJMCR*. Jun 1999a. www.scripps.ohiou.edu/wjmrc/vol02/2-3-B.htm. May 2001.

_____. "Symbolic Politics: Congressional Interest in Television Violence from 1950 to 1996." *Journalism and Mass Communication Quarterly*. Winter, 1999b.

Jones, Christopher. "Music, Violence, and the RIAA." *Wired News*. 3 May 1999. www.wirednews.com/news/print/0,1294,19464,00.html, 2 Oct 2000.

Krattenmaker, Thomas G. and Lucas A. Powe Jr. "Converging First Amendment Principles for Converging Communications Media." *The Yale Law Journal* 104. May 1995.

McAvoy, Kim. "TV Industry to Senate: Self-Regulation, Not Legislation, the Answer to Violence." *Broadcasting and Cable* 123. 24 May 1993.

Mundy, Alicia. "Deja Violence All Over Again." *Mediaweek*. 7 Jun 1999a.

_____. "Youth Ad Plans Scrutinized." *Mediaweek*. 10 May 1999b.

Ossietzky, Carl Von. "Violence and Aggressive Music." *Future Frame News*. Hamburg, Germany: 14 Jul 2000. www.futureframe.de/news/00714-3.htm, 2 Oct 2000.

Ramey, Carl R. "In the Battle Over TV Violence, The Communications Act Should Be Cheered, Not Changed." www.law.indiana.edu/fclj/pubs/v47/no2/ramey.html. May 2001.

Reesman, Bryan. "Hard Music: Thundering into the Millennium — the Metal Class of 2000 Will Rise." *Billboard*. New York, NY: 24 June 2000.

Rhodes, Richard. "The Media-Violence Myth." *Rolling Stone*. 23 Nov 2000.

Simon, Paul. "Independent Audits and Self-Regulation — Not Legislation — Is the Best Answer to TV Violence." *Federal Communications Law Journal* 47. Dec 1994.

Simson, Maria, Genevieve Stuttaford, and Jeff Zaleski. "Review of *Lords of Chaos: The Bloody Rise of the Satanic Underground*." *Publishers Weekly*, 245 (New York): 18 May 1998.

Stack, Steven. "Heavy Metal, Religiosity, and Suicide Acceptability." *Suicide and Life: Threatening Behavior* (New York): Winter, 1998.

University of California Los Angeles. "Web-Report on the History of Congressional Debates on Media Violence." 1995. http://ccp.ucla.edu/webreport95/history.htm, May 2001.

"White House, Congress Examine Media Violence." *News Media and the Law*. Spring, 1999.

Government Documents

Byrd, Robert. "Speech before the President on Violence within the Media." www.senate.gov/ ~byrd/speech-train.htm, 2 Oct 2000.

Feinstein, Dianne. "In Support of the Brownback/Hatch/Lieberman Amendment: Combating Marketing of Unsuitable Material to Our Children." Senate Commerce Committee, 12 May 1999.

Hatch, Orrin G. "Hearing on Marketing Violence to Our Children." Senate Commerce Committee, 4 May 1999.

Hatch, Orrin G., and the Majority Staff. Executive Summary. Senate Committee on the Judiciary, 14 Sep 1999.

Leiberman, Joseph I. "The Social Impact of Music Violence." Governmental Affairs Committee: Subcommittee on Oversight, 6 Nov 1997.

McCain, John. "Lawmakers Praise President for Calling Summit With Entertainment Industry on Media Violence." Secretaries Nancy Ives, Dan Gerstein, and David Moulton. 30 Apr 1998.

Senate Record Vote Analysis. "Juvenile Justice/Media Consent Ratings and Labels." 106th Congress, 1st session, 12 May 1999.

Useful URLS Visited

http://lieberman.senate.gov/~lieberman/press
http://interact.uoregon.edu/MediaLit/FA/MLArticleFolder/vulgarity.html
www.futureframe.de/news/00714-3.htm
www.wirednews.com/news/print/0,1294,19464,00.html
www.alibi.com/alibi/2000-05-18/letters.html
www.abqjournal.com/news/death/default.htm
www.nytimes.com/library/tech/99/04/biztech/articles/26digi.html
www.aclu.org/library/pbr3.html
www.ojp.usdoj.gov/bjs/pub/ascii/llgsfp.txt
www.census.gov/hhes
www.whitehouse.gov/fsbr/ssbr.html
www.senate.gov/member/ct/liberman/releases/r110697c.html
www.senate.gov/~judiciary/mediavio.htm
www.senate.gov/~hatch/littleton.html
www.senate.gov/~feinstein/releases99/videogameamdt.html
Several other www.senate.gov sites

Index

American Civil Liberties Union 144
Angelcorpse 18, 36, 42, 45, 73, 110, 129
Attitudes 116, 119
Autopsy 22, 56, 59

Bolt Thrower 27, 46, 57, 58, 61

Cannibal Corpse 9, 14, 15, 18, 43, 44, 45, 59, 62, 64, 66, 70, 74, 81, 129, 143, 145, 155, 180
Carcass 21, 22, 24, 27, 44, 56, 58, 61, 67
Carnage 22, 27, 45, 61, 95
Cartesianism 124
Celtic Frost 23, 40, 53, 55, 59
Christianity, 41, 42, 62, 166
Columbine 89, 91, 141
Constitution (of the U.S.) 81, 140
Cryptopsy 44, 70, 74, 110, 155

Dark Tranquility 22, 23, 72
Dead Infection 24
Death (the band) 14, 18, 26, 43, 47, 48, 49, 59, 61, 62, 66, 67, 129
Deceased 13, 25, 28, 56, 59, 62, 110, 128, 142
Deeds of Flesh 18, 71
Deicide 18, 27, 42, 43, 57, 58, 62, 64, 66, 70, 71, 125, 165
Demockery 121
Depression 114

Dimmu Borgir 19, 111
Dismember 22, 61
Doom Death Metal 23, 59
Drug Abuse 135
Dying Fetus 9, 11, 12, 13, 15, 19, 28, 31, 41, 46, 71, 72, 111, 121, 128, 129, 143, 144

Earache Records 58, 61
Emperor 19, 43
Entombed 22, 27, 41, 57, 58, 62, 67, 72

Feminism 171, 179, 181, 183
First Amendment 80, 83, 86, 87, 88, 142, 145, 146, 162
Floridian Death Metal 18

Gender 103
General Surgery 24
Gore-Grind Death Metal 24
Gorguts 18, 27
Grave 22, 41, 55, 59, 62, 110
Gut 24, 45, 72

Hate Eternal 18, 74
Hellhammer 40, 53, 55
Hypocrisy 23, 72

Immolation 19, 21, 27, 41, 57, 62, 70, 74, 165

INDEX

Impaled 24, 45
In Flames 15, 22, 23, 72
Incantation 11, 14, 19, 21, 28, 29, 33, 41, 57, 59, 63, 66, 70, 71, 109, 128, 142
Internal Bleeding 9, 19, 72

Lyrical Content 39

Macabre 12, 15, 25, 45, 55, 59, 63, 128
Malevolent Creation 18, 27, 43, 62, 66, 74
Mantas 54
Master 27, 55, 59, 63
Metal Philosophy 123
Misery Index 11, 47, 111, 119, 121, 128, 144
Monstrosity 18, 48, 62, 74
Morbid Angel 14, 18, 26, 27, 40, 42, 43, 56, 57, 59, 62, 64, 66, 70, 72, 164
Morrisound Studio 18, 59
Mortician 19, 21, 28, 43, 45, 59, 63, 70, 71, 100
My Dying Bride 23, 59

Napalm Death 21, 27, 41, 47, 56, 57, 58, 61, 67, 73
Natural Law 125
Necrony 24
Necrophagia 12, 13, 14, 15, 23, 25, 43, 54, 56, 73, 110, 126, 128, 143
New York Death Metal 19
Nihilism 22, 57, 167, 176
Nile 13, 18, 27, 28, 31, 41, 68, 73, 119, 127, 128, 142, 164
Nuclear Blast Records 27

Obituary 18, 26, 27, 48, 57, 58, 62, 66, 67

Origin 11, 12, 13, 15, 29, 36, 71, 75, 110, 129, 131, 143, 157

Paradise Lost 23
Pornography 39, 47, 163, 169, 178, 179, 180, 186
Positivism 125
Possessed 40, 53, 54, 62, 72, 74, 171

Race 105, 106
Rap 106, 107, 108
Regurgitate 24, 72
Relapse Records 27, 28, 59, 63, 71
Relativism 125
Religion 117, 123, 130, 137, 163, 164, 165, 166, 178
Repulsion 27, 43, 55, 63
Roadrunner Records 71

Sepultura 27, 54, 57, 58
Six Feet Under 70
Skinless 19, 28, 36, 71
Subcultural Phenomenon 151
Subjectivism 125
Suffocation 9, 19, 28, 45, 66, 71, 155
Suicide 74
Swedish Death Metal 22, 23, 58, 61

Terrorizer 57

Unleashed 22, 59, 62

Venom 40, 53, 54, 144
Violence 85, 86, 91, 139, 141, 170

With Immortality 111, 129, 144

Zyklon 19, 43